Then strip, lads, and to it, though
sharp be the weather,
And if, by mischance, you should
happen to fall,
There are worse things in life
than a tumble on heather,
And life is itself but
a game at football.

SIR WALTER SCOTT

SATURDAY AFTERNOON

College football and the men who made the day

By Richard Whittingham

Workman Publishing, New York

Library of Congress Cataloging-in-Publication Data

Whittingham, Richard, 1939-
Saturday afternoon.

Includes index.
1. Football—United States—History.
2. College sports—United States—History.
I. Title.
GV950.W47 1985   796.332'0973   85-40522
ISBN 0-89480-933-4

Cover Illustration: Dennis Ziemienski
Cover and Book Design: Kathleen Herlihy Paoli

Back cover: Peter Gowland/FPG (cheerleader),
US Naval Academy (Billy XII), University of Michigan (Gerald Ford),
Mike Sleeper (Doug Flutie).

Workman Publishing Company, Inc.
1 West 39th Street
New York, NY 10018

Manufactured in the United States of America
First printing October 1985

10 9 8 7 6 5 4 3 2 1

Grateful acknowledgment is made for permission to reprint:

Excerpt from *Saturday's America* © 1970 by Dan Jenkins.
Little, Brown, Boston.

"Ten Great Things About College Football" by Beano Cook,
© News Group Chicago, Inc. 1985.
Reprinted with permission of the *Chicago Sun-Times*.

Lyrics from "On Brave Old Army Team" copyright © 1911
Renewed Shapiro, Bernstein & Co. Inc.

Dedication

For
Four Favorite
Former Collegians:
Beth, Charles,
Philip, and Leigh
Whittingham

Acknowledgements

The author and publisher would like to extend their appreciation to the following who made invaluable contributions to this book: Joe Horrigan, curator of the Pro Football Hall of Fame in Canton, Ohio; Jack Clary, noted sports authority who served as general consultant; Wes George, Jim Hargrove, and Frank Shankle. In addition, we are deeply indebted for the cooperation provided by the Sports Information Directors, their staffs, and archivists from the following universities: Alabama, Arizona, Arkansas, Boston College, Brigham Young, Brown, University of California—Los Angeles, University of Chicago, Columbia, Dartmouth College, Duke, Florida State, Georgia Institute of Technology, Grambling State, Harvard, Iowa, Illinois, Indiana, Kansas, Kentucky, Lafayette College, Maryland, Michigan State, Michigan, Minnesota, Nebraska, Northwestern, Occidental College, Ohio State, Oklahoma, University of the Pacific, Penn State, Pennsylvania, Pittsburgh, Purdue, Rutgers, Southern Methodist, Stanford, Syracuse, Texas Christian, Texas, US Naval Academy, Utah State, Virginia, Wake Forest, Whittier College, Wichita State. Special thanks is due to the following for their help and generosity: Cotton Bowl Classic, Pasadena Tournament of Roses, Orange Bowl, Sugar Bowl, Cornell Archives, Notre Dame Sports Information, US Military Academy Archives and Sports Information, University of Southern California Sports Information and Libraries, Yale University Sports Information.

The author would also like to extend his appreciation for exceptional editorial help and guidance from Michael Cader, and for the fine work of designers Kathleen Herlihy Paoli and Susan Aronson Stirling, and photo researcher Frannie Ruch.

The Game

The Warm-Up....8

FIRST QUARTER

SECOND QUARTER

HALFTIME

Famous songs, historic yells, funny incidents, Red Grange's Quarterback Quiz, College Football at the Movies, and a parade of bands, bonfires, cheerleaders and mascots **158**

THIRD QUARTER

The Greatest **170**
The extraordinary games, moments and players, including the Four Horsemen, Grange's Great Day, the Upset of the Decade, National Champions, Ten Great Things About College Football, the Heisman Trophy, and the Greatest Teams of the Century.

FOURTH QUARTER

New Year's Day **222**
When champions are crowned and hearts are broken, as the spectacle of the bowl games unfolds. Recollections of classic games are accompanied by complete statistics on all the season's bowl games.

THE WRAP-UP

The Warm-Up

Saturday afternoon. For more than a century it has stood in passing autumns as the slot of time reserved for one of the most richly colorful, spirited, and vibrantly exciting sports in all the world—college football. Baseball has its summer, pro football its Sunday and Monday nights, basketball its winter indoors, but tradition and college football's legionary following have indisputably claimed that first day of each autumn weekend.

The game's very birth was on a Saturday afternoon, three o'clock to be precise, November 6, 1869, when Rutgers took the challenge laid down by Princeton to meet in a football game that would pit one school's honor and skill against the other. It was really soccer that they played that windy November afternoon, but it is considered the first intercollegiate football contest in America.

Soon after, games were being played among schools like Yale, Columbia, Harvard, Tufts, Amherst, Trinity, Pennsylvania, Williams, Wesleyan, as well as the two progenitors of the sport. And by the 1880s, intercollegiate combat on the football field had become a common diversion in the Midwest, South, and Southwest, and the following decade even in the then remote and sparsely settled far West.

> **"The game of football is to college life what color is to painting. It makes college life throb and vibrate."**
>
> BOB ZUPPKE
> ILLINOIS

In those infant days of college football, students, decked out in coats, vests, ties, and bowlers crowded the boundary lines of the grassy malls or dirt fields where the games were staged. Clutching and waving handmade pennants, they devised spontaneous cheers to urge their compatriots to victory. The spirit was there from the very beginning.

Soon schools began erecting rickety wooden grandstands to accommodate the growing crowds, who chanted across the field at each other in derision and down at the field in support of their own. As time passed the sport began to take on its pageantry with the infusion of cheerleaders, fight songs, mascots, marching bands, bonfires, pep rallies, and tailgate parties.

The bleachers gave way to sturdy stadiums and massive bowls, and the fans eventually traded their derbies and greatcoats for flipbrim hats, raccoon coats, and saddle shoes. Alumni began coming back to their alma maters in droves to watch their former schools compete against lusty rivals, and townspeople joined the throngs for some of the best entertainment to be had. Suddenly, the Saturday afternoon sport that had formerly been witnessed by perhaps a thousand classmates was now, at a given stadium, the focus of tens of thousands of spirited spectators.

The game itself—violent, tactical, demanding of skills, strength, and endurance—evoked the essentials of drama: excitement, suspense, competition, triumph and failure. It is hardly surprising then that it became such a fertile ground for the cultivation of legends. The fathers of the game were the early coaches, who developed it with a panoply of innovations and refinements; men like Walter Camp, Amos Alonzo Stagg, Glenn S. Warner, George Woodruff, Percy Haughton, John Heisman, Fielding Yost, Harry Williams, Gil Dobie, Bob Zuppke, Knute Rockne, and many others.

And the stars came out, sparkling on green fields across the country: a burly Pudge Heffelfinger at Yale, an imposing Hamilton Fish at Harvard, a savagely fleet Willie Heston at Michigan, a corpulent but agile Pete Henry at Washington & Jefferson, a triple-threat Elmer "Ollie" Oliphant at Army, an awesome Jim Thorpe at Carlisle.

By the mid-1920s, more than 50,000 fans would fill Illinois' Memorial Stadium to watch the world's most famous ghost, Red Grange, gallop, while professional football teams like the New York Giants and the Chicago Bears were thrilled if they drew more than 5,000 supporters on a Sunday afternoon. George Gipp died and a nation mourned the Notre Dame star's passing, but would never forget the name of the Gipper, thanks to the most famous locker room pep talk ever made.

It became a stage on which dramas of many natures have been played, from last-second victories to Roy Riegels' wrong-way run, from Woody Hayes' tantrums to Doug Flutie's Hail Mary pass. Besides Grange and the Gipper, it gave us Bronko Nagurski, Don Hutson, Tom Harmon, Sammy Baugh, Blan-chard and Davis, Johnny Lujack, Jim Brown, Dick Butkus, O. J. Simpson, and Herschel Walker. Not to mention the wisdom and wizardries of the likes of Fritz Crisler, Bernie Bierman, Frank Leahy, Bud Wilkinson, Duffy Daugherty, Darrell Royal, Ara Parseghian, John McKay, Bear Bryant, Bo Schembechler, Joe Paterno, and Eddie Robinson.

There are few spectacles in the sporting world to match the ceremony of an Army-Navy game, the color of a Rose Bowl pageant, the emotion when a chorus of thousands rings out with the Notre Dame fight song, the splendor of a tailgate party at a Texas-Oklahoma game, the beauty of USC cheerleaders, or simply the great games that have been played and the extraordinary performances that have been given over the years.

In the words of one of the game's finest coaches, Earl "Red" Blaik, written back in the 1950s, college football is, "a game that through the years has stirred a President to save it, Theodore Roosevelt; another to coach it, Woodrow Wilson; and a third to both play and coach it, Dwight D. Eisenhower." We might add subsequent players, Presidents Richard M. Nixon, Gerald Ford, and Ronald Reagan, the latter even portraying the fabled Gipper on the silver screen. Blaik went on to explain that it is "a game that numbers as legion statesmen, doctors, lawyers, men of finance and business, and thousands of just good citizens who have known the thrill of victory, have experienced the lessons of defeat, and have felt, as few but football players can, the lasting satisfaction that comes from playing on a team."

What he forgot to mention were the particular pleasures of walking with a surging crowd across the fallen amber leaves of autumn into a cavernous stadium where one can cheer and sigh on a noble Saturday afternoon.

FIRST

QUARTER

The Kickoff

Just who were the first to play the game that eventually evolved into what we know as football can never be precisely determined, but the game likely began somewhere between the time men came out of their caves and the age when they began building things like pyramids and Parthenons.

There are hieroglyphic records that show a game like soccer was played in ancient Egypt and that it had something to do with fertility rites, although the exact relationship has never been fully ascertained. The Chinese, it is also recorded, began playing a similar game somewhere around 300 B.C., using a ball stuffed with hair.

In ancient Greece, the game was a popular diversion, written of and played everywhere from Athens to Sparta. Their game was called *harpaston* ("hand ball") and involved two teams, each trying to move a ball-like object across a goal line by kicking or throwing it. The Romans, who conquered the Greeks in the second century before Christ, adopted the game and the name, Latinizing it to *harpastum*.

It is generally believed that the marauding Roman legions spread the game through Europe and to the British Isles. In England it acquired the name "mellay," a predecessor to the term *melee*. It was appropriate because the game as it was played then was riotous and violent, a mob-action scene with no visible restraints or rules of conduct. Legend has it that the first ball used in an English football game was actually the head of a Danish pirate.

Both in Great Britain and on continental Europe the game thrived. Mellays eventually became part of medieval festivals, taking a place alongside such activities as jousting and other knightly pursuits. It became a tradition at the Roman-founded village of Chester in England on Shrove Tuesday, commemorating a day long-past when the people of the area formed a great wedge and drove the legionnaires out of the village. So, on the day before the formal start of Lent, all work would be halted and the townsmen of Chester and the farmers from the surrounding area met on an improvised field of play next to the village's common hall. The event soon became part of the pre-Lenten celebrations in other English towns, which would take on one another in the game that still resembled a raucous mix of kickball and hand-to-hand combat. The ball that was used in those days was ordinarily the inflated blad-

> **"You don't put morale on like a coat, you build it day by day."**
>
> FIELDING YOST
> MICHIGAN

der of a pig, but later, village shoemakers produced balls from hides.

As time passed and pressure was applied by governments and churches to make the game more civilized, it gradually emerged from mayhem to sport and by the 18th century it vaguely resembled the modern version of soccer. It became popular as an intramural activity at most of the secondary schools, from the famous ones like Eton and Harrow to the lesser known in rural England. Previously the game had mostly been the domain of commoners, and was frowned on as undignified by the upper classes. But with its acceptance on the greens of academe, football became respectable in England. There were no rules, however, nor any governing body, and the game itself varied considerably from campus to campus. The only hard-line rule was that the ball could not be carried in the hands or arms. But even that tacit regulation would eventually fall.

The iconoclast responsible for it was a youngster named William Webb Ellis, a student at the Rugby secondary school. The story is told that one day in 1823 in the closing moments of a game of football, the end of which was signaled by the tolling of the five o'clock bell in the school tower, Ellis caught a long kick and in some flight of mad desperation took off running with the ball toward the opposing team's goal.

At first, everyone was stunned at such a breach of tradition, but then players began racing to stop him and to knock him down before he could reach the goal line. The would-be tacklers never did bring down the revolutionary running back, it is told, although the score was not allowed.

Rugby was not born on the spot as the five o'clock bell rang out that afternoon. But afterwards, the idea of running with the ball was discussed frequently around the school and in a while became part of the football games that were played there, and the school imparted its name to the new game.

In the middle of the 19th century, soccer and rugby moved up to the university level in England, and in the cities independent clubs were formed to field teams and compete with each other. From these developments emerged the first sets of organized rules for the games. In October 1863 a set of laws for the soccerlike game of football was written and published at Cambridge. That same year, a similar code of rules was drawn up by representatives of various independent clubs at a meeting at the Freemasons Tavern in London. Shortly thereafter the two codes were combined into a uniform "Rules of the London Football Association" (which, incidentally, is how the term *association football* became synonymous with soccer).

Those clubs and university groups that preferred to play the form of football that allowed running with the ball, which was becoming increasingly popular in the larger cities like London, Manchester, and Liverpool, then took to organizing themselves. The first association of note was the Oxford University Rugby Football Club, which was founded in 1869. Two years later, representatives of various clubs and three universities met at the Pall Mall restaurant in London and formed the Rugby Football Union, drafting bylaws and drawing up a uniform set of rules.

Both soccer and rugby, now organized, flourished in Great Britain. The elements of soccer had been brought to America by the colonists, and those of rugby by the immigrants of the mid-19th century. Elements from the two games were gradually blended and out of the matrix came a new and distinct sport, American football, which would grow from casual intramural games on the malls of the eastern colleges in the mid-1850s to the complex and compelling sport played in the cavernous stadiums of the late 1900s.

1800

Whittingham's All-Americans

Grantland Rice said it was a "mythical" thing to select "the very best" in college football, although he did just that for more than 20 years. There are other terms that come to mind, like controversial or questionable, maybe presumptuous or asinine. Still there are the greats, the stellar figures who shone beyond all others. Maybe some people are reticent about going on the line to say just who stands out as the best ever, but not everybody.

Here are the top players of each decade—you can agree, disagree, or even protest, but they stand undeniably as a roster of greatness in college football.

FIRST TEAM

Position	Player	School
E	Frank Hinkey	Yale
E	Charles Gelbert	Pennsylvania
T	Marshall Newell	Harvard
T	Arthur Hillebrand	Princeton
G	Pudge Heffelfinger	Yale
G	Truxton Hare	Pennsylvania
C	William Lewis	Harvard
B	Edgar Allan Poe	Princeton
B	Charles Daly	Harvard
B	Thomas McClung	Yale
B	Malcolm McBride	Yale
Coach	Amos Alonzo Stagg	Chicago

SECOND TEAM

Position	Player	School
E	Frank Hollowell	Harvard
E	Arthur Poe	Princeton
T	Langdon Lea	Princeton
T	Fred Murphy	Yale
G	Charles Wharton	Pennsylvania
G	Arthur Wheeler	Princeton
C	Peter Overfield	Pennsylvania
B	Knowlton Ames	Princeton
B	Frank Butterworth	Yale
B	George Brooke	Pennsylvania
B	Ben Dibble	Harvard
Coach	George Woodruff	Pennsylvania

1820

A form of association football (soccer) called "ballown" is played at Princeton.

Mid-1800s

A new form of football, combining elements of soccer and rugby, is played at various colleges in the northeastern United States but not on an intercollegiate basis. There are no uniform rules nor any set number of players on a team.

1860

Football is banned at Harvard as being too violent a sport. (The ban is lifted in 1871.)

1866

Beadle's Dime Book of Cricket and Football, the first book on American football, incorporating a definition of terms related to the sport and the "laws" of the game as well as rules for betting on it, is published in New York City.

The First College Game

John W. Herbert of the Rutgers class of 1872 and a member of the Rutgers team that participated in the first intercollegiate football game in the United States wrote this account many years afterwards (reprinted from the football program for the 1968 Cornell-Rutgers game):

"The game was called at 3 o'clock and started with a free kick-off from the tee, the same as now. It was played on the commons (where the Rutgers gymnasium now stands). On the arrival of the players, a few minutes before the game was called, they laid aside their hats, coats and vests. Neither team was in uniform, although some Rutgers players wore scarlet stocking-caps.

"The players lined up on each side, the organization of the twenty-five being the same on both sides. Two men were selected by each team to play immediately in front of the opponent's goal and were known as captains of the enemy's goal.

"The remainder of each team was divided into two sections. The players in one section were assigned to certain tracts of the field which they were to cover and not to leave. They were known as 'fielders.' The other section was detailed to follow the ball up and down the field. These latter players were called 'bulldogs.' They were easily recognizable in the evolution of the game as the forerunners of the modern rush line. I played in this division as I was a good wrestler and fleet of foot.

"The toss of the coin for advantage gave Princeton the ball and Rutgers the wind. Amid a hush of expectancy among the spectators Princeton 'bucked' or kicked the ball, but the kick was bad and the ball glanced to one side."

Parke H. Davis in his "Football, the American Intercollegiate Game," then describes the game as follows:

"The light, agile Rutgers men pounced upon it like hounds and by driving it by short kicks and dribbles, the other players surrounding the ball and not permitting a Princeton man to get near it, quickly and craftily forced it down to Old Nassau's goal, where the captains of the enemy's goal were waiting and these two latter sent the ball between the posts amid great applause.

"The first goal had been scored in five minutes of play. During the intermission, Captain Gummere (William S. Gummere, who later served as Chief Justice of the Supreme Court of New Jersey from 1901 until his death in 1932) instructed Michael (the late Jacob E. Michael,

Princeton '71, who was to become Dean of the Faculty at the University of Maryland), a young giant of the Princeton 25, to break up Rutgers' massing around the ball. Sides were changed and Rutgers 'bucked.' In this period the game was fiercely contested. Time and time again Michael, or 'Big Mike,' charged into Rutgers' primitive mass play and scattered the players like a burst bundle of sticks. On one of these plays Princeton obtained the ball and by a long accurate kick scored the second goal.

"The third goal or 'game,' as it was then called, went to Rutgers, and the fourth was kicked by Princeton, 'Big Mike' again bursting up a mass out of which Gummere gained possession of the ball and, with Princeton massed against him, easily dribbled the ball down and through the Rutgers goal posts, making the score once more a tie.

"The fifth and sixth goals went to Rutgers, but the feature of this latter period of play in the memory of the players after the lapse of many years is awarded to 'Big Mike' and Large (the late State Senator George H. Large of Flemington, a Rutgers player). Someone, by a random kick, had driven the ball to one side, where it rolled against the fence and stopped. Large led the pursuit for the ball, closely followed by Michael. They reached the fence, on which the students were perched, and, unable to check their momentum, in a tremendous impact struck the fence, which gave way with a crash, and over went its load of yelling students to the ground.

"Every college probably has the humorous tradition of some player who has scored against his own team. The tradition of Rutgers dated from this first game, for one of her players, whose identity is unknown, in the sixth period started to kick the ball between his own goal posts. The kick was blocked, but Princeton took advantage of the opportunity and soon made the goal. This turn of the game apparently disorganized Rutgers, for Princeton also scored the next goal after a few minutes of play, thus bringing the total up to four-all.

"At this stage Rutgers resorted to that use of craft which has never failed to turn the tide of every close battle. Captain Leggett had noticed that Princeton obtained a great advantage from the taller stature of their men, which enabled them to reach above the others and bat the ball in the air in some advantageous direction. Rutgers was ordered to keep the ball close to the ground. Following this stratagem the Rutgers men determinedly kicked the ninth and tenth goals, thus winning the match six goals to four and with it the distinction of a victory in the first game of intercollegiate football played in the world."

The Way it Was

John W. Heisman, one of the forefathers of college football and the man for whom the Heisman Trophy was named, played five years at Brown and Pennsylvania from 1887 through 1891. He described what it was like in those days:

"Players of my time had to be real iron men, because we played two games each week—Wednesdays and Saturdays.

"Once a game started, a player could not leave unless he actually was hurt, or, at least, pleaded injury. Accordingly, whenever the captain wanted to put a fresh player into action, he whispered, 'Get your arm hurt, or something.' In one game my captain whispered to me, 'Get your neck broke, Heisman.'

"We wore jerseys and shorts of great variety. We had no helmets or pads of any kind; in fact, one who wore home-made pads was regarded as a sissy. Hair was the only head protection we knew, and in preparation for football we would let it grow from the first of June. Many college men of that day, especially divinity and medical students, permitted their beards to grow. Often they were referred to as 'Gorillas.' . . .

"We didn't have many sweaters in those days, but we all wore snug-fitting canvas jackets over our jerseys.

You see, the tackling in that day wasn't clean-cut and around the legs as it is today. All too often it was wild, haphazard clutching with the hands, and when runners wore loose garments they were often stopped by a defensive player grabbing a handful of loose clothing. Some players wore pants, or jackets, of black horsehair. When you made a fumble grab, you lost your fingernails.

"In those pioneer years, arguments followed most every decision the referee made. The whole team took part, so that half the time the officials scarcely knew who was captain. More than that, every player was privileged to argue as much as he pleased with any and every player of the opposition. The player who was a good linguist always was a priceless asset. . . .

"In the old days, players of one side were permitted to grab hold of their runners anywhere they could and push, pull or yank them along in any direction that would make the ball advance. Sometimes two enemy tacklers would be clinging to the runner's legs, and trying to hold him back, while several team-mates of the runner had hold of his arms, head, hair, or wherever they could attach themselves, and were pulling him in the other direction. I still wonder how some of the ball carriers escaped dismemberment."

1880

With definite possession of the ball as the prevailing mode, the position of quarterback is born and so named. The quarterback receives the ball from a holder who stands at the line of scrimmage and snaps the ball back with his foot.

1880

Other rules changes include the reduction of the size of the playing field to 110 yards in length and 53⅓ yards in width, and restricting the number of players on a side to eleven.

1882

A system of downs is instituted, with teams required to gain five yards in three downs or give up possession of the ball. Previously one team would control the ball for an entire period and the other team would have it for the second period. Now teams have to kick the ball to the opposing team on third down or turn over possession if the five yards is not made.

1882

White lines at five-yard intervals running the width of the field are required. As a result of the pattern, the playing field is called a "gridiron."

1882

Walter Camp's system of signals is adopted by the IFA Rules Committee. Usually coded words or phrases, the signals are shouted to the other players to tell them which play is to be run. (It is believed Camp may have used signals as early as 1880, and that the University of Michigan may have used them in 1881.)

1883

At the now-annual Rules Committee meeting, Walter Camp introduces and obtains enactment for a new numerical scoring system: Five points for a goal kicked from the field during play, four for a goal on the free kick after a touchdown, two for a touchdown, and one for a safety.

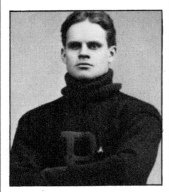

Truxton Hare, Pennsylvania's four-time All-American guard (1897–1900).

1884

The "V-Trick," also known as the wedge, is used by Princeton in a game against Pennsylvania. At the kickoff of a game the two teams line up ten yards apart. To set the ball in play, however, the kicker does not have to kick it ten yards. With the V-Trick, the kicker merely nudges the ball forward, which sets it in play, and he maintains possession. His teammates quickly scramble to form a V-shaped wedge in front of him, providing interference as he advances the ball. The V-Trick is also used by Lehigh the same year.

A scuffle for the ball, taken from a drawing used in a Spalding advertisement in the mid-1880s. The ad highlighted "the lily white regulation rugby ball."

1884

The point value of a touchdown is raised to four, and the goal on a free kick after the touchdown is lowered to two points.

1888

Tackling below the waist is allowed for the first time. To protect the newly vulnerable ball handler, offensive lines, which previously lined up randomly apart, line up shoulder to shoulder. With this potential for mass interference, line plunges become an integral part of the game. The backs also line up close together for added protection, setting the stage for Walter Camp's T Formation, which he introduces in 1889 at Yale.

1889

Caspar Whitney of *Harper's Weekly* magazine selects the first All-American team, published in a New York periodical called *The Week's Sport*. It includes such notables as Amos Alonzo Stagg of Yale at end, William "Pudge" Heffelfinger, also of Yale, at guard, and Edgar Allan Poe (a grandnephew of the famed poet) of Princeton at quarterback. It is believed that Walter Camp assisted Whitney in the selection.

1890

Amos Alonzo Stagg, coach at Springfield (Mass.) College, introduces the "Ends-back" formation. The ends line up a few steps into the backfield, often in tandem with the tackles, to protect the backfield's flanks.

1891

The first game of college football to be played at night is staged under arc lights at Yale.

1891

Coach Stagg devises the "Turtleback" formation for Springfield College. In his words: "This was a formation executed by massing the team into a solid oval against the tackle, and at the snap of the ball into the interior of the oval, rolling the mass around an end and unwinding the runner into a clear field."

First Forward Pass?

Allison Danzig, sportswriter for *The New York Times* for 45 years, made this observation some years ago: "The earliest mention of the use of a forward pass in a game is found in *Athletics at Princeton—A History* (1900), as pointed out by Dr. L. H. Baker. In the 1876 Yale-Princeton game, it states, Walter Camp, when tackled threw the ball forward to Oliver Thompson, who ran for a touchdown. Princeton protested and claimed a foul. The referee tossed a coin to make his decision and allowed the touchdown to stand."

Father of the Game

Walter Chauncey Camp, a "townie" from New Haven, graduate of Hopkins Grammar School there, was 17 years old when he walked onto the campus at Yale in 1876. A handsome, serious-looking young man, his face adorned with a full mustache and muttonchop whiskers, he stood just under six feet tall, weighed somewhere in the vicinity of 160 pounds, and was wiry, strong, fast, and very athletic. His plan was to finish undergraduate work, attend Yale's respected medical school, and then forge a career in the curative arts as a physician. But the game of football got in the way of that plan, and instead Camp, through his innovations and devotion to the game, became the generating source, the true founding father, of American football.

In the 1870s football was just becoming a popular diversion at colleges in the eastern United States, played mostly as an intramural sport. The form of the game was a derivative from Europe of either soccer, or on occasion, the more physical and violent game of rugby. In the four years before Camp's matriculation at Yale, the school had occasionally engaged in football games with other colleges like Rutgers, Princeton, Columbia, and Wesleyan, but they were random encounters.

In 1876, however, the sport suddenly took on the cloak of organization with the creation of the Intercollegiate

Football Association (IFA).

A call for volunteers came from Yale upperclassman Eugene Baker to flesh out a football team that he would be titular captain of, and Walter Camp was among the first to offer his manifold talents.

Camp earned a starting position as halfback his freshman year on the then 15-man Yale squad, and he quickly proved to be one of the most adroit players on the field. It was the beginning of his lifelong marriage to the sport.

The game that emerged from the IFA's first "rules convention" in 1876 was really rugby, the action initiated from a scrum line where the two teams battled for possession of the ball on each play. It would not, however, continue as such because during the next six years, Walter Camp would become the guiding force of the IFA Rules Committee and would steer to enactment new rules that would radically change the nature of the game and create a unique sport.

Foremost among Camp's divergences was the establishment of a "line of scrimmage," instead of a scrum line, from which a team would have definite control of the ball. The team in possession of the ball would snap it into the backfield to set play in motion, and the new position Camp created to receive the snap he called "quarter-back." Within just a few years he added more shape and substance to the sport: the size of a team was reduced to 11 men (seven linemen and four backs); a system of downs was introduced with a set yardage that had to be gained in order to maintain possession of the ball; signals were devised for the quarterback to communicate with his teammates at the line of scrimmage; and a scoring system was designed that eventually evolved into the point values that exist today for touchdowns, field goals, extra points, and safeties.

When Walter Camp was not inventing rules and guiding them to fruition, he was on the field playing the game. For six years, during the last two of which he was in medical school, he was Yale's premier halfback, and twice was honored as the team's captain. He was also captain and pitcher on Yale's baseball team, a member of the school's swimming and tennis teams, a hurdler on the track team, and he held a seat on the crew.

A knee injury in 1882 ended Camp's playing career, but certainly not his life in football. By that time the call of the medical profession had paled considerably, and Camp dropped out of medical school and took a job in sales with the New Haven Clock Company, the firm in which he would eventually rise to the presidency and board chairmanship.

Walter C. Camp, shown below later in life, and to the right posing when he was a pitcher for the Yale baseball team in the late 1870s.

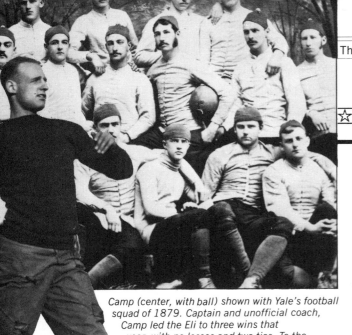

Camp (center, with ball) shown with Yale's football squad of 1879. Captain and unofficial coach, Camp led the Eli to three wins that year, with no losses and two ties. To the left, Camp shows off the winning form.

Despite leaving Yale, he never strayed too far from the Eli football field. He remained a most active member of the IFA Rules Committee and then returned in 1888 as the school's first head coach of football. Previously the coaching of a team had been handled by the captain. With Camp's return in 1888, that changed forever. There was no recompense for the job in those days, but Camp remained there through the 1892 season.

He developed as a coach what came to be called the "Camp System," which he later described to Grantland Rice as being "very simple and very sound. At the end of a season I'd call a meeting at which we'd determine who was graduating and who wasn't. Then we'd screen the returnees. Were they fast? Did they pack power? The type material we would have pretty much determined our mode of offense. We moved the ball with more authority because, as a team, we worked much harder on signals than our adversaries. As far as I know we also had the distinction of being the first team to develop the cutback—where a back starts at one point in the rival line and hits at another. This got us many, many yards. Remember, however, that everything and anything we tried in those days was new."

It was also informal and definitely improvisational. Just how much so is evident in the words of William "Pudge" Heffelfinger, one of the most luminous of Yale's early football stars, quoted by sportswriter John McCallum in his book *Ivy League Football Since 1872*: "In 1888, Yale actually had *two* coaches—Camp and his earnest young bride, Allie. . . . They were newlyweds and Walter was sales manager in the New York office of the New Haven Clock Company. His superiors wouldn't let him attend our afternoon practices, so he sent his wife to stand in for him. I can still see her pacing up and down the sideline, taking notes of our scrimmages. Walter kept in touch with our progress by reading her notebook. Then, several nights a

week some of us on the team would go over to the Camps' home in New Haven for a review of strategy.

"Allie Camp could spot the good points and the weaknesses in each man's play. Her woman's intuition helped Walter suggest the right man for the right position to the team captain. Remember, in those pioneer days at Yale, the head coach made no decision without first consulting the captain."

Walter Camp's name is, of course, deeply associated with the All-America teams which he selected, starting in 1889, when he collaborated with Caspar Whitney (whose byline appeared on the listings). Camp started making the selections by himself in 1897 when Whitney went abroad. Two years later, Whitney took over again at *Harper's Weekly,* and Camp started publishing his picks under his own name at *Collier's*. From that point forward, Camp's choices were considered the standard for outstanding performance on the gridiron until his death in 1925.

Premier All-Americans

The first All-American team, for 1889, selected by Caspar Whitney and Walter Camp, and published in *The Week's Sport*:

Position	Player	School
E	Amos Alonzo Stagg	Yale
E	Arthur Cumnock	Harvard
T	Hector Cowan	Princeton
T	Charles Gill	Yale
G	Pudge Heffelfinger	Yale
G	Jesse Riggs	Princeton
C	William George	Princeton
B	Edgar Allan Poe	Princeton
B	Roscoe Channing	Princeton
B	Knowlton Ames	Princeton
B	James Lee	Harvard

Among Camp's pupils in the game of American football were Amos Alonzo Stagg, Henry Williams, and Howard Jones, all Yale graduates who in turn went out and established themselves as legends when they coached, contributing creatively to the sport. Camp also wrote three books about the game he loved so dearly, that became the gospel of the sport in their time: *Football: How to Coach a Team* (1886), *American Football* (1891), and *Walter Camp's Book of College Sports* (1893).

The man who gave American football its own uniqueness died on the evening of March 14, 1925, while he was attending a Rules Committee meeting in New York City. Being there was hardly new for him; he had attended the meetings regularly since 1878, guiding the actions and polishing the product. He was indeed Father of the Game.

The Harvard Wedge, ready to go.

1894

Playing time is reduced from two 45-minute periods to two 35-minute periods.

1894

Linemen, who heretofore could line up in the backfield for interference on what were then called "mass momentum plays," are required to remain on the line of scrimmage.

1892

Lorin F. Deland of Harvard creates the "flying wedge," a play he first uses in the game against arch-rival Yale. At the kickoff, five players on the kicking team line up at each sideline about 20 yards behind the kicker. On a signal, they race toward the kicker and, as they converge on him, form a wedge in front. With the wedge moving at full speed, the kicker nudges the ball into play and follows his flying wedge interference into the opposing team.

1892

The first intercollegiate game in the West is played between the University of California and Stanford.

1893

Amos Alonzo Stagg, with Henry L. (Harry) Williams, authors *A Scientific and Practical Treatise on American Football for Schools and Colleges,* published by the Case, Lockwood & Brainard Company of Hartford, Connecticut.

Amos Alonzo Stagg at Yale, circa *1889.*

1894

The Southern Intercollegiate Athletic Association (SIAA), forerunner of the Southern Conference, which later spawns both the Atlantic Coast Conference and the Southeastern Conference, is formed at a meeting called for and directed by Dr. William L. Dudley of Vanderbilt. Charter members of the conference are Alabama, Auburn, Georgia, Georgia Tech, Sewanee, and Vanderbilt.

1894

The flying wedge is in effect outlawed when a new rule requires a kickoff to travel at least ten yards before the ball is deemed to be in play.

1895

What will become the Big Ten conference is organized. At its inauguration, the conference has seven charter members: Chicago, Illinois, Michigan, Minnesota, Northwestern, Purdue, and Wisconsin.

1897

The touchdown is given a point value of five, and the goal after touchdown is reduced to one point.

1898

The first of Walter Camp's "official" All-America teams is published in *Collier's* magazine and will appear in that periodical annually and be recognized as the official selection through 1924.

1900

Whittingham's All-Americans

FIRST TEAM

Position	Player	School
E	Thomas Shevlin	Yale
E	John Kilpatrick	Yale
T	Hamilton Fish	Harvard
T	Jim Hogan	Yale
G	Dutch Goebel	Yale
G	Ham Andruss	Yale
C	Germany Schultz	Michigan
B	Walter Eckersall	Chicago
B	Willie Heston	Michigan
B	Ted Coy	Yale
B	Bill Hollenback	Pennsylvania
Coach	Fielding Yost	Michigan

SECOND TEAM

Position	Player	School
E	Casper Wister	Princeton
E	David Campbell	Harvard
T	Horatio Biglow	Yale
T	Jim Cooney	Princeton
G	William Warner	Cornell
G	Francis Burr	Harvard
C	Henry Holt	Yale
B	Foster Rockwell	Yale
B	Henry Torney	Army
B	Pete Hauser	Carlisle
B	Wallie Steffen	Chicago
Coach	John Heisman	Clemson/Georgia Tech

Walter Eckersall of Chicago (above) displays his running skills. Harvard's Hamilton Fish (right) later became a U.S. congressman.

1902

The first Rose Bowl game is played on New Year's Day at Tournament Park in Pasadena, California. Michigan, coached by Fielding Yost, with a regular season record of 12-0, defeats Stanford, coached by Charles Fickert and with a record of 3-1-2, by the score of 49–0. Wolverine fullback Neil Snow scores five touchdowns.

Fielding Yost, Michigan's coach from 1901–23 and 1925–26, famed for his Point-a-Minute teams during the years 1901–05.

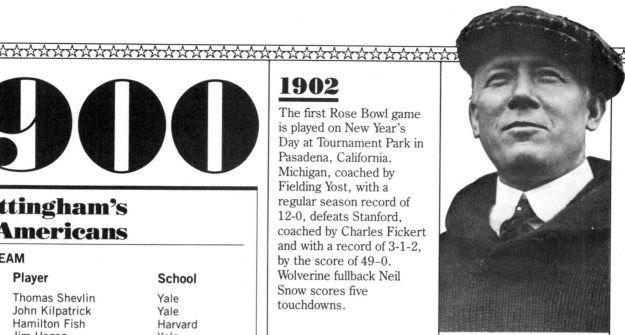

Dr. Harry Williams, Minnesota's legendary coach and one of the prime innovators of the game.

1902

A backfield formation shift is devised by Amos Alonzo Stagg for his University of Chicago team, considered to be the first use of a shift. Some historians suggest, however, that Harry Williams may have used his Minnesota shift a year or two earlier.

1903

John Heisman, coach of Clemson, recommends to Walter Camp that the forward pass be legalized, but the Rules Committee rejects it.

The Hidden Ball Trick

Famed coach Glenn S. "Pop" Warner of Carlisle in 1903 claims to be the first to have used the hidden ball trick, when his team received the opening kickoff in a game against Harvard. He described it in an article he wrote for *Collier's Weekly* 28 years later.

"The ball sailed far and high down the center of the field, and was caught on the five-yard line by Jimmie Johnson, our little quarterback, who was an All-America that year.

"The Indians gathered at once in what now would be called a huddle, but facing outward, and Johnson quickly slipped the ball under the back of Charlie Dillon's jersey. Charlie was picked as the 'hunchback' because he stood six feet and could do a hundred yards in ten seconds. Besides, being a guard, he was less likely to be suspected of carrying the ball.

"'Go!' yelled Johnson. And the Carlisle players scattered and fanned out toward the side lines, each back hugging his helmet to his breast, while Dillon charged straight down the center of the field. Talk about excitement and uproar! The Indian backs were chased and slammed, but when the tacklers saw that it was only headgear they were cuddling, not the ball, they began to leap here and there, yelping like hounds off the scent. Nobody paid any attention to Dillon, for he was running with both arms free, and when he came to Carl Marshall, safety man, the Harvard captain actually sidestepped what he thought was an attempt to block and dashed up the field to join the rest of his team in a frantic search for the ball.

"The stands were in an uproar, for everybody had seen the big lump on Dillon's back, but the Harvard players were still scurrying wildly around when Charlie crossed the goal line. One of his mates jerked out the ball and laid it on the turf and, as I had warned the referee that the play might be attempted, he was watching carefully and ruled that the touchdown had been made within the rules."

1903

The hidden ball trick, or "hunchback play," is used by Glenn S. "Pop" Warner's Carlisle team against Harvard for the first time on record. It results in a touchdown.

1903

Harvard builds a concrete stadium seating 30,000 for football games.

A photograph believed to be the earliest shot of Carlisle's star, Jim Thorpe.

Glenn S. "Pop" Warner, who coached at six different schools during his 44-year career (Georgia, Cornell, Carlisle, Pittsburgh, Stanford, Temple), shown here while at Carlisle.

1905

The publication of statistics on the violent nature of the game of football causes a nationwide furor. According to the reports, 18 deaths and 159 serious injuries were directly attributable to the sport.

1906

Pop Warner, coaching at Cornell, begins developing the single wing formation. The next year he moves to Carlisle and uses it often, and it becomes known as the Carlisle formation. A few years later Warner improvises further, bringing the other halfback up in line with the wingback to create the double wing formation.

This drawing, taken from The Illustrated London News *from 1910, shows the perceptions of "American football" as a "rough-and-rumble game" requiring players to be protected heavily with "armour."*

1906

The IFRC then formally adopts a set of new rules designed to make the game safer. Among them are:
★Legalization of the forward pass (with a variety of restrictions).
★Creation of a neutral zone at the line of scrimmage.
★Raising the yardage required for a first down from five to ten yards.
★Reducing the playing time of a game from two 35-minute periods to two 30-minute periods.
★Calling for the disqualification of players guilty of "fighting with or kneeing an opposing player."

1908

Amos Alonzo Stagg devises the "Statue of Liberty" play for his Chicago team. The quarterback raises his arm as if to throw a forward pass, but instead a halfback runs behind him, snatches the ball from his uplifted arm, and races around end. The "Statue of Liberty" play, from a forward pass formation, was based on the principles of the "Old 83" play, an end-around play from a "semipunt" formation, developed by Fielding Yost at Ohio Wesleyan in 1897.

Chicago's coach, Associate Professor Amos Alonzo Stagg.

1906

President Theodore Roosevelt summons representatives of Princeton, Yale, and Harvard to the White House for a meeting at which he insists they take steps to reform the sport to make it less brutal and dangerous. If not, he warns, it might have to be banned altogether.

1906

Representatives of 28 colleges that are not members of the Intercollegiate Football Association meet in New York City to establish their own rules committee. Called simply the "Conference Committee," it is headed by Captain Palmer E. Pierce of Army. Subsequently Pierce meets with Walter Camp, leader of the IFA Rules Committee, and the two agree to merge. The resulting organization is called the Intercollegiate Football Rules Committee (IFRC), the forerunner of the National Collegiate Athletic Association (NCAA).

1909

The value of a field goal is reduced from four to three points.

1910

Whittingham's All-Americans

FIRST TEAM

Position	Player	School
E	Tack Hardwick	Harvard
E	Guy Chamberlain	Nebraska
T	Fats Henry	Washington & Jefferson
T	Josh Cody	Vanderbilt
G	Stan Pennock	Harvard
G	Joe Alexander	Syracuse
C	Henry Ketcham	Yale
B	Jim Thorpe	Carlisle
B	Chic Harley	Ohio State
B	Elmer Oliphant	Army
B	Eddie Mahan	Harvard
Coach	Pop Warner	Carlisle/ Pittsburgh

SECOND TEAM

Position	Player	School
E	Doug Bomeisler	Yale
E	Paul Robeson	Rutgers
T	Harold Ballin	Princeton
T	Wally Trumbull	Harvard
G	Clarence Spears	Dartmouth
G	Bob Fischer	Harvard
C	Bob Peck	Pittsburgh
B	Gus Dorais	Notre Dame
B	Fritz Pollard	Brown
B	Charlie Brickley	Harvard
B	Charles Barrett	Cornell
Coach	Bob Zuppke	Illinois

Jim Thorpe (left), and Paul Robeson, All-American end at Rutgers in 1917 and 1918. A phi beta kappa, Robeson went on to become an internationally famous singer and actor.

1910

The NCAA offers some new rules. Among them:
★Changing the segments of play from two 30-minute periods to four 15-minute periods.
★Outlawing the flying tackle.
★Making only backs and ends eligible to receive a forward pass (formerly, any lineman could receive one if he lined up behind the line of scrimmage).
★Requiring seven men on the line of scrimmage at the start of any play.
★Banning interlocked interference, wherein linemen interlocked arms to form a single block of interference.

1910

The Intercollegiate Football Rules Committee changes its name to the National Collegiate Athletic Association.

1911

Jack Marks, new head coach at Notre Dame, designs and uses what is to become known as the Notre Dame box formation, adapted from a formation Marks developed as a coach at Dartmouth with head coach Frank Cavanaugh, in which the four backs form the corners of a box. Two years later, Notre Dame's new head coach, Jesse Harper, introduces the Notre Dame shift, which he had developed with Amos Alonzo Stagg at Chicago, in which the backfield lines up in a T formation and on a signal shifts into the box.

Elmer "Ollie" Oliphant, consensus All-American back in 1916 and 1917 at Army. Ollie actually played seven years of college football, three at Purdue (1911–13) and four at West Point (1914–17).

1912

A touchdown is given the value of six points and the onside kick is eliminated.

1912

The length of the football field is reduced to 100 yards, with the provision of a ten-yard end zone behind each goal line.

Teams are allowed four downs instead of three to gain the ten yards necessary for a first down.

1912

Some restrictions on the forward pass are removed, except that only one such pass can be thrown during a single four-down series of plays, and the pass has to be thrown from at least five yards behind the line of scrimmage.

1914

The Southwest Conference is founded, with eight charter members: Arkansas, Baylor, Oklahoma, Oklahoma A&M (today Oklahoma State), Rice, Southwestern, Texas, and Texas A&M.

1916

The conference that will become the PAC-10 is formed; charter members are California, Oregon, Oregon State, and Washington.

The First Homecoming

Homecoming, that grand tradition which is so much a part of the college football milieu, originated at the University of Illinois in 1910. Two seniors, Elmer Ekblaw and C. F. Williams, were waxing sentimental that spring as their graduation neared, and wondering if ever they would return to their *alma mater*.

Between them they came up with the idea of designating a certain weekend in the autumn, focused around an Illini football game, on which all grads would be invited back to socialize with each other and cheer on the old Orange and Blue. Enterprising youngsters that they were, the two mustered support from some of the university's honorary societies and fraternities and took their case to the school authorities.

Permission was granted to stage a Homecoming the following autumn on a trial basis. Word of the plan went out and on October 14, 1910, approximately 5,000 Illinois grads returned to campus to watch their team defeat the University of Chicago 3–0. Among the other festivities devised for that first Homecoming weekend were a "hobo parade" and a stunt show.

Fritz Pollard, a five-foot-eight-inch, 150-pound dynamo of a back, starred for Brown from 1914–16, and was the first black player selected for the first team of Walter Camp's All-American selections.

1916

The most lopsided victory in college football history is posted by Georgia Tech, under Coach John Heisman, when his prolific eleven drub Cumberland 222–0. In that game Tech kicker Jim Preas boots 18 extra points in the first half alone.

1917

Coaching from the sideline, which includes sending in a substitute with a play, is prohibited.

George Halas played end for Illinois (1915–17) and on the Great Lakes Naval Training Station team that triumphed in the 1919 Rose Bowl. In 1920, Halas, as player/coach/owner of the then Decatur Staleys (later Chicago Bears), was one of the founding fathers of the National Football League.

Halas Remembers

Prior to his more than 60-year career in professional football as a player, coach, and owner of the Chicago Bears, George Halas served his apprenticeship as an end, first at Illinois and, after World War I broke out, with the Great Lakes Naval Base team, which played against college teams in 1917 and 1918.

"One of the games I remember best from those days was when I was at Great Lakes. We traveled to Annapolis to play the Naval Academy team. They had a lot of pride and looked on us as a bunch of upstarts.

"Navy scored on us and were leading six to nothing. Much later in the game, they were about to score again. They were near our goal and their fullback Bill Ingram tried to smash through. But we hit him on the one yard line and he fumbled the ball. It popped right into the arms of one of our players, Dizzy Eilson.

"Well, Dizzy took off toward the other end of the field. Jimmy Conzelman (who would go on to become a great pro player and coach) and myself blocked for him. By the time he reached midfield, there wasn't a player between him and the goal line. Jimmy and I, at this point, just turned around to protect him, to stop anybody who might be chasing him.

"Gil Dobie, the Navy coach that year, almost went insane as he saw his game slipping out from under him. 'Stop him! Stop him!' he shouted.

"Bill Saunders, a substitute who later went on to coach at Denver, was alongside Dobie waiting to enter the game. He took Gil at his word, dashed onto the field, and made a perfect tackle of Eilson. There was a big to-do on the field, everybody shouting at everybody else—coaches, players, referees.

"Finally the Academy superintendent, a man named Captain Edward Eberle, came marching out onto the field and demanded order. He wanted to know what in hell was going on. The officials told him they had decided that Navy would be penalized halfway to the goal for the infraction. We were all screaming that we should be awarded a touchdown.

"The captain decreed that we should be given the touchdown. The officials said that was not the rule. The rule was a penalty, halfway to the goal. Captain Eberle said that was a ridiculous rule, and he didn't give a damn about it. 'It would have been a touchdown if that idiot hadn't run onto the field,' he said. 'I run this place and a touchdown it is.'

"Well, we made the conversion and won the game 7-6. Captain Eberle went on to become an admiral and chief of naval operations."

1920

Whittingham's All-Americans

FIRST TEAM

Position	Player	School
E	Bennie Oosterbaan	Michigan
E	Wes Fesler	Ohio State
T	Century Milstead	Yale
T	Ed Weir	Nebraska
G	Frank Schwab	Lafayette
G	Chuck Hubbard	Harvard
C	Ben Ticknor	Harvard
B	Benny Friedman	Michigan
B	Red Grange	Illinois
B	Ernie Nevers	Stanford
B	Bronko Nagurski	Minnesota
Coach	Knute Rockne	Notre Dame

SECOND TEAM

Position	Player	School
E	Brick Muller	California
E	Eddie Anderson	Notre Dame
T	Ralph Scott	Wisconsin
T	Frank Wickhorst	Navy
G	Jim McMillen	Illinois
G	Carl Diehl	Dartmouth
C	Mel Hein	Washington State
B	Harry Stuhldreyer	Notre Dame
B	George Wilson	Washington
B	Ken Strong	New York
B	George Gipp	Notre Dame
Coach	Wallace Wade	Alabama

Ernie Nevers, one of the greatest fullbacks of all-time, carried the ball for Stanford from 1923 through 1925. His coach, Pop Warner, said of him, "He could do everything Thorpe could do and he tried harder."

The Watch-Charm Guard

If ever there was a football player who symbolized the difference between college football as it was played in the days prior to World War II and the modern game, it had to be Bert Metzger of Notre Dame. He played guard from 1928 through 1930, made All-American his senior year, stood five-feet-nine-inches tall and weighed 145 pounds most of the time although it is said he got up to 149 occasionally.

He was called the "Watch-Charm" guard because of his diminutive size, not presence. He held forth in the line like a 245-pounder today, played sixty minutes a game, and in 1930 was one of the key figures, along with Frank Carideo and Marchy Schwarz, who brought an unofficial national championship to Notre Dame. He came to be one of Notre Dame's most famous players, right up there with George Gipp, the Four Horsemen, Johnny Lujack, George Connor, and Paul Hornung.

It is a safe bet there will never again be a 145-pound All-American guard in college football.

1921

Coach Hugo Bezdek introduces his Penn State shift.

1925

The first East-West Shrine game is played in San Francisco; each team is composed of selected college all-stars. The West wins, 6–0.

1926

The first electronic scoreboard is installed by the University of Wisconsin, first used in their game against Iowa.

1927

The goal posts are moved ten yards back from the goal line to the end line.

1927

Illegal use of the hands by a defender is defined to include striking a player. The penalty for such an infraction is disqualification of the player from the game and a penalty of half the distance to the goal line, regardless of where the line of scrimmage is.

1928

The Big Six conference (later to become the Big Eight) is formed at a meeting in Lincoln, Nebraska. Charter members include Iowa State, Kansas, Kansas State, Missouri, Nebraska, and Oklahoma.

The First Team to Fly

It was back in 1929 that a football coach first decided to *fly* his team to a game.

"Fly?" everyone asked. "Golly, where's he going to get all the planes? It would take the Graf Zeppelin to fly a whole football squad. And why fly? No sensible coach wants to field a team that's airsick!"

No, but you didn't build an athletic program in a little cow college by being *too* sensible, either. When Coach Roy Johnson came to the University of New Mexico in 1920, the enrollment was 227, and the football field didn't have any grass. The first day of practice each September was devoted to removing tumbleweeds, cacti, and some of the larger rocks. By 1927, Coach Johnson got tired of this; so, he borrowed a plow and a team, and planted grass. He watered it himself every morning. In his spare time, he taught Phys. Ed., coached boxing, baseball, track, golf, basketball, and—when there was water in the fire department pond—swimming.

The football team played nearby schools like Montezuma Seminary and occasionally got as far west as Arizona. Then came the big invitation from Occidental College to play in the huge new bowl in Pasadena!

Oxy was evidently reaching far for an opponent. Stanford and UCLA had the Rose Bowl booked for the afternoon of October 12, so Occidental had to settle for Friday night. Few coaches wanted to play under the lights, which were a novelty at the time. (Newsmen were still writing columns with titles like: "Night Baseball and the Mosquito.")

New Mexico had never played at night, but Coach Johnson agreed to try. He felt that a trip to California—the first one in the school's history—would be very educational for his ranch kids . . . and it might help recruiting, too.

His decision came just at the time that Albuquerque was delirious with "airline fever." In the summer of 1929, Charles A. Lindbergh helped organize Transcontinental Air Transport (T.A.T.), the first line with a coast-to-coast schedule. The passengers travelled by train at night and by plane in the daytime, and the segment from Clovis, N. M., to Albuquerque and on to Los Angeles was entirely by air. The line had four or five huge Ford Tri-Motors that carried 12 passengers each.

Caught up in the fever, Coach Johnson decided that the team should fly to the big game, but as a wily strategist, he prepared public opinion by calling several press conferences to say that flying was out of the question. That started the citizens talking, and soon they were all begging him to reconsider. Slowly he gave in, and he finally agreed that every boy who brought a note from his parents—and promised to study on the trip—would have an airplane ride.

Yet T.A.T. didn't have enough space. Even by adding its one spare plane, it could provide only about 18 seats. You see, it did have a few other paying passengers.

"Eighteen seats will be fine," said the coach. "Because of the risk of air-sickness, we'll send our best eleven boys to Los Angeles by train, and the subs will go in the planes. Then for the return trip, they will switch, and everyone will get a plane ride."

The train group left town quietly that Thursday at 3:45 a.m., and the subs assembled at the Albuquerque Airport before a cheering crowd the same morning at 10. One-fifth of the town's adult population was on hand to see history in the making.

The pilots took them across Arizona, buzzing herds of antelope and detouring over the Grand Canyon for fun, and the boys reached Los Angeles in time to motor out to Pasadena for a little practice under the lights. But where was the first team? Still on the train! They did not encounter the lights (henceforth described in school annals as "those glaring lights") until the night of the game itself.

Coach Johnson's precautions against air-sickness led to the great strategic error of the trip. The New Mexico starters had difficulty adjusting to the lights. Not once did they manage to catch and hold a punt.

The Oxy team was notably stronger, too, and the New Mexico boys were awed by the size of the Rose Bowl and the huge crowd of 17,000.

Most troublesome was the fact that the ball was white and the Occidental jerseys were white, too. When Oxy carried the ball, it was well-nigh invisible. (Coach Johnson later persuaded his old coach, Fielding Yost of Michigan, to get the rules changed so that the ball makes a contrast.)

The game ended with a 26 to 0 loss for New Mexico, but everyone enjoyed the trip and the University was proud to have the first aerial team in history.

The business manager on that flight, Tom Popejoy, later became president of the University. T.A.T. eventually became Trans World Airlines, and now has much bigger planes. The trip across the West is much faster, but the pilots don't buzz antelope anymore.

(The preceeding article first appeared in a Michigan State program.)

1930

Jay Berwanger of Chicago, the first recipient of the Downtown Athletic Club's Heisman Trophy in 1935.

Whittingham's All-Americans

FIRST TEAM

Position	Player	School
E	Don Hutson	Alabama
E	Larry Kelley	Yale
T	Ed Widseth	Minnesota
T	Nick Drahos	Cornell
G	Ralph Heikkinen	Michigan
G	Bill Corbus	Stanford
C	Alex Wojciechowicz	Fordham
B	Sammy Baugh	Texas Christian
B	Tom Harmon	Michigan
B	Jay Berwanger	Chicago
B	Marshall Goldberg	Pittsburgh
Coach	Howard Jones	USC

SECOND TEAM

Position	Player	School
E	Wayne Millner	Notre Dame
E	Gaynell Tinsley	Louisiana State
T	Ed Beinor	Notre Dame
T	Ernie Smith	USC
G	Biggie Munn	Minnesota
G	Harry Smith	USC
C	Chuck Bernard	Michigan
B	Harry Newman	Michigan
B	Whizzer White	Colorado
B	Clint Frank	Yale
B	Marchy Schwarz	Notre Dame
Coach	Jock Sutherland	Pittsburgh

Tom Harmon of Michigan, All-American in 1939 and 1940, and Heisman Trophy honoree in 1940.

1932

The Southeastern Conference comes into being. Its original members: Alabama, Auburn, Florida, Georgia, Georgia Tech, Kentucky, Louisiana State, Mississippi, Mississippi State, Sewanee, Tennessee, Tulane, and Vanderbilt.

1934

The first College All-Star game is played at Soldier Field in Chicago. More than 79,000 people watch the college stars under coach Nobel Kizer of Purdue battle to a scoreless tie against the 1933 NFL champs, the Chicago Bears, coached by George Halas.

1935

The first Heisman Trophy is awarded to Jay Berwanger, right halfback for the University of Chicago. The first Coach of the Year Award, selected by vote of the American Football Coaches Association, goes to Lynn Waldorf of Northwestern.

1935

The first official Orange Bowl game is played in Miami, with Bucknell demolishing Miami (Fla.) 26–0.

1935

The first Sugar Bowl game is played at Tulane Stadium in New Orleans, where Tulane defeats Temple by the score of 20–14.

1937

The first Cotton Bowl game is held in Dallas, where Texas Christian defeats Marquette 16–6.

1938

The first official Blue-Gray game, with selected all-stars from Northern colleges on the Blue and those representing Southern colleges on the Gray, is played in Montgomery, Alabama. The Blue win 7–0.

Camp's Last All-Americans

What a group they were. The illustrious eleven that Walter Camp selected as his 1924 All-America team were among the finest ever to toil on a football field. What a difficult time he must have had in choosing from that season of prime players; the backs alone toll the bells of legend. At Notre Dame there were the Four Horsemen, at Illinois Red Grange, at Stanford Ernie Nevers, at Alabama Johnny Mack Brown, at Michigan Benny Friedman, and at Washington Wildcat Wilson.

Many of them didn't make Camp's select group, and some that did stirred a little controversy. But they were a special group, gridiron greats who were destined for success in life after football as well. What happened to Walter Camp's last All-America team?

E Charlie Berry (Lafayette). After college he played two years of pro football with the Pottstown Maroons, then changed sports and signed on as a catcher for the Philadelphia Athletics and later played for the Boston Red Sox and the Chicago White Sox. After 13 years in the

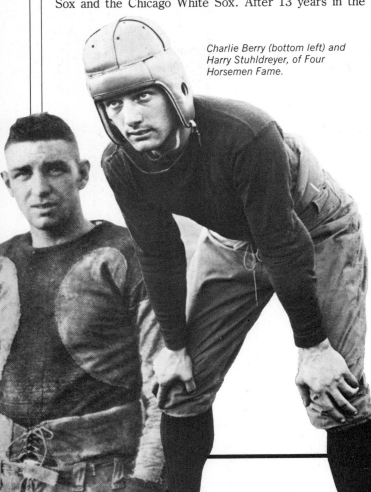

Charlie Berry (bottom left) and Harry Stuhldreyer, of Four Horsemen Fame.

majors, he retired with a lifetime batting average of .267. Later he worked for 19 years as an umpire in the American League and as a referee in the National Football League.

E Henry Bjorkman (Dartmouth). He chose Wall Street and became a successful stockbroker and analyst in New York.

T Ed Weir (Nebraska). He joined the pros and served with the Frankford Yellow Jackets for two years. Then he returned to his alma mater as track coach, where his teams won ten outdoor and indoor collegiate titles.

T Ed McGinley (Pennsylvania). He joined the banking world and rose to be a top executive with New York's Chemical Bank and Trust Company.

G Ed Slaughter (Michigan). He stayed in the college sports world, ending up on the football staff of the University of Virginia and as head golf coach.

G Babe Horrell (California). He invested widely in real estate in California, operated an apple farm and an orange orchard, owned a produce company, and had major financial interests in two golf courses.

C Ed Garbisch (Army). After marrying the daughter of Walter P. Chrysler, he worked his way up to the board chairmanship of the Grocery Store Products Company of New York, and also became a major collector of primitive American art.

QB Harry Stuhldreyer (Notre Dame). He played a year with the Brooklyn franchise in the fledgling American Football League, then went into coaching, for 12 years at Villanova and 11 at the University of Wisconsin. After that he became an executive with the U.S. Steel Corporation.

HB Red Grange (Illinois). He joined the Chicago Bears and went with them on a nationwide pro football junket, earning somewhere in the vicinity of $250,000 for the two months of the tour. After his pro career ended years later, he remained for a while as an assistant coach, ran a successful insurance business, and forged another career as a radio and television commentator on football.

HB Walt Koppisch (Columbia). He became the player/coach of the Buffalo Bisons in the NFL his first year out of college, and the next year moved cross-state to play for the New York Giants. After that he became a stockbroker on Wall Street and later an investigator for the Securities and Exchange Commission.

FB Homer Hazel (Rutgers). He became a football and basketball coach and eventually athletic director at the University of Mississippi. He also became a golf pro and worked as a labor relations manager.

1940

Whittingham's All-Americans

FIRST TEAM

Position	Player	School
E	Leon Hart	Notre Dame
E	Hub Bechtol	Texas
T	George Connor	Notre Dame
T	Leo Nomellini	Minnesota
G	Alex Agase	Illinois
G	Bill Fischer	Notre Dame
C	Chuck Bednarik	Pennsylvania
QB	Johnny Lujack	Notre Dame
RB	Glenn Davis	Army
RB	Charlie Trippi	Georgia
RB	Doc Blanchard	Army
Coach	Frank Leahy	Notre Dame

SECOND TEAM

Position	Player	School
E	Barney Poole	Army/Mississippi
E	Hank Foldberg	Army
T	Al Wistert	Michigan
T	Dick Wildung	Minnesota
G	Rod Franz	California
G	Joe Steffy	Army
C	Clayton Tonnemaker	Minnesota
QB	Bobby Layne	Texas
RB	Frank Sinkwich	Georgia
RB	Doak Walker	SMU
RB	Steve Van Buren	Louisiana State
Coach	Earl Blaik	Army

George Connor played tackle for Holy Cross (1942–43) and Notre Dame (1946–47).

1940

On October 5, Maryland meets Pennsylvania in the first televised college football game. (The first television coverage of college football actually occurred the year before when NBC telecast a Fordham practice session in New York, with Bill Stern handling the commentary.)

1941

Free substitution is allowed, and substitutes are permitted to communicate immediately with their teammates on the field, and therefore can bring in plays from the sideline.

1945

Cecil Isbell of Purdue becomes the first coach in history to direct his team from the press box, and his Boilermakers defeat Ohio State 35–13.

1946

The first Gator Bowl game is played in Jacksonville, Florida, with Wake Forest beating South Carolina by the score of 26–14.

Johnny Lattner of Notre Dame, Heisman Trophy winner for 1953 and a consensus All-American in both his junior and senior year.

1946

The Outland Award, a trophy to honor the outstanding interior lineman of the year, with the selection made by a vote among the members of the Football Writers Association of America, is instituted. The first recipient is George Connor, tackle for Notre Dame.

1947

The Tangerine Bowl begins in Orlando, Florida, with Catawba beating Maryville, 31–6. In 1983, the name of the game is changed to the Florida Citrus Bowl.

1949

Tom Nugent, head coach at Virginia Military Institute, introduces the I formation, which features all the running backs lined up in a row behind the quarterback. Nugent goes on to success at Florida State and the University of Maryland, while his new formation gains fame when used by Frank Leahy at Notre Dame in 1951.

1950

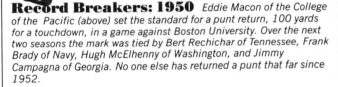

Whittingham's All-Americans

FIRST TEAM

Position	Player	School
E	Bill McColl	Stanford
E	Ron Kramer	Michigan
T	Alex Karras	Iowa
T	Dick Modzelewski	Maryland
G	Les Richter	California
G	Jim Parker	Ohio State
C	Bob Pellegrini	Maryland
QB	Babe Parilli	Kentucky
RB	Billy Cannon	Louisiana State
RB	Johnny Lattner	Notre Dame
RB	Jim Brown	Syracuse
Coach	Bud Wilkinson	Oklahoma

SECOND TEAM

Position	Player	School
E	Ron Beagle	Navy
E	Dan Foldberg	Army
T	Bob Gain	Kentucky
T	Jim Weatherall	Oklahoma
G	Calvin Jones	Iowa
G	Bob Ward	Maryland
C	Jerry Tubbs	Oklahoma
QB	Jack Scarbath	Maryland
RB	Paul Giel	Minnesota
RB	Howard Cassady	Ohio State
RB	Alan Ameche	Wisconsin
Coach	Duffy Daugherty	Michigan State

Jim Parker (left) played guard and linebacker for Woody Hayes at Ohio State. Parker received the Outland Trophy in 1956. Howard "Hopalong" Cassady, Ohio State's great halfback of the mid-1950s, won the Heisman and Maxwell trophies in 1955.

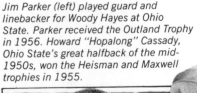

Record Breakers: 1950 *Eddie Macon of the College of the Pacific (above) set the standard for a punt return, 100 yards for a touchdown, in a game against Boston University. Over the next two seasons the mark was tied by Bert Rechichar of Tennessee, Frank Brady of Navy, Hugh McElhenny of Washington, and Jimmy Campagna of Georgia. No one else has returned a punt that far since 1952.*

1951

The televising of college football games on Saturday afternoons is approved by the NCAA, but restricted to only one game in each area per Saturday.

1953

The Atlantic Coast Conference is founded with seven charter members: Clemson, Duke, Maryland, North Carolina, North Carolina State, South Carolina, and Wake Forest.

1953

Free substitution is eliminated, and the game of college football reverts to one of single platoon.

1956

The Ivy League is formally organized as an athletic conference, consisting of eight universities: Brown, Columbia, Cornell, Dartmouth, Harvard, Pennsylvania, Princeton, and Yale. Winner of the first Ivy League crown is Yale, under head coach Jordan Olivar, with a conference record of 7-0 and an overall record of 8-1.

1958

The two-point conversion after a touchdown in lieu of the kicked extra point is introduced.

1959

The first Bluebonnet Bowl is held in Houston Texas, on December 19. Visiting Clemson easily beats the natives from Texas Christian, 23–7.

1959

The first Liberty Bowl game is played on December 19 in Philadelphia, Pennsylvania, as Penn State beats Alabama 7–0. By 1965 the game makes a permanent home for itself in Memphis, Tennessee.

Record Breakers:
1956 *Jim Brown of Syracuse, consensus All-American in 1956, holds the record for the most points scored in a college football game, a total of 43, on six touchdowns and seven extra points, playing against Colgate.*

1960

Whittingham's All-Americans

OFFENSE

Position	Player	School
E	Howard Twilley	Tulsa
E	Mike Ditka	Pittsburgh
T	Ralph Neely	Oklahoma
T	Ron Yary	USC
G	Rick Redman	Washington
G	Dick Arrington	Notre Dame
C	Lee Roy Jordan	Alabama
QB	Roger Staubach	Navy
RB	O. J. Simpson	USC
RB	Gale Sayers	Kansas
RB	Ernie Davis	Syracuse

DEFENSE

Position	Player	School
E	Bubba Smith	Michigan State
E	Ted Hendricks	Miami (Florida)
T	Bob Lilly	Texas Christian
T	Carl Eller	Minnesota
G	Jim Stillwagon	Oklahoma
LB	Dick Butkus	Illinois
LB	Tommy Nobis	Texas
LB	Steve Kiner	Tennessee
DB	Jack Tatum	Ohio State
DB	George Webster	Michigan State
DB	Johnny Roland	Missouri
Coach	Ara Parseghian	Notre Dame

Tommy Nobis, two-time All-American linebacker from Texas (1964–65) won the Outland Trophy his senior year and was one of only a few linemen ever to be awarded the Maxwell Trophy.

Record Breakers: 1963 *A halfback with seemingly superhuman moves, Gale Sayers of Kansas earned All-American honors in 1963 and 1964. He averaged 6.5 yards a carry over three seasons, and set the record for the longest run from scrimmage when he raced 99 yards for a touchdown against Nebraska (since tied by Max Anderson of Arizona State, Ralph Thompson of West Texas State, and Kelsey Finch of Tennessee).*

1962

The Western Athletic Conference is inaugurated, initially comprising Arizona, Arizona State, Brigham Young, New Mexico, Utah, and Wyoming.

1964

Unlimited substitution is restored, and platooning becomes the accepted mode of play.

1968

Coach Darrell Royal of Texas perfects the wishbone, or triple option offense. A staple of college football in the seventies and early eighties, the formation gives the quarterback the option of handing off to the fullback or rolling out with the ball and running it himself or pitching out to the halfback.

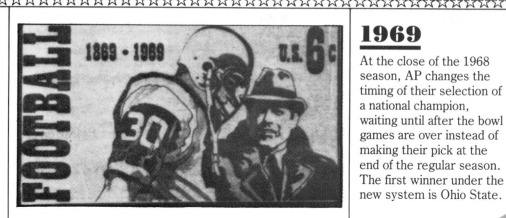

1969

At the close of the 1968 season, AP changes the timing of their selection of a national champion, waiting until after the bowl games are over instead of making their pick at the end of the regular season. The first winner under the new system is Ohio State.

1968

Atlanta, Georgia hosts the first Peach Bowl game on December 30, as LSU beats Florida State 31–27.

1969

The Pacific Coast Athletic Association is formed. Charter members: California/Long Beach, California/Los Angeles, California/Santa Barbara, Fresno State, Pacific, San Diego State, and San Jose State.

1969

Intercollegiate football celebrates its one-hundredth anniversary. Commemorations of the event include a special stamp, issued in a ceremony in New Brunswick, New Jersey, site of the first game.

Record Breakers:
1966 *Quarterback Virgil Carter of Brigham Young set the current record for total offense yards in a single game in 1966 when he racked up 599 yards, 86 rushing and 513 passing, against Texas-El Paso.*

1970

Whittingham's All-Americans

OFFENSE

Position	Player	School
WR	Johnny Rodgers	Nebraska
WR	Lynn Swann	USC
TE	Kellen Winslow	Missouri
T	Jerry Sisemore	Texas
T	Chris Ward	Ohio State
G	Chip Kell	Tennessee
G	Mark Donahue	Michigan
C	Jim Ritcher	North Carolina State
QB	Jim Plunkett	Stanford
RB	Tony Dorsett	Pittsburgh
RB	Archie Griffin	Ohio State

DEFENSE

Position	Player	School
E	Ross Browner	Notre Dame
E	Hugh Green	Pittsburgh
T	Randy White	Maryland
T	Lee Roy Selmon	Oklahoma
LB	Randy Grandishar	Ohio State
LB	Jerry Robinson	UCLA
LB	Tom Cousineau	Ohio State
DB	Dennis Thurman	USC
DB	Johnie Johnson	Texas
DB	Ken Easley	UCLA
DB	Dave Brown	Michigan
Coach	Paul Bryant	Alabama

Notre Dame's defensive end Ross Browner (left) won the Outland Award in 1976 and took the Vince Lombardi Trophy in 1977. Lee Roy Selmon, defensive tackle for Oklahoma, preceeded him as recipient of both the Outland and Vince Lombardi trophies in 1975.

1971

The first Fiesta Bowl game is held on December 27 in Tempe, Arizona. The local favorites prevail as Arizona State beats Florida State 45–38.

1975

UPI joins AP in waiting until after the bowl games are over to select a national champion. They don't agree on their selections though, as UPI picks USC and AP chooses Oklahoma.

1976

The first Independence Bowl game is played in Shreveport, Louisiana, on December 13. McNeese State edges out Tulsa 20–16.

Record Breakers:

1978 Eddie Lee Ivery of Georgia Tech used moves like this to set the single game rushing standard when he ran for 356 yards on 26 carries against the Air Force Academy. Rueben Mayes of Washington State passed him in 1984 with a 357-yard rushing effort, but Mayes carried the ball 39 times, averaging far below Ivery's record-setting 13.7 yards per carry.

Record Breakers:

1977 Both Steve Little (right) of Arkansas and Russell Erxleben of Texas booted record-setting field goals of 67 yards in 1977. Their mark was tied the next year by Joe Williams (left) of Wichita State.

1978

Sunny San Diego, California hosts the first Holiday Bowl, on December 22. The visitor from the East, Navy, beats Brigham Young 23–16.

1980

Whittingham's All-Americans

OFFENSE

Position	Player	School
WR	Anthony Carter	Michigan
WR	Irving Fryar	Nebraska
TE	Gordon Hudson	Brigham Young
T	Mark May	Pittsburgh
T	Don Mosebar	USC
G	Dean Steinkuhler	Nebraska
G	Mike Pitts	Alabama
C	Dave Rimington	Nebraska
QB	Jim McMahon	Brigham Young
RB	Herschel Walker	Georgia
RB	Marcus Allen	USC

DEFENSE

Position	Player	School
E	E. J. Junior	Alabama
E	Billy Ray Smith	Arkansas
T	Ken Sims	Texas
T	Reggie White	Tennessee
LB	Lawrence Taylor	North Carolina
LB	Mike Singletary	Baylor
LB	Rick Hunley	Arizona
DB	Terry Kinard	Clemson
DB	Ronnie Lott	USC
DB	Russell Carter	SMU
DB	Mike Richardson	Arizona State
Coach	Joe Paterno	Penn State

Nebraska's two-time Outland Trophy winner (1981 and 1982), center Dave Rimington.

1982

On December 29, Alabama defeats Illinois 21–15 in the Liberty Bowl, giving coach Paul "Bear" Bryant his final triumph. With 323 career victories, Bryant retires as the winningest college football coach ever.

1982

In a major restructuring, the NCAA splits its Division 1 into two parts. Ninety-seven schools remain in the newly created Division 1-A, while forty others choose to join the somewhat less intense Division 1-AA.

1982

Christmas Day sees the first Aloha Bowl game, held in Honolulu, Hawaii. The game is no gift as Washington works hard to earn a 21–20 victory over Maryland.

Record Breakers:

1980 *Dave Wilson of Illinois, holder of the mark for most yards passing in a single game, 621, against Ohio State. He also accounted for 585 total offense yards (sacks accounted for his 36-yard loss rushing) in the same game, second only to Virgil Carter's record of 599.*

1985

The Missouri Valley Conference, forerunner of the Big Eight, announces it will no longer sponsor college football after the 1985 season. Only two schools, Tulsa and Wichita State, will remain in Division 1-A, as the others move on to 1-AA level competition.

Record Breakers:

1982 *Sandy Schwab, a freshman at Northwestern, broke the record for pass completions in a single game in 1982 when he completed 45 against Michigan.*

they haven't come close to a national title and have conquered the SEC only once. That was in 1950 when Bear Bryant was their head coach, and All-Americans Vito "Babe" Parilli and Bob Gain respectively led the offense and defense. Bryant, incidentally, is the only coach in Kentucky's history with a winning record in the SEC (22-18-4 within the conference and 60-23-5 overall).

Ole Miss had its good years from 1947 to 1970 under John Vaught, who won the conference crown his first year as head coach. He won it five more times while compiling an impressive record of 190-60-12. That first year, his Mississippi Rebels were blessed with All-Americans like quarterback Charlie Conerly and all-purpose end Barney Poole.

Arch-rival of Ole Miss, Mississippi State has only been able to claim the conference championship once in its history, in 1941 under Allyn McKeen. But they have had some of the game's more famous coaches, such as Darrell Royal and Murray Warmath.

Florida is the only team in the conference yet to win an official title. The Gators did in fact take the SEC crown in 1984 but it was vacated because of recruiting violations, and the NCAA took them off the list of champs. Coach Charley Pell was forced to leave as a result of the scandal. Florida had also come close several times during the reign of Red Graves in the 1960s, Florida's winningest coach, when Steve Spurrier was their quarterback. In the 1980s the Gators have had a winning season and gone to a bowl game each year, except for their ill-fated 1984 season.

Southeastern Conference Champions

Year	School	Year	School
1933	Alabama	1959	Georgia
1934	Alabama	1960	Mississippi
	Tulane	1961	Alabama
1935	LSU		LSU
1936	LSU	1962	Mississippi
1937	Alabama	1963	Mississippi
1938	Tennessee	1964	Alabama
1939	Georgia Tech	1965	Alabama
	Tennessee	1966	Alabama
	Tulane		Georgia
1940	Tennessee	1967	Tennessee
1941	Mississippi State	1968	Georgia
1942	Georgia	1969	Tennessee
1943	Georgia Tech	1970	LSU
1944	Georgia Tech	1971	Alabama
1945	Alabama	1972	Alabama
1946	Georgia	1973	Alabama
	Tennessee	1974	Alabama
1947	Mississippi	1975	Alabama
1948	Georgia	1976	Georgia
1949	Tulane		Kentucky
1950	Kentucky	1977	Alabama
1951	Georgia Tech	1978	Alabama
	Tennessee	1979	Alabama
1952	Georgia Tech	1980	Georgia
1953	Alabama	1981	Alabama
1954	Mississippi		Georgia
1955	Mississippi	1982	Georgia
1956	Tennessee	1983	Auburn
1957	Auburn	1984	Florida*
1958	LSU		

*vacated

SOUTHWEST CONFERENCE

ARKANSAS
BAYLOR
HOUSTON
RICE
SMU
TEXAS
TEXAS A&M
TEXAS CHRISTIAN
TEXAS TECH

No state dominates a single major collegiate conference as Texas does the Southwest Conference. Eight of the nine universities currently enrolled in the conference are from the Lone Star State; only alien Arkansas crosses the border to challenge them.

In recent decades, however, the Razorbacks from Fayetteville, Arkansas, have provided plenty of competition for the Texas cartel, especially the University of Texas Longhorns. The rivalry between the two is probably as fierce as any in the country.

On the other hand, there is little doubt that the state of Texas has an adequate supply of football talent to populate a major conference. A survey conducted by the NCAA in the mid-1970s showed that Texas had produced more All-American football players in the previous quarter century than any state in the Union. As a regional proving ground for football excellence, Texas has proved itself, but its evolution toward national prominence was gradual.

The roots of today's Southwest Conference date back to 1911. In that year, spectator violence broke out in a game between Texas A&M and their rival, the University of Texas. Following the fracas, officials from both schools ordered an immediate stop to athletic events between the two universities. Largely as a result of that unpleasantness, representatives of the eight schools that became charter members of the Southwest Athletic Conference held two meetings at Dallas in 1914 to get the athletic program back on the right path.

The original members of the conference were Arkansas, Baylor, Oklahoma, Oklahoma A&M (today Oklahoma State), Rice, Southwestern of Texas, Texas, and Texas A&M. There was no conference champ in 1914; in 1915 Oklahoma and Baylor tied for the title, but Baylor was disqualified because of an ineligible

SOUTHWEST CONFERENCE NATIONAL CHAMPIONS		
Year	**Team**	**Coach**
1938	Texas Christian	Dutch Meyer
1939	Texas A&M	Homer Norton
1963	Texas	Darrell Royal
1964	Arkansas	Frank Broyles
1969	Texas	Darrell Royal

player. Over the next decade, however, Oklahoma, Southwestern, and Oklahoma A&M withdrew from the conference. Southern Methodist gained entry in 1918, Texas Christian in 1923, and Texas Tech in 1956 (but Tech did not start playing football until 1960).

The University of Houston, the youngest member of the Southwest Conference, entered, with authority in 1976, showing the kind of play that might be expected from a team that had its home field in the cavernous Astrodome. In its first year of official conference play, the Houston Cougars took the conference title, winning it again in 1978 and sharing the title in 1979 and 1984.

The most remarkable of the early Southwest Conference teams was undoubtedly Texas A&M, under head coach Dana Xenophon Bible. From 1917 through 1928, he turned much of the Southwest into his personal Bible Belt, winning five conference titles, giving a new dimension to the word *xenophobia,* in this case a well-warranted fear of the Texas Aggies.

In the eight-game schedule of 1917, the Aggies went undefeated, untied, and unscored upon. Bible might have repeated the feat the following season, but had to take time out to fly airplanes for the United States in World War I. But by 1919 he was back at the Aggies' helm and, astonishingly, once again moved through a season in which Texas A&M neither lost a game nor gave up a single point.

In the final game of the 1920 season, the Texas Longhorns finally managed to become the first team to score against the Bible-led Aggies—and the first team to beat them as well, winning 7–0. During Bible's remaining eight years at Texas A&M, only Texas, Baylor, and SMU provided significant competition.

Although Baylor's sole Southwest Conference championship in recent years came in 1980, the Bears were a powerhouse in the early years of the conference. Under Harvard-educated head coach Frank Bridges, featuring the high-scoring runner Wesley Bradshaw, Baylor captured conference titles in 1922 and again in 1924. Morley Jennings, coaching the

Dana Xenophon Bible on the sidelines for Texas during the last game of his 45-year college coaching career. His most notable tenures were at Texas A&M (1917, 1919–28), Nebraska (1926–36), and Texas (1937–46). His Longhorns gave him a departure gift that afternoon, defeating Bible's former employer, the A&M Aggies, 24–7.

Doak Walker, SMU's three-time All-American back (1947–49) prepares to hand off to fullback Dick McKissick during a "dummy scrimmage" down in Dallas.

Bears from 1926 through 1940, amassed the most wins at Baylor, 83, against 60 losses and 6 ties. In 1980, under Grant Teaff, they were 10-1 and then lost to Alabama in the Cotton Bowl, 30–2.

In the mid-1920s, Southern Methodist quarterbacks Logan Stollenwreck and Gerald Mann, under coach Ray Morrison, the winningest coach in Mustang history (82-31-20), introduced a high-powered passing attack while everyone else was concentrating on running the ball. As a result they copped conference titles in 1923 and 1926. In that four-year period, SMU lost only one conference game. In 1935, aided by the fine running of Bobby Wilson, the Mustangs went 12-0 for the season, but their most memorable days were when Doak Walker and Kyle Rote led the Mustang offense. Walker, a consensus All-American three years running, led SMU to conference championships in 1947 and 1948. Replacing Walker at tailback, Rote grabbed All-American honors in 1950. And then there was 1982, when Bobby Collins, in his first year as head coach, brought the Mustangs the closest they had ever come to a national championship. With an 11-0-1 record and a 7–3 victory over highly regarded Pittsburgh in the Cotton Bowl, Southern Methodist ended up second only to undefeated Penn State in the final AP rankings. Collins's success that year was due in large part to the

explosive running of consensus All-American Eric Dickerson.

The conference's renowned "aerial circus" came to fame in the late 1930s under Dutch Meyer at Texas Christian. "The Saturday Fox," as Meyer came to be known, practiced endless drills for every passing pattern and opened up opposing defenses by introducing the use of two split ends. The execution of his attack came at the hands of tailback Sammy Baugh.

"They said I had my ends sitting in the stands," Meyer once joked, "spread out so wide they could sell soda water between plays." Actually they were never spread out more than two or three yards, but it enabled them time and time again to get free to grab the pinpoint passes of Slingin' Sammy or Davey O'Brien.

While Baugh was the better known of the two, TCU won its only national championship under the passing of five-foot-six-inch, 150-pound O'Brien, the heir to Baugh's tailback slot. O'Brien was an elusive runner, fine passer, and superb team leader. In Meyer's tenure as the head of the Horned Frogs (1934–52), his teams won 109 games against 79 losses and 13 ties, capturing three conference crowns.

Dana Xenophon Bible, who had brought the Texas A&M Aggies to prominence earlier, was appointed head coach of the Texas Longhorns in 1937,

TCU's two immortal backs: Sammy Baugh (left) and Davey O'Brien, who is squirming in for a touchdown at the 1939 Sugar Bowl, a game in which he led the Horned Frogs to a 15–7 win over Carnegie Tech.

after having coached for eight years at Nebraska. But before Bible accepted the position, the entire Texas state legislature had to ponder his salary demands. The $15,000 annual salary agreed upon by Bible and university officials was higher than that being paid to the university president. The legislative body solved the dilemma by raising the president's pay.

With the question of remuneration behind him, Bible set to work building champions out of the Longhorns, who had fallen on hard times (the year before they were 2-6-1). The first two years under Bible were no better, but the cagey coach had put into effect what he called the "Bible Plan." In this plan, the entire state of Texas was divided into districts, and an alumnus was assigned to each with the task of recruiting the best high school athletes in it. It began to pay off in 1939 with the Longhorns' first winning season in five years. From 1940 through 1946, Bible's last year on the Texas sideline, his teams won 53 games against only 13 losses and 1 tie, with three conference crowns to boot. What Bible left his successor Blair Cherry was Bobby Layne, converted to the Southwest's first T-formation quarterback and a consensus All-American in 1947.

But the most gilded era of Longhorn football began with the arrival of Darrell Royal in 1957. During his 20 years as sideline commander, Texas won 167 games, lost but 47, tied 5, took two national championships, and won or shared 12 conference titles.

The kind of resurrection Bible wrought for the Longhorns in the 1940s was brought to the Texas A&M Aggies in the 1950s by Paul "Bear" Bryant. When the Bear came to College Station, Texas (today's mailing address is Aggieland, Texas), to assume head coaching duties in 1954, the Aggies hadn't won a

Timmy Trible (0), SMU's mascot and waterboy, does his job on the Mustang sideline. Slaking his thirst is Timmy's idol, 1948 Heisman honoree Doak Walker.

conference championship since 1941. Bryant's debut was awful (1-9-0), but over the next three years he won 24 games, lost just 4, tied 2, and gave A&M a conference crown before moving on to Alabama.

The interloper, Arkansas, had won conference titles under Fred Thomsen in 1936, John Barnhill in 1946, and Bowden Wyatt in 1954, times when they had featured All-Americans of the caliber of end Jim Benton and back Clyde "Smackover" Scott. But it was after 1958, the year Frank Broyles signed on as head coach, that the Razorbacks surged to national acclaim. Broyles guided the destinies of 19 Arkansas teams and stoked a rivalry with the University of Texas and Darrell Royal that was not only incendiary but provided some of the finest college football games in history. In 1964, the two teams met midway through the season, both undefeated and ranked in the top five in the nation, both gunning for the national championship. It was a game that went back and forth down to the final seconds. Before a frenetic mob of hometown fans, the Texas Longhorns came back to score with just a little

Clyde "Smackover" Scott was not only an All-American back for Arkansas in 1948, but also a silver-medal hurdler at the Olympic Games in London that year.

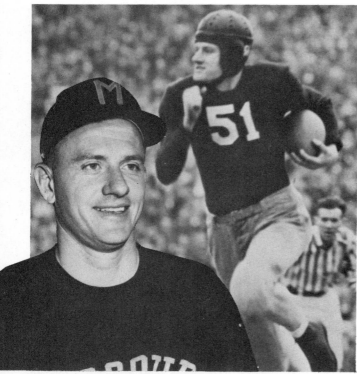

Frank Broyles as coach (left) and player, toting the ball for Georgia Tech in the 1944 Sugar Bowl—his Yellow Jackets came from behind to beat Tulsa 20–18 and his winning ways continued in his coaching career.

Southwest Conference Champions

Year	School	Year	School
1914	No champion	1953	Rice
1915	Oklahoma		Texas
1916	No champion	1954	Arkansas
1917	Texas A&M	1955	TCU
1918	No champion	1956	Texas A&M
1919	Texas A&M	1957	Rice
1920	Texas	1958	TCU
1921	Texas A&M	1959	Arkansas
1922	Baylor		Texas
1923	SMU		TCU
1924	Baylor	1960	Arkansas
1925	Texas A&M	1961	Arkansas
1926	SMU		Texas
1927	Texas A&M	1962	Texas
1928	Texas	1963	Texas
1929	TCU	1964	Arkansas
1930	Texas	1965	Arkansas
1931	SMU	1966	SMU
1932	TCU	1967	Texas A&M
1933	No champion	1968	Arkansas
1934	Rice		Texas
1935	SMU	1969	Texas
1936	Arkansas	1970	Texas
1937	Rice	1971	Texas
1938	TCU	1972	Texas
1939	Texas A&M	1973	Texas
1940	SMU	1974	Baylor
	Texas A&M	1975	Arkansas
1941	Texas A&M		Texas
1942	Texas		Texas A&M
1943	Texas	1976	Houston
1944	TCU		Texas Tech
1945	Texas	1977	Texas
1946	Arkansas	1978	Houston
	Rice	1979	Arkansas
1947	SMU		Houston
1948	Rice	1980	Baylor
1949	Rice	1981	SMU
1950	Texas	1982	SMU
1951	TCU	1983	Texas
1952	Texas	1984	Houston
			SMU

more than a minute to play in the game, putting them within a point of Arkansas, 14–13. Royal chose not to go for the tie and instead gambled on the two-point conversion. It failed. Arkansas won, then went on to triumph in the rest of their games that year, ending with a record of 10-0-0. AP and UPI, however, ranked unbeaten Alabama ahead of them at season's end, but on New Year's Day, Texas beat Alabama in the Orange Bowl while Arkansas whipped Nebraska in the Cotton Bowl, showing who truly was number one.

Broyles-led teams won or shared seven conference championships, and his record of 144-58-5 endeared him forever to Arkansans everywhere (the athletic complex on campus is named for him).

Five different teams have won the Southwest Conference title in the ten years from 1975 to 1984, illustrating just how competitive the Texans and their intruder from "up-country"—as Arkansas is referred to by some of the down-home boys from the Lone Star State—really are.

The spectacular Eric Dickerson (19) of SMU overruns Arkansas' Nathan Jones in a 1982 Southwest Conference contest. The game ended in a 17–17 tie, the only blemish on the Mustangs 11-0-1 record that year, and the game that forced them to settle for second place in the national rankings.

BIG EIGHT CONFERENCE

COLORADO
IOWA STATE
KANSAS
KANSAS STATE
MISSOURI
NEBRASKA
OKLAHOMA
OKLAHOMA STATE

Dynasties come and go in all the major conferences, but two teams—Nebraska and Oklahoma—have almost universally dominated the Big Eight since its inception. Of the 86 conference titles that have been claimed over the years, those two schools have collected or shared 63. Only Missouri has won more than can be counted on your hands, 12, while Kansas has five to its credit, Iowa State and Oklahoma State two, and Colorado and Kansas State one apiece.

The Big Eight as it stands today was not formed until the closing years of Bud Wilkinson's dynasty at Oklahoma, 1958 to be precise. It evolved from other conferences, comprising most of the same schools.

Early in 1907, Iowa, Kansas, Missouri, Nebraska, and Washington University (St. Louis) gathered to form the Missouri Valley Intercollegiate Athletic Association. The following year, Drake and Iowa State (then known as Ames College) joined. But in 1911, Iowa moved to the Big Ten. Kansas State came aboard in 1913, Grinnell in 1919, Oklahoma in 1920, and Oklahoma State (then Oklahoma A&M) in 1925.

At a meeting in Lincoln, Nebraska, in 1928, six of the seven state schools in the association (Oklahoma State abstaining) organized a new conference and called it the Big Six. It became the Big Seven in 1947 when Colorado was admitted, and the Big Eight in 1957 when Oklahoma State rejoined.

Ultimate success on the national level, to which Oklahoma and Nebraska have become so accustomed in the latter half of the 20th century, was not achieved until 1950 when Bud Wilkinson and his Sooners brought the crown to the Big Eight for the first time. This is not to say, however, that there weren't superb teams, coaches, and players before that.

In his book *Big Eight Football*, John D. McCallum described one of the conference's early contributions to the game of football: "Generally unrecognized, Oklahoma played a considerable role in popularizing the forward pass. Having lost all their regulars following a 6-2-0 record in 1913, the Sooners decided to pin their hopes on an aerial circus the next season. Coach Bennie Owen adopted what was described as 'a wide-open, reckless attack,' and it paid off handsomely.

Oklahoma scored the most points (435) of any major team in the nation on the way to nine wins, one loss, and one tie."

Unfortunately, because of the isolation of the Southwest in those days, Oklahoma's novel offense was scarcely noticed by the rest of the nation. By 1915, the explosive Sooners were averaging between 30 and 35 passes a game, high even by modern standards.

During the same era, Ewald "Jumbo" Stiehm was building powerful teams at Nebraska. From 1911 to 1915, his Cornhuskers won 35 games, lost 2 (both to Minnesota), tied 3, and collected four Missouri

Byron "Whizzer" White, Colorado's All-American back (1937), Rhodes Scholar, and U.S. Supreme Court Justice (appointed in 1962 by another football enthusiast, John F. Kennedy).

Valley Association championships. Nebraska crowned its first golden era in 1915 when, largely due to the leadership and exploits of the great end and back Guy Chamberlain, they beat a highly regarded Notre Dame team, 20–19. The victory brought national attention to "Champ" Chamberlain and the rest of the Nebraska team. "With the win over Notre Dame, Nebraska has definitely come of age," *The New York Times* declared. "It must be ranked with the major powers." And Chamberlain was a consensus All-American.

In 1921, Nebraska and Oklahoma played a game in the mud that was to have special significance in football lore. The Cornhuskers, then coached by Fred T. Dawson, walloped the Sooners 44–0 that afternoon despite the muck and mire. The reason for Nebraska's success in such conditions was given in a newspaper account of the game: "The Huskers had specially designed conical mud spikes, three inches in length, on their shoes, which prevented them from sinking in and gave them a fairly firm hold in the mud. . . . Rubber soles kept the mud from sticking to the shoes." Soon after, specially cleated shoes, often called "mudders" in those days, were added to the equipment stock of many major colleges.

Colorado had one of its most exciting periods in the 1930s, before it was a conference member, although the Buffalos regularly played some

Gale Sayers of Kansas steps out against Nebraska in 1963, the first of his two All-American seasons.

BIG EIGHT NATIONAL CHAMPIONS		
Year	**Team**	**Coach**
1950	Oklahoma	Bud Wilkinson
1955	Oklahoma	Bud Wilkinson
1956	Oklahoma	Bud Wilkinson
1970	Nebraska	Bob Devaney
1971	Nebraska	Bob Devaney
1974	Oklahoma	Barry Switzer
1975	Oklahoma	Barry Switzer

of the Big Six teams. That was the time when Byron "Whizzer" White lugged the ball for them, earning consensus All-American honors before taking his Rhodes Scholarship to Oxford, and eventually, a seat on the bench of the U.S. Supreme Court.

It took Colorado 14 years to win the Big Seven after joining it in 1947. That was in 1961, under Sonny Grandelius, a team that also ranked seventh in the nation. In 1976, with Bill Mallory as head coach, they shared the title with Oklahoma and Oklahoma State.

Kansas won its first conference crown all the way back in 1908, but did not win another until 1930. Under George Sauer in his only two years at Kansas, the Jayhawks shared back-to-back titles with Oklahoma in 1946 and 1947. Again they shared a championship in 1968 when Pepper Rodgers was at the helm. But some of the most memorable afternoons were in non-title years in the sixties, first under quarterback John Hadl and subsequently when Gale Sayers dazzled opponents and spectators alike with his remarkable running.

Missouri won three conference titles in the 1920s under Gwinn Henry, and another three between 1939 and 1942 when Don Faurot was the Tiger coach. Probably the two finest teams ever to play at Missouri were the 1939 Tigers, ranked sixth in the country, with All-American tailback Paul Christman, and the 1960 team under Dan Devine, which claimed the fifth spot.

Kansas State earned a title in 1934 under Lynn "Pappy" Waldorf; Oklahoma A&M won one in 1926 and not another until Jim Stanley guided them in 1976. Iowa State, coached by Clyde Williams, shared Missouri Valley Association titles with Nebraska back in 1911 and 1912, but has never reached the conference summit since.

Oklahoma, on the other hand, has merited 29 titles since its first in 1920. Jim Tatum got the Sooners to the top of the conference in 1946, then turned over the reins to Bud Wilkinson the next year, and the fabulous Oklahoma dynasty was launched. During the ten years that the conference stood as the Big Seven

Dan Faurot is hoisted in triumph after his last game as head coach of Missouri in 1956, which his Tigers won over Kansas 15–13.

and the first year of the Big Eight, Wilkinson's Sooners not only triumphed easily each year but never lost a *single* conference game during those 11 years. His 1950 team, with Billy Vessels and Leon Heath in the backfield, won the national title; and the squads of 1955 and 1956, which featured the great running of Tommy McDonald, repeated that honor.

If the 1950s belonged to the Oklahoma Sooners, the period from the mid-60s into the early '70s surely was the prize possession of Nebraska. Coached by Bob Devaney, the Cornhuskers won or shared eight conference titles in the ten years between 1963 and 1972. In 1970 and 1971, behind the quarterbacking of Jerry Tagge, Nebraska won consecutive national titles. In the second, the Cornhuskers edged out conference colleagues Oklahoma (number two) and Colorado (number three) for the crown. Devaney coached one more year after that and then in 1973 he turned the job over to Tom Osborne, who would keep Nebraska in the nation's top ten for eight of the next ten years.

In 1974 and 1975, Oklahoma rode back to the number one ranking behind the deft piloting of Barry Switzer. And between 1973 and 1980, Switzer's Sooners won or shared the conference championship every year. Then Nebraska revived and gave Tom Osborne successive conference titles from 1981 through 1983.

Since 1961 either Oklahoma or Nebraska has been at the top of the Big Eight Conference at the end of the season.

Big Eight Conference Champions

MISSOURI VALLEY

Year	School
1907	Iowa
	Nebraska
1908	Kansas
1909	Missouri
1910	Nebraska
1911	Iowa State
	Nebraska
1912	Iowa State
	Nebraska
1913	Missouri
	Nebraska
1914	Nebraska
1915	Nebraska
1916	Nebraska
1917	Nebraska
1918	No champion because of World War I
1919	Missouri
1920	Oklahoma
1921	Nebraska
1922	Nebraska
1923	Nebraska
1924	Missouri
1925	Missouri
1926	Oklahoma A&M
1927	Missouri

BIG SIX

1928	Nebraska
1929	Nebraska
1930	Kansas
1931	Nebraska
1932	Nebraska
1933	Nebraska
1934	Kansas State
1935	Nebraska
1936	Nebraska
1937	Nebraska
1938	Oklahoma
1939	Missouri
1940	Nebraska
1941	Missouri
1942	Missouri
1943	Oklahoma
1944	Oklahoma
1945	Missouri
1946	Kansas
	Oklahoma
1947	Kansas
	Oklahoma

BIG SEVEN

Year	School
1948	Oklahoma
1949	Oklahoma
1950	Oklahoma
1951	Oklahoma
1952	Oklahoma
1953	Oklahoma
1954	Oklahoma
1955	Oklahoma
1956	Oklahoma
1957	Oklahoma

BIG EIGHT

Year	School
1958	Oklahoma
1959	Oklahoma
1960	Missouri
1961	Colorado
1962	Oklahoma
1963	Nebraska
1964	Nebraska
1965	Nebraska
1966	Nebraska
1967	Oklahoma
1968	Kansas
	Oklahoma
1969	Missouri
	Nebraska
1970	Nebraska
1971	Nebraska
1972	Nebraska*
1973	Oklahoma
1974	Oklahoma
1975	Nebraska
	Oklahoma
1976	Colorado
	Oklahoma
	Oklahoma State
1977	Oklahoma
1978	Nebraska
	Oklahoma
1979	Oklahoma
1980	Oklahoma
1981	Nebraska
1982	Nebraska
1983	Nebraska
1984	Nebraska
	Oklahoma

*Oklahoma forfeited championship after player ruled ineligible.

BIG TEN CONFERENCE

ILLINOIS
INDIANA
IOWA
MICHIGAN
MICHIGAN STATE
MINNESOTA
NORTHWESTERN
OHIO STATE
PURDUE
WISCONSIN

American football was born on the eastern college campuses, but midwestern schools were quick to take it up, and some, like Chicago, Michigan, Minnesota and Illinois, were instrumental in bringing the sport to its highest level of competition. When Illinois coach Bob Zuppke called his conference "the anchor of amateur athletics in America," it was a statement of veracity, not a boast.

Just after the turn of the 20th century, the Michigan teams of Fielding Yost were the first to snatch the national championship from the great eastern schools. Over the first few decades of the 1900s, the Big Ten produced eight unofficial national champions, and since the rankings received an NCAA imprimatur in 1936 there have been nine national titles bestowed on Big Ten teams. Lately, in the 1970s and '80s, conferences to the south and the west have produced most of the champions, but the tradition of Big Ten football still stands with the very best in college competition.

Part of the reason for the conference's success has been its consistency. When the president of Purdue University, James H. Smart, convened a meeting in early 1895 with the presidents of six other midwestern colleges, five current Big Ten members were in attendance. The Intercollegiate Conference of Faculty Representatives (ICFR), the organization spawned by that 1895 meeting and a second one the following year, did much to eliminate amateur athletic abuses in the early days of college football.

The brutal nature of midwestern football prior to

Walter Eckersall of Chicago, All-American end and consummate kicker (he booted five field goals against Illinois in 1905 and another five in a game against Nebraska in 1906).

the organization of the ICFR is exemplified by an incident in a game between the University of Chicago and Purdue in 1893. The district attorney of Indiana's Tippecanoe County walked onto the field and threatened many of the players with indictments for assault and battery. The same charge could have been made during many other midwestern games of that era, sports historians note. The final resolution adopted at the university presidents' meeting of 1895 addressed that very subject: "We call upon the expert managers of football teams to so revise the rules as to reduce the liability of injury to a minimum."

The rules for collegiate athletics drawn up by the university administrators at that time included sanctions against payments or gifts of any sort to college athletes and stipulated that players be bona fide students on the campus for which they played. The rules also prohibited students delinquent in their studies from participating in team sports.

The charter members of ICFR, which soon became popularly known as the Western Conference, were Chicago, Purdue, Minnesota, Wisconsin, Illinois, Northwestern, and Michigan (which replaced Lake Forest, a participant in the first presidents' meeting).

BIG TEN NATIONAL CHAMPIONS

Year	Team	Coach
1936	Minnesota	Bernie Bierman
1940	Minnesota	Bernie Bierman
1941	Minnesota	Bernie Bierman
1942	Ohio State	Paul Brown
1948	Michigan	Bennie Oosterbaan
1952	Michigan State	Biggie Munn
1954	Ohio State	Woody Hayes
1965	Michigan State	Duffy Daugherty
1968	Ohio State	Woody Hayes

Of those seven universities, only Chicago would permanently leave the conference, after the 1939 season.

Iowa and Indiana joined the conference on December 1, 1899, and Ohio State followed on April 6, 1912. During the 1940s and early '50s, after the departure of Chicago, the conference was known as the Big Nine, not reaching its current quota until the Michigan State Spartans came aboard in 1953. The newcomer, incidentally, in its premiere season, also shared the conference championship with Illinois.

The earliest of the great coaches in the conference was the "Grand Old Man" of football himself— although he was a very young man then—Amos Alonzo Stagg. Before coming to the University of Chicago, Stagg had been a star player at Yale (1886–90). He arrived in Chicago in 1892 as a hired coach for the Maroon, but he also played for two years on the team, something one could do in those days of undefined eligibility.

As a coach, Stagg's gentlemanly approach to the game would, at times, limit the success of the Maroon. Not until 1905, when he had the great Walter Eckersall in his backfield, did Chicago have a team that claimed to be the best in the nation.

In the earliest days of the conference, the major powers were Wisconsin, Michigan, and Chicago. Wisconsin took the first two conference titles in 1896 and 1897, followed the next year by Michigan, then Chicago in 1899, and Minnesota at the turn of the century.

It was following the 1900 season that Fielding Yost and several of his top Stanford players packed their bags and headed back east for Ann Arbor and the Michigan maize and blue, where they ruled the conference imperiously for several seasons. Yost's spectacular Wolverines were universally considered the finest in the nation in 1901. From the beginning of that season through 1904, Yost's Point-a-Minute teams, as they appropriately came to be called, were undefeated, tied only once, and outscored their opponents 2,326 to 40.

The single tie occured in 1903 in a game between Michigan and Minnesota. In that historic match, the Golden Gophers, coached by the legendary Dr. Harry Williams, adopted a defensive pattern employing, for the first time, a four-man secondary, leaving just seven players at the line of scrimmage. Until that time, in an age when the forward pass was virtually unheard of, almost all defenses deployed a nine-man line. Dr. Williams' unusual defense was able to stop Michigan's superstar back Willie Heston, something no other team had been able to do during that four-year period.

When the game ended in a tie, Yost was in such a hurry to get his players out of town that he left behind the brown plaster jug used to hold fresh spring water for the Michigan supermen. "Yost left his yug," one Minnesotan spoofed. Then the Gophers' trainer sent a note to the trainer at Michigan, informing him of the oversight and challenging the Wolverines to "come and try to get it back" the next year. And so was born the battle for the Little Brown Jug, the trophy that has ever since gone to the winner of the annual Gopher-Wolverine game.

From 1901 to 1969, teams from today's Big Ten have appeared consistently at the top of various national polls. During those 69 years, Michigan, Chicago, Illinois, Iowa, Ohio State, Minnesota, and Michigan State have all laid claim to at least one national championship. Indiana, Northwestern, Purdue and Wisconsin are the only Big Ten teams that have yet to rule college football.

A decade before Howard Jones moved to USC to mastermind the great Trojan dynasty, he was the head

The Galloping Ghost, Red Grange, taking off his legendary #77 for the last time, as a collegian at least, after his Illini beat Michigan 14–9.

Michigan great Bob Chappius, carrying the ball here, was one of the prime reasons the Wolverines were undefeated in 1947 (10-0-0) and routed USC 49–0 in the Rose Bowl.

coach at Iowa, where he produced two perfect seasons in 1921 and 1922. From the fifth game of 1920 to the fourth game of 1923, Iowa never lost. It took an Illinois powerhouse, guided by Bob Zuppke, featuring sophomore halfback Red Grange, to finally defeat the Hawkeyes. The Galloping Ghost from Wheaton, Illinois, destined to make the name Red Grange synonymous with football, as Babe Ruth was with baseball, carried the Fighting Illini to their first undisputed national championship that same year.

In the mid-1930s and again in the early '40s, the Minnesota Gophers, under head coach Bernie Bierman, ruled the Big Ten. Minnesota's string of 28 games without a loss was finally broken by Northwestern in 1936. The Wildcats, coached by Lynn "Pappy" Waldorf, were in the running for the national title that year. The game was played in a veritable swamp at Northwestern's Dyche Stadium, and predictably turned into a defensive battle. But Northwestern finally moved the ball through the mud and scored on a one-yard plunge. The final score was 6-0, handing Minnesota its only loss of the year. At season's end, Northwestern had an identical record of 7-1-0, having lost to Notre Dame earlier. When AP came out with its first official ranking that year, the Gophers were at the top, despite the loss to Northwestern. The Wildcats were not even mentioned in the poll's top five, although many observers felt they should have been awarded the title. Northwestern did earn the confer-

ence title that year, which proved to be the last one it has been able to claim so far. Minnesota won another pair of national crowns early in the 1940s, and took the title again in 1960 under coach Murray Warmath, though they lost to Washington in the Rose Bowl, 17-7. During the years from the end of World War II until 1953, the conference had a diversity of champions, as no fewer than seven universities won or shared the crown. During that era, the well-rounded conference gave Californians and other West Coasters ample opportunity to view a wide sampling of midwestern football power. The reason, of course, was that in 1947 the Big Ten and the PAC-10 conferences signed a formal agreement specifying that the champions of each were to meet in the annual Rose Bowl game, a New Year's Day tradition that had been initiated back in 1902. Until the 1947 agreement, West Coast teams played whomever the bowl committee chose to invite. Big Ten teams won the first six encounters under the new system, then after USC nipped Wisconsin 7–0, they won the next six straight, too.

After Woody Hayes came to Ohio State in 1951, the Buckeyes became the team to beat in the Big Ten.

Bernie Bierman (right) led Minnesota to three national championships (1936, 1940, 1941) and ten Big Ten titles.

During his stormy career, he and OSU won or shared 13 Big Ten titles. In 1969, Bo Schembechler took command at Michigan and from that day forward, the rivalry between Ohio State and Michigan has stood as one of the greatest in football, the climax of every Big Ten season. As a point of fact, from 1968 through 1982, either Ohio State or Michigan has won or shared the Big Ten title, and six times during that period the two shared the title with each other.

With Willie Heston (Michigan), Red Grange (Illinois), Bronko Nagurski (Minnesota), Duke Slater (Iowa), Benny Friedman (Michigan), Tom Harmon (Michigan), Buddy Young (Illinois), Crazylegs Hirsch (Wisconsin), Bob Chappius (Michigan), Otto Graham (Northwestern), Alan Ameche (Wisconsin), Dick Butkus (Illinois) and Archie Griffin (Ohio State), the Big Ten has presented an endless parade of gridiron greats. Dynasties have come and gone, but the intense competition among Big Ten teams has never cooled.

Willie Heston, the best back in the game in the early 1900s, was the focal point of Fielding Yost's Point-a-Minute team and was a consensus All-American in 1903 and 1904.

Big Ten Conference Champions

WESTERN CONFERENCE

Year	School	Year	School
1896	Wisconsin	1918	Illinois
1897	Wisconsin		Michigan
1898	Michigan		Purdue
1899	Chicago	1919	Illinois
1900	Iowa	1920	Ohio State
	Minnesota	1921	Iowa
1901	Michigan	1922	Iowa
	Wisconsin		Michigan
1902	Michigan	1923	Illinois
1903	Michigan		Michigan
	Minnesota	1924	Chicago
	Northwestern	1925	Michigan
1904	Michigan	1926	Michigan
	Minnesota		Northwestern
1905	Chicago	1927	Illinois
1906	Michigan	1928	Illinois
	Minnesota	1929	Purdue
	Wisconsin	1930	Michigan
1907	Chicago		Northwestern
1908	Chicago	1931	Michigan
1909	Minnesota		Northwestern
1910	Illinois		Purdue
	Minnesota	1932	Michigan
1911	Minnesota	1933	Michigan
1912	Wisconsin	1934	Minnesota
1913	Chicago	1935	Minnesota
1914	Illinois		Ohio
1915	Illinois	1936	Northwestern
	Minnesota	1937	Minnesota
1916	Ohio State	1938	Minnesota
1917	Ohio State	1939	Ohio State

THE BIG NINE

Year	School	Year	School
1940	Minnesota	1964	Michigan
1941	Minnesota	1965	Michigan State
1942	Ohio State	1966	Michigan State
1943	Michigan	1967	Indiana
	Purdue		Minnesota
1944	Ohio State		Purdue
1945	Indiana	1968	Ohio State
1946	Illinois	1969	Michigan
1947	Michigan		Ohio State
1948	Michigan	1970	Ohio State
1949	Michigan	1971	Michigan
	Ohio	1972	Michigan
1950	Michigan		Ohio State
1951	Illinois	1973	Ohio State
1952	Purdue		Michigan
	Wisconsin	1974	Ohio State
			Michigan

THE BIG TEN

Year	School	Year	School
1953	Illinois	1975	Ohio State
	Michigan State	1976	Michigan
1954	Ohio State		Ohio State
1955	Ohio State	1977	Michigan
1956	Iowa		Ohio State
1957	Ohio State	1978	Michigan
1958	Iowa		Michigan State
1959	Wisconsin	1979	Ohio State
1960	Iowa	1980	Michigan
	Minnesota	1981	Iowa
1961	Ohio State		Ohio State
1962	Wisconsin	1982	Michigan
1963	Illinois	1983	Illinois
		1984	Ohio State

PAC-10 CONFERENCE

ARIZONA
ARIZONA STATE
CALIFORNIA
OREGON
OREGON STATE
STANFORD
UCLA
USC
WASHINGTON
WASHINGTON STATE

When Rutgers and Princeton played the first game of intercollegiate football in 1869, the completion of the nation's first transcontinental railroad in that same year was considered a much bigger news story. When the final golden spike was driven into the ground at Promontory Point, Utah, the Pacific coast was at last linked by rail with the rest of the nation. It would not seem surprising to find that in that then sparsely populated, undeveloped region, college football developed a bit more slowly than in the East and the Midwest.

But not all that much slower. By 1892, Stanford and the University of California met for the first organized game of intercollegiate football on the West Coast. The student manager of that Stanford team, incidentally, was a young engineering student named Herbert Hoover, who eventually became the thirty-first president of the United States.

The organization of a conference, however, did not come about until 1915. In December of that year, the Pacific Coast Conference was founded at a meeting in Portland, Oregon, with four charter members: California, Oregon, Oregon State, and Washington. Conference competition began the next autumn, and over the next two years Washington State and Stanford joined. By 1922, the conference admitted USC and Idaho, and by 1928 was up to ten members with the admission of Montana and UCLA.

Montana left for the Mountain States Conference in 1950. Then, in 1959, the PCC was dissolved and in its place was formed the Athletic Association of Western Universities, a five-school conference (California, USC, Stanford, UCLA, and Washington). In the 1960s, Washington State, Oregon, and Oregon State signed on, and the name was changed to the Pacific-8 Conference. With the admission of Arizona and Arizona State in 1978, it became the PAC-10.

College football in the West has always been a colorful affair, and the most attention has usually been focused on the teams that do battle within the state boundaries of California. But the first legitimate West Coast dynasty was developed out of state, up at the University of Washington in Seattle, by Gilmour

"Gloomy Gil" Dobie. Throughout his long coaching career, Dobie demonstrated an uncommon talent for developing winning football teams as well as entrenched enemies. In 1908, on his first day at Washington, Dobie nearly came to blows with both Seattle's former mayor and its postmaster, who had decided to come out and watch practice, something Dobie frowned on. Gloomy Gil then called the team captain, a local hero, "yellow." For Wee Coyle, the Washington quarterback, he had this: "You play like a man devoid of a brain," and added that Coyle wouldn't even be allowed to suit up "if I didn't have so many cripples."

Gil Dobie managed to inspire so much animosity during his first year at Washington that he was con-

Lynn Swann (22) goes up to grab one, a step ahead of Notre Dame's Tom Lopienski, in a 1973 contest. But it was not enough that day as the Irish ended the Trojans' 25-game winning streak with a 23–14 victory.

ciate professor and director of the department of Physical Culture as well as head coach).

As schools began to bring aboard coaches for their teams, the game of football began to change significantly. Tactics, new formations and plays, and organization were infused into the sport. Among the great innovators, besides Camp and Stagg, there were other important architects of the game: Percy Haughton at Harvard, George Woodruff of Pennsylvania, Harry Williams at Minnesota, John Heisman, Pop Warner, Fielding Yost—the list is long and gilded.

It was from these imaginative minds that American football developed into the game as it is known today. As technically complex and sophisticated as football is in the 1980s, with teams of coaches, encyclopedic play books, films, communications systems, computers, scouting programs, aids *ad infinitum,* the basics of the game are really no different from the formations, shifts and plays that were dreamed up in the late 1800s and early 1900s by the game's first masterminds.

There have been so many wonderful coaches in the first century of college football, so many contributions to the game by them, such imprint on the players they have guided. We have chosen fifteen for special recognition here, the criteria including not just their successes but also the impact they have had on the game as a result of their football creativity and unique legacies to the game.

Unincluded biographically, but not overlooked either in anecdotes, statistics, or the heart of the author are such legends in their own right as (in no particular order and identified with the school(s) they were most associated with) Jess Neely (Clemson and Rice), Warren Woodson (Arkansas State, Hardin-Simmons, Arizona, New Mexico State), Dana Xenephon Bible (Texas A&M, Nebraska, Texas), Dan McGugin (Vanderbilt), John Vaught (Mississippi), Carl Snavely (Cornell, North Carolina), Gil Dobie (Washington, Navy Cornell, Boston College), Ben Schwartzwalder (Syracuse), Bob Neyland (Tennessee), Frank Thomas (Alabama), Jock Sutherland (Pittsburgh), Fritz Crisler (Princeton, Michigan), Jim Crowley (Michigan State, Fordham), Andy Smith (California), Frank Cavanaugh (Dartmouth, Boston College, Fordham), Jim Tatum (Maryland, North Carolina), Bill Roper (Princeton), T.A.D. Jones (Yale), Bobby Dodd (Georgia Tech), Red Sanders (UCLA), Biff Jones (Army, Louisiana State, Oklahoma, Nebraska), Bob Devaney (Nebraska), Frank Kush (Arizona State), John McKay (Southern Cal), Dan Devine (Missouri, Notre Dame), Frank Broyles (Arkansas), Vince Dooley (Georgia), Bobby Bowden (West Virginia, Florida State), Barry Switzer (Oklahoma), Joe Paterno (Penn State), Tom Osborne (Nebraska), Bo Schembechler (Michigan), and LaVell Edwards (Brigham Young). And those are just the best known.

AMOS ALONZO STAGG

"All modern football stems from Stagg," said Knute Rockne, who came to know and admire football's Grand Old Man, when Stagg was at the University of Chicago, in the first decade of his 56-year tenure as a college football coach. Few will disagree with the Rock's assertion.

Amos Alonzo Stagg was a pioneer in developing so many elements of the game, including diagrammed playbooks, the huddle, various backfield shifts, men in motion, the spiral pass, onside kick, fake kick, and reverses, among many others. He was also the first coach to take a team cross-country to play a game.

Head coach at Chicago for 41 years, Stagg battled other legendary coaches from the neighborhood, such as Fielding Yost of Michigan and Bob Zuppke of Illinois.

As an active coach, he outlasted generations of competitors, and did not make a lasting retirement from the game until 1960, at the age of 98. He reigned as the winningest coach in the history of college football, his 314 victories just topping the 313 of Glenn "Pop" Warner, until Paul "Bear" Bryant set a new record in 1982 of 323.

Born when Abe Lincoln was president, Stagg's career and teams were a testament to clean living. As both a star pitcher and a football mainstay at Yale, he refused to drink, smoke, or swear. He rejected a flurry of professional baseball offers after graduation because he objected to the sale of alcoholic beverages at professional baseball games. "The whole tone of the game was smelly," he said some years later.

Even during the heat of many gridiron battles, Stagg would never swear. His strongest epithet to a player was "jackass," and, in particularly flagrant situations, "double jackass." Many of his players felt that

An aged but very active Amos Alonzo Stagg (center) pensively watches a roaring fire with some of his players at the College of the Pacific in Stockton, California, his last coaching assignment. Stagg won Coach of the Year honors there in 1943 at age 81.

Stagg instructs some of his players on their home field at the University of Chicago. The stadium, named for Stagg, was not used for football after Chicago dropped the sport in 1940, but it became famous when physicist Enrico Fermi produced the first controlled nuclear reaction in tests within the structure in 1942.

The Evils of Pro Football

Amos Alonzo Stagg worried a lot about college football players being corrupted. The more he worried, the angrier he got. Finally, in 1923, he gave a statement to the press venting his wrath on the many evils he saw lurking in the shadows of the college game.

"For years, the colleges have been waging a bitter warfare against the insidious forces of the gambling public and alumni and against overzealous and shortsighted friends, inside and out, and also not infrequently against crooked coaches and managers, who have been anxious to win at any cost. . . . And now comes along another serious menace, possibly greater than all others, viz. Sunday professional football.

"Under the guise of fair play but countenancing rank dishonesty in playing men under assumed names, scores of professional teams have sprung up in the last two or three years. . . . These teams are bidding hard for college players in order to capitalize not only on their ability but also and mostly on the name of the college they come from. . . . The well-known Carlinville and Taylorville incident of 1921 is likely to be repeated in essence on different occasions this fall."

The Carlinville-Taylorville game to which Stagg referred has become somewhat of a notorious landmark in football lore, a contest waged between two Illinois towns for football prestige, not to mention a few dollars wagered among the townspeople. The star of the game, Joey Sternaman, the five-foot-six-inch 150-pound quarterback for Illinois earlier in the year, tells about the contest.

"Doug Simpson (a fellow Illini player) came up after the season and said, 'How would you like to play in a game and make fifty dollars, maybe a hundred dollars?' He said

Carlinville was going to come over and play Taylorville—these were two football-crazy towns in central Illinois. A lot of money was being bet on the game and therefore the towns could afford to pay the players some good money for playing in the game. He said that Laurie Walquist and Oscar Knop, who had been in the backfield with me at Illinois that year, were going down; so were a lot of other players. I didn't think there was any chance of the people at the university finding out, so I said okay.

"Well, that day, lo and behold, there were all kinds of players there in Taylorville: college, pros, semipros. I didn't play in the first half, Charlie Dressen of the old Decatur Staleys did for Taylorville. He later went on to become a well-known baseball manager with the Brooklyn Dodgers. Anyway we got messed up somehow and so I went in for the second half at quarterback. We had some of the other Illinois boys in there, too, and Carlinville had most of the Notre Dame team playing for them. They had Hunk Anderson and Eddie Anderson and Chet Wynne, the whole doggone team. The score was 0–0 at halftime. I was able to move the ball down the field and then I dropkicked a field goal. I got two more later and we won 9–0. And the story they told afterward was that they had to move the First National Bank of Carlinville over to Taylorville. . . .

"There's always been the story going around that I wore paint on my face and adhesive bandages to disguise who I was, but that wasn't really so. . . . I guess it made for a better story."

Word did get back to Illinois officials and Joey Sternaman and a few other Illinois football players were booted off the team. Sternaman went on to an illustrious career with the Chicago Bears, playing in a backfield that included Taylorville alumni Oscar Knop and Laurie Walquist, and later another Illini back, Red Grange.

their college careers could not be complete until they had joined, at least once, the coveted "Jackass Club."

Throughout his career, Stagg felt that sportsmanship and honor were more important than victories. A longtime member of college football's rules committee, he once refused to send in a substitute with a badly needed play when Chicago's offense had faltered on its opponent's one-yard line. "The rules committee deprecates the use of a substitute to convey information," he explained. Chicago went on to lose the game. During his tenure at Chicago from 1892 through 1932, the school won only six Big Ten titles.

Soon after Robert Maynard Hutchins was named president of the University of Chicago, Stagg, at the age of 70, was forced to obey university rules and retire. But the very next year he became head coach at the College of the Pacific where, until the age of 84, he

compiled a respectable record against often larger and more powerful rivals. Two other positions there kept him active in college football until the age of 98.

Stagg's 100th birthday was celebrated from coast to coast in 1962, a time when football's Grand Old Man was beginning to feel the effects of advancing age. "I would like to be remembered," he said at the time, "as an honest man."

SCHOOLS	RECORD
Springfield 1890–91	Won 314
Chicago 1892–1932	Lost 199
Pacific 1933–46	Tied 17
	Pct. .605

GLENN S. "POP" WARNER

Until Bear Bryant came along, only Amos Alonzo Stagg had won more football games than Glenn Scobey Warner, known to the football world as Pop. In coaching assignments at Georgia, Cornell, Carlisle, Pittsburgh, Stanford, and Temple he compiled a record of 313 victories against 106 losses and 32 ties.

Like Stagg, Warner is known as one of the great innovators of the game. He introduced the single wing and double wing formations, the spiral punt, rolling body blocks, numbers on players' jerseys, and blocking dummies. In his career of nearly half a century, he coached a total of 47 consensus All-Americans, including two of football's greatest athletes, Jim Thorpe at Carlisle and Ernie Nevers at Stanford.

Also like Stagg, Warner was a stickler for good sportsmanship. "You cannot play two kinds of football at once, dirty and good," he once said. Red Smith described him as a "gruff old gent, kind and forthright and obstinate and honest."

Warner was also spectacularly successful. Between 1915 and 1918, his teams at Pittsburgh went undefeated for four consecutive seasons. By the early 1920s, his nationwide reputation attracted considerable interest even on the West Coast, where Stanford officials began courting his services.

Accepting the Stanford head coaching position prior to the 1923 season, Warner insisted on honoring the remaining two years of his contract at Pittsburgh. In the interim he sent assistants Andy Kerr and Tiny Thornhill to Stanford to begin implementing his system.

Once he arrived at Stanford, Warner coached some of his greatest players and engaged in one of college football's all-time great rivalries. His finest athlete was All-American back Ernie Nevers, still regarded as the greatest player ever to wear a Stanford uniform. Comparing Nevers to Thorpe, Warner gave the edge in overall performance to Nevers. Thorpe, he felt, did not always give his best effort. "If their skill is about the same," he once said, "I'll take the all-outer over the in-and-outer every time."

The historic rivalry with the University of Southern California began in 1925, coach Howard Jones' first

Warner on the Record

Writing to football historian H.A. Applequist in 1943, Pop Warner tried to set straight the innovations in the game which he claimed as his own.

"The things which I *did* originate are as follows:

"The crouching stance of the backs on offense. In 1908 I started this innovation, having the backs stand with one or both hands on the ground. This practice has since been almost universally used by teams with the exception of the teams using a shifting backfield. This stance gives nearly the same advantage in starting as that used by modern trackmen over the old standing start of early days.

"The unbalanced line. I am quite sure that I was the first coach of football to use the *four* and *two* line which is so commonly used by teams today. I started this offensive method in 1906.

"The single wing formation. I started this type of offensive formation in 1906, when the rules prohibited helping the ball carrier by pushing or pulling of a player in order to advance the ball. This formation was alluded to by Walter Camp and other noted writers and coaches of football as the 'Carlisle Formation'. This formation or its variations is probably used at the present time by at least three-fourths of all the football teams in the country.

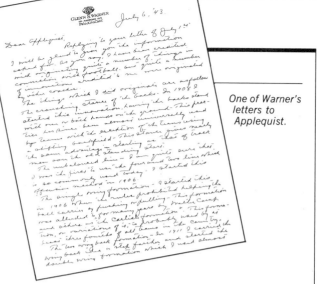

One of Warner's letters to Applequist.

"The two wing-back formation. In 1911, I carried the wing back idea a step further and started the double wing-back formation which I used almost exclusively throughout the rest of my coaching career.

"The direct pass from the center to the ball carrier. I am quite certain that I was the first to use this method of getting the ball to the runner instead of having the quarterback handling the ball on every play.

"The screen forward pass. I used such a pass very successfully along about 1920, and it is my belief that I was the first football coach to make use of this type of forward pass. Such a pass, as you know, becomes illegal except when the screen is formed on or behind the scrimmage line."

Pop Warner shows his Temple players how it's done in 1934. It was his second year there, a long way football-wise as well as in miles from Stanford, in the ever-darkening twilight of his long career.

season at USC. Warner won the first two meetings and tied the third, but beginning with the fourth contest, USC took five straight games from Stanford.

Depressed and disgusted by his inability to defeat Southern Cal, Pop Warner resigned from Stanford at the end of the 1932 season. In a move he later described as "the worst mistake of my life," he became head coach at Temple, where his teams never achieved glory. But his legacy at Stanford, directed by Tiny Thornhill, thrived with the famed Vow Boys, who pledged never to be defeated by USC.

Despite his lackluster years at Temple, Warner is regarded as one of the most influential collegiate coaches of all time. Grantland Rice once wrote that it would be difficult to determine whether Pop Warner or Knute Rockne had the greatest overall effect on the game of college football.

SCHOOLS	RECORD
Georgia 1895–96	Won 313
Cornell 1897–98	Lost 106
Carlisle 1899–1903	Tied 32
Cornell 1904–1906	Pct. .729
Carlisle 1907–14	
Pittsburgh 1915–23	
Stanford 1924–32	
Temple 1933–38	

Warner enjoys a football-shaped cake given to him by his players in 1937. The next year was his last in football, retiring at age 67 after a brilliant 44-year career.

FIELDING YOST

"**Y**ou're not movin' out there. Ya think we got all day?" he would holler, clapping his hands at a player who dared to enter a scrimmage somewhat slower than the speed of light. "Hurry up! Let's go! Hurry up!" To his parents, Peremenus and Elzena Yost, he was known by the name of Fielding, but to everyone connected with college football, he was "Hurry Up" Yost, the master of rapid motion on and off the field.

"Horrible Nightmare" screamed a West Virginia newspaper headline after Yost's Michigan team destroyed West Virginia by the incredible score of 130–0 at a game played in Ann Arbor in 1904. But even in the most lopsided of games, Yost was sure to point out that forty or more players had participated in the drubbing.

His coaching career developed early. After earning a law degree from either Lafayette or West Virginia (historians are not certain which school holds the

Yost and Lardner

Fielding Yost, Michigan's fabled coach, was not always the easiest man to get along with. Ring Lardner, while traveling with Yost in the early 1920s, got caught in a little argument regarding the Michigan-Pennsylvania game of 1906.

"Penn won that one, 17–0," Lardner said.

"No, Michigan won it," Yost said. "That was the year we had Garrels, a great fullback."

"Penn won it," Ring repeated. "That was the year they had Scarlett and Greene."

Finally Yost bet Lardner five dollars, a tremendous bet for Yost. They looked it up in a record book. Score: Pennsylvania 17–Michigan 0.

"I told you Pennsylvania won," Yost said. And then he told Lardner it was not necessary for him to pay up.

A pair of classics in college football, Fielding Yost (right) and Bob Zuppke (left) sport posters of each other, presented in 1942 by the American Football Coaches Association in recognition of their accomplishments.

honor), Yost began coaching college football teams. In the next four years, he won four championships with four different schools, Ohio Wesleyan, Nebraska, Kansas, and Stanford. By the time he reached California, a single coaching job during the football season was simply not enough for his restless nature. In 1900, he guided the Stanford varsity, the Stanford freshman team, the Lowell high school team, and assisted at San Jose College. All four teams won championships, but by the close of the season Yost apparently grew bored with the pace of life in California. With three of his top players in tow, he moved to the University of Michigan in 1901, where he established one of the greatest dynasties in the history of Big Ten football.

Yost's Wolverines responded immediately, all but destroying their opponents, ending the season with a crushing victory over Stanford in what was the first Rose Bowl Game. When C.M. Fickert, the overwhelmed Stanford coach, asked that the game be stopped, Yost replied, "No sirree, let's get on with it." The Michigan captain finally agreed to end the rout with nearly 10 minutes left to play, the score standing at 49–0.

Yost was named athletic director at Michigan in 1921 and retired as head coach after an undefeated season in 1923. But when the Wolverines committed the unspeakable sin of losing two games in the 1924 season, Yost was back at the helm in 1925. That year, Michigan defeated everyone but Northwestern, losing 3–2 (the only points the Wolverines gave up all season), beating even the Illinois team led by Red Grange. Yost regarded that 1925 team as his greatest and

retired again in 1926, but for several years, the head coach's position would be "questionable," with Yost always ready to step in.

There could be little question, however, about Yost's remarkable record at Michigan: 164 victories against only 29 defeats; eight undefeated teams, seven Big Ten titles, and four national championships.

SCHOOLS	RECORD
Ohio Wesleyan 1897	Won 196
Nebraska 1898	Lost 36
Kansas 1899	Tied 12
Stanford 1900	Pct. .828
Michigan 1901–23	
1925–26	

John William Heisman: The Man Behind the Trophy

John William Heisman was born the same year that the first intercollegiate football game was played, in 1869, when Princeton faced Rutgers on the latter school's commons in New Brunswick, New Jersey. He played his first game 17 years later for Titusville High School in western Pennsylvania, against the wishes of his father, who described the game as "beastial."

That introduction began a love affair with the sport that would last almost 50 years. He went to Brown in 1887, where he played for three years, then to Pennsylvania for another two years of varsity ball. In 1892, he abandoned his study of law and took up coaching at Oberlin College. It was the beginning of a 36-year, peripatetic career that would take him to eight different colleges. As a grand strategist and innovator, his name would come to rank in football lore with those of Camp, Stagg, and Warner.

Heisman was a short man, a little stumpy at about 155 pounds, who usually wore a high turtleneck sweater and a baseball cap when he walked the sidelines. At Oberlin, his team won all seven of their games. Then he moved to Akron for the 1893 season and returned to Oberlin in '94.

He experimented with the hidden ball trick, instituted a shouted signal (sometimes "Hike," sometimes "Hep") to snap the ball from center, and developed a double lateral pass that was much copied. To the rules committee, he advocated the division of the game into quarters and campaigned for three years for the legalization of the forward pass, which he saw come to fruition in 1906.

After coaching at Oberlin, he moved to Auburn for a five-year stint, then to Clemson for four seasons, and finally to Georgia Tech in 1904 where he made his biggest impact over the next 16 years. At Tech he was a noted taskmaster: long practices, tight training rules (including no hot-water baths or use of soap during the week because they were, in his opinion, "debilitating"), and stern dealings with players. He often lectured his team in booming stage tones, replete with Shakespearean quotes.

It was also at Tech where he coached one of the game's all-time greats, Indian Joe Guyon, who had come from Carlisle, where he had played in the backfield with Jim Thorpe, under the tutelage of Pop Warner. Besides remembering Guyon as a wonderful football player, Heisman always liked to tell the story of taking Guyon to New Orleans to play Tulane. He told Guyon that the oysters in that town were a special treat. The afternoon of the game Heisman noticed his star back sitting in a corner of the dressing room and looking a little ill. "The oysters," he told Heisman when the coach asked him what was the

matter. "Raw oysters," he said, grimacing.

"They didn't agree with you?" Heisman asked.

"Well, the first four or five dozen did. I think I got some bad ones after that."

It was also at Georgia Tech where Heisman was accused, legitimately, of running up the score against weak opponents. In 1916, Cumberland College traveled to Atlanta to face Tech and was beaten by Heisman's team 222-0, the most points ever scored in a college football game. Thirty-two touchdowns and 30 extra points were all that Heisman needed that afternoon.

Heisman also lent his name to a shift, one he invented while at Georgia Tech. It was described in the *New York Sun* by sportswriter George Trevor this way: "On the ingenious shift Heisman originated in 1910, the entire team, except the center, dropped behind the scrimmage zone. The four backs took their post in Indian file at right angles to the rush line, forming the letter T." The Heisman shift, along with the Minnesota shift, developed by Dr. Harry Williams, and the Notre Dame shift of Knute Rockne, became the most famous shifts in the early years of organized American football. And Heisman's was unorthodox, although, everyone agreed, it was effective.

As Trevor noted with enthusiasm, "one virtue of the balanced formation was that it could attack either flank with equal force. There were no strong- or weak-side plays as the shift swung left or right. At the shift signal the phalanx deployed with the startling suddenness of a Jeb Stuart cavalry raid, catching the defense off balance. No pause was required by the more lenient rules of that period, the absence of any momentary stop making it difficult for the defense to countershift in time."

Heisman himself shifted to Pennsylvania in 1920, remained there three seasons, and then moved on to Washington & Jefferson in 1923. The following year he took the head coaching job at Rice and held it until 1927, when he retired at the age of sixty.

When his coaching career closed, Heisman could claim 185 victories against 70 defeats and 17 ties, one of the twenty winningest coaches in college football history. He had also been elected president of the American Football Coaches Association twice and was one of the founders of the New York Touchdown Club.

The year he died, 1936, the Downtown Athletic Club of New York named their annual award for excellence, begun the year before, in honor of their accomplished member, and Larry Kelley of Yale was given the first trophy bearing the name Heisman.

The Season's First Lesson

During his coaching career from the late 1800s into the 1920s, Heisman traditionally would face his recruits at the beginning of the football season, holding a football in his hands.

"What is it?" he would ask rhetorically.

"A prolate spheroid, an elongated sphere," he would answer himself, "one in which the outer leathern casing is drawn up tightly over a somewhat smaller rubber tubing."

Then, after a melodramatic pause, "Better to have died as a small boy than to fumble this football."

HOWARD JONES

U ntil the last decade of his life, Howard Harding Jones was an unsung hero, an innovative and highly successful coach known chiefly by football experts. It shouldn't have been so. After relatively brief coaching experiences at Syracuse, Yale, and Ohio State, the one-time Yale end became Iowa's head coach in 1916. By 1922 he could boast of two undefeated and untied seasons for the Hawkeyes and two consecutive Big Ten championships, the second of which was shared with Michigan.

At Iowa, Jones developed his first superstar, quarterback Aubrey Devine, who the coach described as "the greatest all-around backfield man I have ever coached or seen in the modern game." Howard Jones' innovations at Iowa included an offensive shift in which both ends dropped back into the backfield to block for the quarterback and the fullback rush, a move that caused considerable confusion among opponents. Be-

fore Illinois finally defeated Iowa in the fourth game of the 1923 season, the Hawkeyes had won 20 consecutive games. Jones then left for Duke at the end of the season, where he won only four of nine games.

In 1925 he was installed as the head coach at the University of Southern California where, half a decade later, he finally established a national reputation. At Southern Cal he won seven Pacific Coast Conference titles, two national championships, and his teams were invited to the Rose Bowl five times, winning on each occasion. But even before his second appearance in the Pasadena classic, *The New York Times* would describe him as "the most under-recognized coach, from a national standpoint, the game has had in many years. It seems incomprehensible that Jones should have received so little attention as has been accorded him."

By leading his Trojans to three Rose Bowl victories

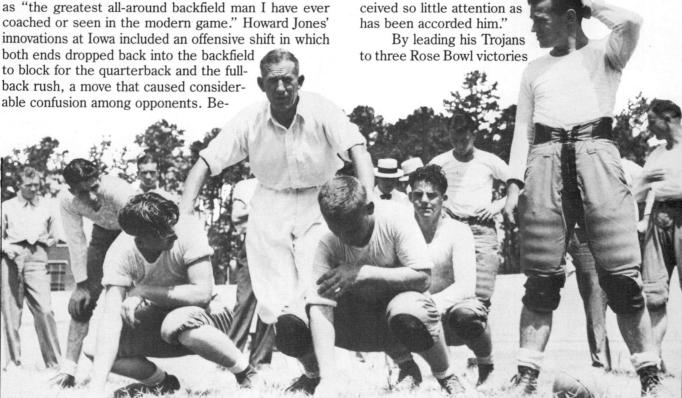

Howard Jones oversees the training of a few of his Southern Cal players at a pre-season workout in 1933. That season USC lost a game and tied another—a letdown, Jones said, but it was the last championship-caliber team he would enjoy until 1938.

Jones poses here with back Ford Palmer in 1932. Besides Palmer, Jones had the diminutive Cotton Warburton in his backfield, who led USC through an undefeated season to a national championship, albeit unofficial in those days.

in four years, however, Jones became a phenomenon that no one could ignore. One of his quarterbacks at USC, Ambrose Schindler, described Jones this way:

"He was just such a genius at football. He believed in knowing the opponent by having them well scouted. That way his team could properly set up a defense. And by controlling them, his team could beat them with their own selected offensive patterns.

"He preferred to win with his system. . . . He liked to win by seeing that his techniques prevailed, and that his methods were superior. . .

"Howard Jones believed in running directly at the other team's best linemen. Jones would pick their All-American and concentrate the attack on him to prove to his own men that you had to beat their best man, and that when you did, you had the game. He had us do that against everybody."

After his Rose Bowl victories in 1930, 1932, and 1933, Jones' teams were eclipsed in 1934 and 1935 by the Vow Boys at Stanford. But his strict, often unfor-

giving, demands never ceased. A player for Jones always knew that if he made one critical mistake, a chance to redeem himself might never come.

The 1938 and 1939 teams, called the Thundering Herd, made a strong comeback, winning the Rose Bowl at the close of each season. After a 3-4-2 season in 1940, Jones died suddenly of a heart attack at the age of 46. He left behind several books on football and libraries of memories for Southern Cal fans.

SCHOOLS	RECORD
Syracuse 1908	Won 194
Yale 1909	Lost 64
Ohio State 1910	Tied 21
Yale 1913	Pct. .733
Iowa 1916–23	
Duke 1924	
Southern Cal 1925–40	

KNUTE ROCKNE

The Rock, as he was known to every football fan, masterminded one of football's greatest dynasties, bringing Notre Dame national championships in 1924, 1929, and 1930, and guiding some of the most famous players ever to wear college football uniforms, among them George Gipp and the fabled Four Horsemen.

In 1913, playing end for Notre Dame, he teamed with quarterback Gus Dorais to develop the use of the forward pass in a game against Army. But it is coaching genius and his inspirational pre-game and halftime talks that are best remembered.

The Rock would say whatever he felt was needed to inspire—or goad—his Irish on to victory. Actor Pat O'Brien immortalized Rockne's "Win one for the Gipper" speech in the film *Knute Rockne—All American,* but there were dozens of other inspired anything-for-a-win locker room talks. It is said Notre Dame's locker room still rings with his pre-game chants: "Go out there and hit 'em," he would yell. "Crack 'em! Fight to live! Fight to win! Fight to win, win, win, WIN!"

He frequently used sarcasm to bring his troops to life. Opening the locker room door after a disappointing first-half performance, he peered in at his team, shook his head, and said, "I beg your pardon. I thought this was a Notre Dame team." That was all. Rock's halftime invectives could fly like a 50-yard kick in the pants. "Remember girls," he once said to his team after another lackluster first half, "let's not have any rough stuff out there." But when the game was over, Rockne always showed his team that there was nothing personal in his remarks. After berating the team as a whole, he would then shower with the players, forsaking his personal locker room. Few of his troops missed the point. But, by the next game, he would be back at work, exhorting them to win, bending the truth if necessary, threatening to quit, even using the phlebitis that plagued him late in his career to explain why a loss might kill him.

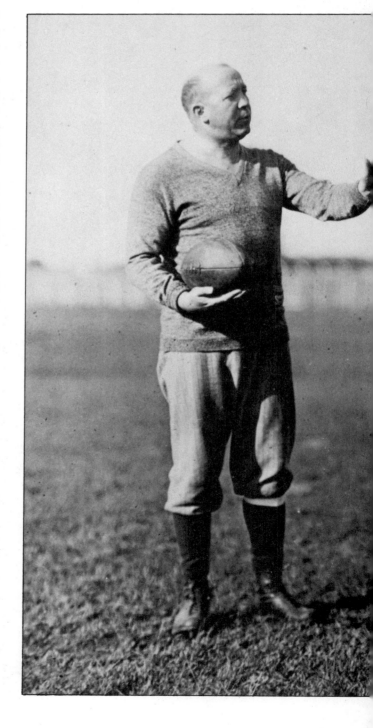

From the sidelines, squeezing an unlit cigar and often gesticulating with it wildly, Rockne marshaled the Irish's winning strategy. His innovations included the Notre Dame shift, a refinement of a system that he inherited from former Irish coach Jesse Harper, in which the backfield lined up in a T formation and

Rockne (second from right) poses with fellow Notre Dame players who served as lifeguards at Cedar Point beach in 1914, including quarterback Gus Dorais (far left).

Knute Rockne has a few words for Jack Elder on the field at South Bend in 1929. With backs like Elder, Frank Carideo, Joe Savoldi, and Moon Mullins, the Irish went 9-0-0 and were the top team in the nation.

A Moral Force

Paul Gallico, sports editor for the *New York Daily News* in the 1920s and 1930s before becoming a noted fiction writer, described how the force of college football was pervasive enough to influence the social structures in which it existed. As proof, he told this story of Knute Rockne in the Roaring 20s:

"He closed down a *maison de joie* known as 'Sally's,' above a feed store on La Salle Street in South Bend, as having a deteriorating effect on the neighborhood. The police dragged their feet when requested to cooperate, since apparently some kind of profit-sharing plan was in operation. When repeated appeals failed, Rockne made another suggestion. Either Sally's closed, or he would bring his football team down and take the place apart. The threat of this kind of publicity shook the city fathers to the soles of their shoes, and Madame Sally's establishment took over premises in another town."

shifted into a single wing. He developed the "Shock Troop" system, using his second-string players to start the game to absorb the initial blows of the opponents, then bringing in his first string to face a tired opponent. He was the first to advocate and implement what was then known as a "suicide schedule," a game with a major opponent every week.

Rockne was highly respected throughout the country for his public speaking skills, inspirational thoughts and suggestions, and legion of friends and followers, establishing him as a legend in his time.

"Rockne sold football to the men on the trolley, the elevated, the subway," said pupil Harry Mehre, "to the baker, the butcher, the pipe fitter who never went to college. He made it an American mania."

SCHOOL	RECORD
Notre Dame 1918–30	Won 105 Lost 12 Tied 5 Pct. .881

up his sleeve, such as his controversial fake injury play, to use when his time-outs were expended. "A team feels better if it believes it has something in reserve," the master pointed out.

When emotional strain and poor health forced Leahy to retire in 1953, it took the Irish more than a decade to fully recover. Not until 1964 and the start of the Ara Parseghian era would the Irish truly get back on the track to glory.

Leahy is pictured (left) with one of the finest players he ever coached, Heisman winner Johnny Lujack, shown here in his new job as Leahy's line coach.

SCHOOLS	RECORD
Boston College 1939–40	Won 107
Notre Dame 1941–43	Lost 13
1946–53	Tied 9
	Pct. .864

On the sidelines with Leahy. Liked by some players, disliked by others, he never let either attitude get in the way of winning games for the Fighting Irish.

Wojciechowicz on Leahy

Alex Wojciechowicz, one of Fordham's Seven Blocks of Granite, a two-time All-American there and later one of the finest centers ever to play professional football, remembers well Frank Leahy, who was a line coach at Fordham before becoming head coach at Boston College.

"I liked Jim Crowley, our coach at Fordham, but my personal coach there was Frank Leahy, his assistant who handled the center and the guards. Every day with him it was snap the ball and block, snap the ball and block, hours on end.

"There's a little story about Leahy and myself which happened my senior year (1937). The way we used to practice, I'd center the ball and he'd go after me and bang me around the head, really give me a whack. After an hour of it, I'd have a headache. Well, in my last year, I said to him, 'Frank, if you keep hitting me around the head like that, I'll probably flunk all my courses.' Then I told him, 'You know, coach, I never block against you in practice like I do in a game. I go easy on you. In a game I block like a wild man.'

"He looked at me very astonished. 'What?' he shouted.

"'What the heck, you're older and my coach. I don't want to hurt you.'

"He was furious. 'From now on, you go after me just like you do in a ball game. Even more so!'

"Well, I didn't for the next three or four blocks, and he knew it, and he reminded me of it. 'Are you really sure?' I asked. He was, he said.

"So I went at him as hard and as fast as I could. I don't think he knew what hit him. I got him just right. They carried him off the field, and for a long time after that he had to go up to Mayo Clinic for treatments for his back. I felt bad about that but that's the way Frank Leahy was. We remained good friends after I left Fordham and he went on to Notre Dame."

The Word on Fritz Crisler

Before his legendary years as head coach at Michigan, Fritz Crisler led Princeton's Tigers from 1932 to 1937. Writing for the *Princeton Athletic News* in 1932, Amos Alonzo Stagg had this to say about him:

"It is a pleasure to write a few lines about Herbert Orrin Crisler. Having had considerable to do with Fritz during his kindergarten, primary, secondary, and collegiate education in football at the University of Chicago, I am able to write, I believe, understandingly about him as a coach.

"Fritz proved to be a wonderfully apt student in football, and he easily qualified for a doctor's degree in this sport long before he left the University of Chicago. For eight years he was my assistant coach... Finally he regretfully left to become athletic director and football coach at the University of Minnesota... Besides being a master of the fundamentals of offense and defense in football, Fritz possesses a rare breadth of knowledge of various systems of play... By nature and by training Fritz measures up to the moral and spiritual leadership of a great coach. He possesses splendid human traits in his personality. He has plenty of warmth of heart along with forcefulness and will power. He possesses excellent balance and good judgment. He has principles and he isn't afraid to stand up for them... Princeton will find him a real man, a natural leader, and prospectively a great coach."

Crisler was a skilled writer himself. The following is taken from a letter sent to his players before the beginning of the school year, outlining exactly what was expected of a Princeton football player.

"The following qualities are demanded of the candidates for the Princeton University football team of 1934. Unless you can offer these qualities on a hundred percent basis do not come out for practice for I do not want anybody on the field who cannot give one hundred percent interest, one hundred percent enthusiasm, and one hundred percent fighting courage while on the squad. Further, a fellow who becomes self-satisfied and thinks that he is so good that he cannot improve will be better off not to report. We must have:

1. Men who are loyal, who are fighters, who have a superabundance of courage, determination and perseverance.

2. Men who are conscientious, serious-minded, hard workers.

3. Men who have continuous interest, prolonged enthusiasm, and unending ambition to make the team.

4. Men who have the capacity to think, study and work to develop every feature of their position and technique of play and imagination to translate it into team work.

5. Men who will be supremely interested in perfecting the technique of their own play, but will be equally interested in cooperating for the perfection of team play results.

6. Men who will work to understand and perfect every detail of their assignment on every play.

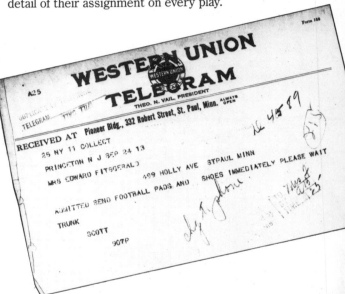

7. Men who are selfish to produce the highest rate of individual performance of play but absolutely unselfish where the team's interests are concerned.

8. Men who will have a broad friendship and companionship with the other men on the squad and be interested in the development of the team's morale and esprit de corps.

9. Men who have predominant will power to do their level best and to stimulate others to give their best in order to produce team spirit, team enthusiasm, and the will to win.

10. Men who are masters of themselves who will make personal sacrifices in eating, smoking, sleeping, drinking, and in social events in order to train honestly and faithfully to get themselves in the best physical condition possible so that individually and cooperatively they can always do their best.

11. Men who have an earnest desire to strive for perfection and realize that there is always something that can be done to improve themselves."

In response to another of Crisler's letters, this one a questionnaire seeking advice, alumnus and former college football player F. Scott Fitzgerald wrote him the letter reproduced on the next page in 1934.

F. Scott Fitzgerald, would-be Princeton Tiger football player (lower left) poses with his freshman buddies in their dinks (known elsewhere as beanies). To the left is Fitzgerald's eloquent telegram to his mother, noting his acceptance on the team.

Dear Fritz:

You write me again demanding advice concerning the coming season. I hasten to answer—again I insist that using a member of the Board of Trustees at left tackle . . . would be a mistake. My idea is a backfield composed of Kipke, Eddie Mahan, President Lowell and anybody we can get for the left side . . . and then either bring back Light-Horse Harry Lee, or else you will fill in yourself for the last place. . . .

Now Fritz, I realize that you and Tad know more about this thing than I do—nevertheless I want to make my suggestion: all the end men and backfield men and members of the Board of Trustees start off together—then they all reverse their fields, led by some of the most prominent professors and alumni—Albie Booth, Bob Lassiter, etc.—and almost before we know it we are up against the Yale goal—let me see, where was I? I mean the Lehigh goal —anyhow some goal, perhaps our own. Anyhow the main thing is that the C.W.A. is either dead, or else just beginning, and to use again that variation of the "Mexican" shift that I suggested last year will be just disastrous. Why? Even I can follow it! Martineau comes out of the huddle—or topples back into it—he passes to some member of past years' teams—(who won't be named here because of the eligibility rules) and then—well, from there on we go on to practically anything.

But not this year, Fritz Crisler, if you take my advice!

Best,

F. Scott Fitzgerald

CHARLES "BUD" WILKINSON

Bud Wilkinson had plenty to smile about in his 17 years as head coach at Oklahoma, with national championships and record-shattering victory streaks among his many accomplishments.

He owns one of the game's most prestigious records, one that many claim may never be broken. It started during the third game of the University of Oklahoma's 1953 season, when the Sooners, led by Charles "Bud" Wilkinson, defeated Texas 19–14. That started a record-shattering streak that ended on November 10, 1957, with a 7–0 upset by Notre Dame—the Wilkinson-coached Sooners had won 47 games in a row. No other college team has ever come close.

It is hard to describe how completely Bud Wilkinson's team dominated college football in both the Plains states and the entire United States.

Between 1948 and 1957, the Big Seven Conference (now the Big Eight) had but a single champion—Wilkinson's Oklahoma Sooners.

Wilkinson was no stranger to winning streaks, having played guard on an undefeated Minnesota team in 1934. On that Gopher line, he lined up against a stocky but powerful center for Ohio State named Gomer Jones, who went on to become one of Wilkinson's assistants and eventually succeeded him as the Oklahoma head coach.

At Oklahoma, Wilkinson compiled one of the best win-loss records of modern times: 145 wins, 29 losses, and 4 ties, for an enviable winning percentage of .826. Normally dressed in a white shirt and loosely knotted tie, the gray-haired wizard of Norman looked more like an executive than a football coach as he paced up and down the sidelines during Sooner games.

On the field he was noted for popularizing a number of split-T modifications, but to the delight of his fans and the chagrin of his opponents, there was little mystery to his crushing ground attacks. Oklahoma was a testament to the efficacy of bone-jarring power, and Wilkinson had a natural ability to inspire desire and effort from his players. His all-business style, devoid of affectations, seemed just right for his time and place.

Had Wilkinson continued his college coaching career, he would probably rank among the winningest coaches of all time. But he left the game after the 1963 season at age 50 to make an unsuccessful bid for the U.S. Senate in 1964. Wilkinson did head John F. Kennedy's renowned Physical Fitness Program and later served in an executive post for Richard Nixon.

Despite his relatively brief career, Wilkinson left behind a memorable legacy: three national championships, a 6-2 bowl record (including four Orange Bowl victories), and the longest winning streak in the century-old history of college football.

SCHOOL	RECORD
Oklahoma 1947–63	Won 145
	Lost 29
	Tied 4
	Pct. .826

PAUL "BEAR" BRYANT

"**T**his must be what God looks like," said George Blanda describing the towering six-foot-three-inch Bear Bryant, his coach at Kentucky. The Bear went on to become a living legend with Alabama's Crimson Tide, and, although Grambling's Eddie Robinson is relentlessly stalking his record, Bryant has reigned as the winningest coach in the history of college football, with 323 victories.

What is it that separates Bryant from mere mortals in his profession? "I'm just a plow hand from Arkansas," he said in a *Time* magazine article near the end of his final season in 1982. "But I've learned over the years how to hold a team together. How to lift some men up, how to calm down others, until finally they've got one heartbeat together, a team."

Although he coached such high-spirited superstars as Kenny Stabler and Joe Namath, his ability to mold a team out of raw individual talents was the secret of his success. The awe he inspired in his players must have made the formidable task somewhat easier.

Once before a game with Texas A&M, John David Crow, who went on to win the Heisman Trophy, stood outside Bryant's closed office door for more than an hour, anxious for a brief talk with his coach, but afraid to knock. People around Bryant treated him with the sort of respect usually reserved for divinity. Once when the coaching staff was ordered to appear in his

Bear Bryant (right) and Woody Hayes party it up on New Year's eve before the 1978 Sugar Bowl game in New Orleans. The next day Bryant's Alabama team overwhelmed Hayes' Ohio State squad 36-6.

office for an early morning meeting, an assistant coach slept on the office floor the night before because he was unsure of the exact hour of the appointment.

Bryant's personal life was filled with contradictions. While many of the game's greatest coaches emphasized clean living and total sportsmanship, the Bear followed a more tortuous path. He fought a long but eventually successful battle against alcohol; he was a gambler, and spent many hours at the craps tables in Las Vegas; and, while coaching at Texas A&M, he was at the center of a recruitment scandal involving cash payments and gifts of cars to athletes. He did not coach a black player until the class of 1974. At all times, he seemed to test the limits of the rules so fiercely that NCAA officials kept a constant and well-trained eye on him.

His technical coaching was not original. He added a passing attack to the wishbone formation, which he borrowed from Darrell Royal. When he challenged NCAA rules with his tackle-eligible pass play, officials banned it. But he won football games, more often than

anyone else. Bum Phillips once said that Bryant won "because he coached people, not football."

Late in his career, the Bear insisted that when he stopped coaching football he would die. During the 1982 season, the Tide lost four games. "I'm going to alert the president of the university and anybody who wants to know that we need to make some changes, and we need to start at the top, and I'm at the top," Bryant said before the season was over.

He passed away less than a month after his final game, a 21–15 victory over Illinois in the Liberty Bowl.

SCHOOLS	RECORD
Maryland 1945	Won 323
Kentucky 1946–53	Lost 85
Texas A&M 1954–57	Tied 17
Alabama 1958–82	Pct. .780

DARRELL ROYAL

The coach who found fame with the Texas Longhorns understood well the potential dangers of the forward pass. As an All-American defensive back for Oklahoma in the late 1940s and 1950s, Darrell Royal set a school career record with 17 interceptions.

"When you pass, three things can happen, and two of them are bad," he said, after he had been firmly installed at Texas. Little wonder that Royal's teams were noted for their outstanding rushing attacks. But when Royal first came to Texas, few people realized what kind of glory-maker had arrived.

One who seemed to understand Royal's talent early on was Bear Bryant. In 1956, while he was still at Texas A&M, a sportswriter asked the Bear if he could see any stars looming on the college coaching horizon.

"There are three great young ones right now," Bryant answered, and one of them was Darrell Royal.

Following brief assignments at Mississippi State and Washington, Royal came to Texas after the Longhorns' disastrous 1-9 season in 1956. He quickly provided a glimpse of things to come early on when Texas upset previously top-ranked Arkansas in 1957, thus fueling a great Southwest Conference rivalry.

By 1959, the Longhorns shared the conference championship with Arkansas and TCU, and went on to the Cotton Bowl. Royal always regarded the 1961 Texas team as one of his finest, comparing it favorably with his 1963 national championship team. In 1961, the Longhorns sported Royal's new "flip-top" offense, which featured running back James Saxton who, helped along considerably by Royal's novel plays, averaged almost eight yards per carry and won All-American honors. Throughout much of the season, Texas was ranked first in both the AP and UPI polls, but Royal's

A jubilant Darrell Royal congratulates Drew Morris (20) and Mike Dowdle (33) after Texas defeated arch-rival Oklahoma 19-12 in 1959. Royal's Longhorns were fourth in the nation that year, with a 9-1-0 record.

dreams of a national title were dashed when underdog TCU defeated them in a defensive war. Much to Royal's chagrin, TCU's only score came on a 50-yard touchdown pass.

For Royal, of course, there would be plenty of conference championships and number one rankings to come. He found considerable support for his suspicion of the forward pass when the Longhorns defeated Joe Namath's top-ranked Alabama team, 21–17, in the Cotton Bowl. Yet despite his obvious misgivings, a Royal-coached team could use the pass effectively if it was absolutely necessary.

His most lasting contribution to football strategy was unquestionably the wishbone offense, which he introduced in 1968 and used to propel the Longhorns to the top of the college ranks. In the wishbone, the quarterback could pass—if he had to. Bear Bryant was

so impressed by the triple option the formation afforded the quarterback that he almost immediately installed the wishbone at Alabama, as did coaches across the country.

Perhaps Darrell Royal's personal philosophy was best summed up in his own words, when he saw a magazine illustration of his bitter 1961 defeat to TCU. "There's that damn pass," he said.

SCHOOLS	RECORD
Mississippi State 1954–55	Won 184
Washington 1956	Lost 60
Texas 1957–76	Tied 5
	Pct. .749

ARA PARSEGHIAN

When Ara Parseghian assumed command at South Bend in 1964, the fortunes of Notre Dame football were at an all-time low. The Fighting Irish compiled a pathetic record of 19 wins against 30 losses from 1959 through 1963. Even the announcement of Ara's new role at South Bend began on a sour note.

With an impressive record of 74-31-2 with Miami (Ohio) and Northwestern University, including four consecutive victories against Notre Dame, Parseghian was negotiating for the head coaching position with the Irish when he walked out of a press conference called, it was thought by all, to announce his appointment. Apparently, a last-minute disagreement with one of the school's athletic administrators, Father Edmund Joyce, had brought about the debacle. The flustered coach, son of an Armenian father and French mother, returned for several days to Northwestern. A few days later, Parseghian was back in South Bend to reach a new agreement, refusing forever to divulge the true nature of the previous row. "Father Joyce wanted a shamrock on the new helmets," Ara joked later about the incident, "and I wanted a camel crossing the desert."

"He should be with us for a long time," said athletic director Moose Krause, "after all, he signed twice." Parseghian seemed to agree, because he immediately departed from the conventional wisdom of new head coaches and built a house in Indiana.

From his very first season, Ara fashioned a new dynasty in South Bend, at once rekindling the beloved memories of Knute Rockne and Frank Leahy. Taking control of essentially the same team that had managed only two victories the previous season, Parseghian juggled assignments until he had an imposing passing attack and a solid defense. Then he began a series of tough drills for every member of the team, including workouts at four o'clock on Sunday afternoons, which must have made the ground shake around South Bend.

As an example of Parseghian's skillful manipulation, John Huarte went from being a third-string quarterback in 1963 to winning the Heisman Trophy in 1964.

Parseghian came to Notre Dame with a plan to make the lackluster team into national champions in four years and came within seconds of doing the impossible in his first season. After winning their first nine games in 1964, only USC stood between Notre Dame and a national championship. When the showdown came, the Irish took a 17–0 lead into the locker room at halftime. But with less than two minutes to go in the second half, the Trojans managed to pull out a 20–17 victory. "I prefer to think of our record as 9¾ to ¼," the new Irish coach said of his first season, "not 9 and 1."

Ara Parseghian pounds a point across in the Notre Dame locker room.

Parseghian talks with four stalwarts from his national championship Notre Dame team of 1966: (from the left) defensive tackle Kevin Hardy, end Jim Seymour, quarterback Terry Hanratty, and halfback Rocky Bleier.

For another full decade, his teams pounded out the victories, showing totally new offensive looks virtually every season, winning a national championship in 1966 (one year ahead of Parseghian's bold prediction) and again in 1973, but the pressure-packed job took its toll on the high-strung coach. Parseghian often fought the pressure by scrimmaging right along with his players, absorbing the blows along with the youngsters. But by the end of his eleventh season, he had had enough. After one of the most successful coaching careers in the proud Fighting Irish history, he resigned at the relatively young age of 51. But the excitement of the gridiron continues to beckon and he is a familiar commentator on television broadcasts of the game he mastered so thoroughly from the sidelines.

SCHOOLS	RECORD
Miami (Ohio) 1951–1955	Won 170
Northwestern 1956–63	Lost 58
Notre Dame 1964–74	Tied 6
	Pct. .739

The photogenic Parseghian, urging his players on.

The Cradle of Coaches

One university, Miami (Ohio), has an unparalleled record in turning out successful football coaches.

All the following played football for Miami, then went to make their marks as head coaches with major colleges or NFL teams, with the exception of Paul Brown, who simply attended the school and cheered the team on.

Coach	Graduated from Miami	Best known for coaching
Earl Blaik	1917	Dartmouth (1934–40) Army (1941–58)
Paul Brown	1930	Cleveland Browns (1948–62) Cincinnati Bengals (1968–73)
Weeb Ewbank	1930	Baltimore Colts (1954–1962) New York Jets (1963–73)
Ara Parseghian	1947	Miami (1951–55) Northwestern (1956–63) Notre Dame (1964–73)
Paul Dietzel	1948	Louisiana State (1955–61) Army (1962–65) South Carolina (1966–74)
Bill Arnsparger	1950	Kentucky (1954–61) New York Giants (1974–76)
Bo Schembechler	1951	Miami (1963–68) Michigan (1969–)
John Pont	1951	Miami (1956–62) Indiana (1965–72) Northwestern (1973–77)
Carmen Cozza	1952	Yale (1965–)
John McVay	1953	Dayton (1964–71) New York Giants (1976–78)
John Mackovic	1966	Kansas City Chiefs (1983–)

Other coaches who served their apprenticeships on Miami coaching staffs include Woody Hayes of Ohio State, Stu Holcomb of Purdue, and Sid Gillman of the San Diego Chargers.

Distinguished Miami alumnus, Bo Schembechler, whose name is now synonymous with Michigan football.

WOODY HAYES

For three decades at Ohio State, Wayne Woodrow Hayes was the winningest coach in the Big Ten. Considering his attitude, it should come as no surprise. "Without winners," he flatly asserted once, "there wouldn't be any civilization."

Despite his unparalleled success on the field, there were many detractors who found it odd that Hayes, of all people, should talk about being civilized. He was a loner, who one associate said "lived without friends happily." Woody's career was characterized by his frequent, and often violent, temperamental explosions. During a 1971 game against arch-rival Michigan, Hayes demonstrated his anger against the officials by grabbing the yard markers and breaking them over his knee, then tossing the scraps onto the field.

Often, Hayes also used living targets to vent his displeasure. In 1973, a *Los Angeles Times* photographer claimed that the Ohio State coach shoved the camera back into his face when he tried to take a picture at a practice session before that season's Rose Bowl game, and then shouted, "That ought to take care of you, you son-of-a-bitch." The photographer dropped a criminal battery charge after Hayes sent him "an appropriate communication." In 1977, near the end of a game with Michigan, after a crucial Ohio State turnover, which in effect gave the game and a Rose Bowl trip to the Wolverines, an impetuous television cameraman stepped in front of Hayes to capture a close-up of the coach's anguish. Hayes punched him in the face.

The Buckeye coach often treated the working press, even the locals from Columbus, as wartime enemies. He was notorious for making them wait inordinately long for interviews, threatening them with physical violence on occasion, and sometimes even following through on the threat if things were going

A typical sideline scene featuring Woody Hayes berating an official during a 1962 game. Hayes actually had a lot to complain about that year, with his Buckeyes finishing in a tie for third place in the Big Ten.

Hayes was very proud of this halfback, Howard "Hopalong" Cassady. In 1955, when this picture was taken, Cassady was a consensus All-American and winner of the Heisman trophy, and Ohio State was ranked fifth in the nation.

badly. His aggressive instincts and legendary temper were not just reserved for sportswriters, but extended to everyone, players included.

"You became very wary of Woody at practice," said one of his star ends. "You left his practices with scars on your helmet."

Throughout his career, Hayes was surrounded by criticism as well as accolades. Some people complained that his "three yards and a cloud of dust" style of offense was outdated, and more than one writer called Ohio State's play monotonous. Other critics pointed to an Ohio State schedule that year after year excluded such non-conference powerhouses as Notre Dame, Oklahoma, and Nebraska. But by the end of 1978, Hayes could point to three national championships, 1954 (AP), 1957 (UPI), and 1968 (AP and UPI), and fourteen Big Ten titles (a number of them shared with his nemesis, Michigan). In the history of the sport only Bear Bryant, Eddie Robinson, Amos Stagg, and Pop Warner have won more games. Even his harshest critics had to admit that there was nothing outdated about being a winner.

For all his success, Hayes has lived a simple and Spartan life. Although he made considerable money from a television show, hundreds of lectures and clinics, and three books, he rejected several offers of a raise in pay, insisting that the additional money go to his assistants instead. "I had a Cadillac offered to me a couple of times," he recalled. "You know how that works. They give you a Cadillac one year and the next year they give you the gas to get out of town."

The gruff genius of Ohio State football doomed his career at the Gator Bowl in late December 1978. In the last two minutes of that game, with Woody's Buckeyes trailing 17–15, Clemson linebacker Charlie Bauman intercepted an OSU pass and was knocked out of bounds not far from Hayes. Enraged at the turn of events, Hayes rushed at Bauman, shouting and swinging his fists, striking him on the face mask. When a Buckeye player tried to restrain Hayes, Woody turned and punched him just below the face mask. The next day Ohio State fired Hayes, and his frenetic career was over.

SCHOOLS	RECORD
Denison 1946–48	Won 238
Miami (Ohio) 1949–50	Lost 72
Ohio State 1951–78	Tied 10
	Pct. .759

EDDIE ROBINSON

On the warm evening of September 25, 1982, a chant echoed back and forth in Florida A&M's Bragg Stadium. "Not here, Eddie, not here! Not here, Eddie, not here!" the fans taunted. But it did happen there. When Eddie Robinson's Grambling Tigers came from behind in the fourth quarter to defeat the home team, Coach Robinson joined the most select club in the proud annals of collegiate football. That night, he won his 300th game. Only Stagg, Warner, and Bryant had done it before.

Robinson is the only living member of the 300 Club and he is still actively coaching, masterminding victory after victory at Grambling, a small, predominantly black university in northern Louisiana. Going into the 1985 season, the 65-year-old coach has 320

victories to his credit, every one at Grambling. By the time Louisiana law compels him to retire at age 70, he is likely to have surpassed Bear Bryant to become the winningest coach in the history of college football. That record should stand for a long, long time—few people become head coach at the age of 22 any more, as Robinson did in 1941 when he was installed as head coach of Grambling (enrollment 320), just after it was renamed from Louisiana Negro Normal and Industrial Institute. He suffered a losing record his first year but came back with a vengeance the next year, posting a 9-0 record and shutting out every opponent. Since the early 1950s, Grambling has won more than seventy-five percent of its games.

Some may quibble with Robinson's record because of the NCAA's varying classifications of Grambling over the years, which have included Small College, Division II and Major College, and the smaller college opposition they have faced. Grambling is cur-

Eddie Robinson joins in the celebration as Grambling defensive tackle Gary Johnson shows off his awards as Defensive Player of the Year among black college players in 1974.

rently in Division II and a member of the Southwestern Athletic Conference.

But NCAA officials share no such qualms or prejudices. "If he gets to 324," NCAA Associate Director of Statistics Steve Boda has said, "we'll consider him the winningest college football coach of all time, regardless of division, pure and simple."

Those who would accuse Robinson of winning at least a portion of his honor in the bush leagues might, however, consider that Eddie Robinson has sent as many players to the pros as any other coach.

For all his success, Robinson has changed little over nearly half a century of coaching. He has always cautioned his students about the dangers of drugs, loose women, and a lackadaisical attitude toward education. At 6 a.m. every school day, he walks up and down the corridors of the Grambling dorm, ringing an old-fashioned school bell to be certain that all students wake early enough to attend their first class.

The tradition remembered best by Grambling players is Robinson's ritual of bringing back former students to help train newcomers each year. "When I was at Grambling," USFL star wide receiver Trumaine Johnson said, "I got to work with former players like Frank Lewis, Sammy White, and Charlie Joiner."

And all of his former players remember with a touch of reverence Eddie Robinson, the carefully dressed, patriotic, raspy-voiced football genius who is standing on the edge of history.

SCHOOL*	RECORD
Grambling 1941–	Won 320
	Lost 106
	Tied 15
	Pct. .743
*Still actively coaching	

Coach of the Year

Each year the American Football Coaches Association (AFCA) and the Football Writers Association of America (FWAA) poll their members to determine a Coach of the Year. Prior to 1957, only the AFCA made such an award. When the two organizations selected different coaches for the award, both are given here.

Year	Coach	School	Year	Coach	School
1935	Lynn Waldorf	Northwestern	1964	Ara Parseghian (AFCA & FWAA)	Notre Dame
1936	Richard Harlow	Harvard		Frank Broyles (AFCA)	Arkansas
1937	Ed Mylin	Lafayette	1965	Tommy Prothro (AFCA)	UCLA
1938	Bill Kern	Carnegie Tech		Duffy Daugherty (FWAA)	Michigan State
1939	Eddie Anderson	Iowa	1966	Tom Cahill	Army
1940	Clark Shaughnessy	Stanford	1967	John Pont	Indiana
1941	Frank Leahy	Notre Dame	1968	Joe Paterno (AFCA)	Penn State
1942	Bill Alexander	Georgia Tech		Woody Hayes (FWAA)	Ohio State
1943	Amos Alonzo Stagg	Pacific	1969	Bo Schembechler	Michigan
1944	Carroll Widdoes	Ohio State	1970	Charles McClendon (AFCA)	Louisiana State
1945	Bo McMillin	Indiana		Darrell Royal (AFCA)	Texas
1946	Earl Blaik	Army		Alex Agase (FWAA)	Northwestern
1947	Fritz Crisler	Michigan	1971	Paul Bryant (AFCA)	Alabama
1948	Bennie Oosterbaan	Michigan		Bob Devaney (FWAA)	Nebraska
1949	Bud Wilkinson	Oklahoma	1972	John McKay	USC
1950	Charlie Caldwell	Princeton	1973	Paul Bryant (AFCA)	Alabama
1951	Chuck Taylor	Stanford		Johnny Majors (FWAA)	Pittsburgh
1952	Biggie Munn	Michigan State	1974	Grant Teaff	Baylor
1953	Jim Tatum	Maryland	1975	Frank Kush (AFCA)	Arizona State
1954	Red Sanders	UCLA		Woody Hayes (FWAA)	Ohio State
1955	Duffy Daugherty	Michigan State	1976	Johnny Majors	Pittsburgh
1956	Bowden Wyatt	Tennessee	1977	Don James (AFCA)	Washington
1957	Woody Hayes	Ohio State		Lew Holtz (FWAA)	Arkansas
1958	Paul Dietzel	Louisiana State	1978	Joe Paterno	Penn State
1959	Ben Schwartzwalder	Syracuse	1979	Earle Bruce	Ohio State
1960	Murray Warmath	Minnesota	1980	Vince Dooley	Georgia
1961	Paul Bryant (AFCA)	Alabama	1981	Danny Ford	Clemson
	Darrell Royal (FWAA)	Texas	1982	Joe Paterno	Penn State
1962	John McKay	USC	1983	Ken Hatfield (AFCA)	Air Force
1963	Darrell Royal	Texas		Howard Schnellenberger (FWAA)	Florida
			1984	Lavell Edwards	Brigham Young

Best Winning Percentages

Coach	Team most associated with	Percentage and Record
Knute Rockne	Notre Dame	.881 (105-12-5)
Frank Leahy	Notre Dame	.864 (107-13-9)
George Woodruff	Pennsylvania	.846 (142-25-2)
Percy Haughton	Harvard	.832 (96-17-6)
Bob Neyland	Tennessee	.829 (173-31-12)
Fielding Yost	Michigan	.828 (196-36-12)
Bud Wilkinson	Oklahoma	.826 (145-29-4)
Barry Switzer*	Oklahoma	.824 (115-23-4)
Jock Sutherland	Pittsburgh	.812 (144-28-14)
Tom Osborne*	Nebraska	.810 (118-27-2)
Bob Devaney	Nebraska	.806 (136-30-7)
Joe Paterno*	Penn State	.802 (176-43-1)
Frank Thomas	Alabama	.795 (141-33-9)
Harry Williams	Minnesota	.787 (139-34-10)
Gil Dobie	Cornell	.781 (180-45-15)
Paul Bryant	Alabama	.780 (323-85-17)
Fred Folsom	Colorado	.779 (106-28-6)
Bo Schembechler*	Michigan	.768 (186-54-6)
Fritz Crisler	Michigan	.768 (116-32-9)
Charley Moran	Texas A&M	.766 (122-33-12)
Wallace Wade	Alabama/Duke	.765 (171-49-10)
Frank Kush	Arizona State	.764 (176-54-1)
Dan McGugin	Vanderbilt	.762 (197-55-19)
Jim Crowley	Fordham	.761 (78-21-10)
Andy Smith	California	.761 (162-32-13)
Woody Hayes	Ohio State	.759 (238-72-10)
Earl Blaik	Army	.759 (166-48-14)
Darrell Royal	Texas	.749 (184-60-5)
John McKay	USC	.749 (127-40-8)

*Still actively coaching

All-Time Winningest Coaches

Coach	Team most associated with	Wins
Paul Bryant	Alabama	323
Eddie Robinson*	Grambling	320
Amos Alonzo Stagg	Chicago	314
Glenn Warner	Carlisle/Stanford	313
Woody Hayes	Ohio State	238
Jess Neely	Rice	207
Warren Woodson	New Mexico State	207
Eddie Anderson	Holy Cross	201
Dana Bible	Texas	198
Dan McGugin	Vanderbilt	197
Fielding Yost	Michigan	196
Howard Jones	Southern Cal	194
John Vaught	Mississippi	190
Bo Schembechler*	Michigan	186
John Heisman	Georgia Tech	185
Darrell Royal	Texas	184
Carl Snavely	North Carolina	180
Gil Dobie	Cornell	180
Ben Schwartzwalder	Syracuse	178
Joe Paterno	Penn State	176
Ralph Jordan	Auburn	176
Frank Kush	Arizona State	176
Bob Neyland	Tennessee	173
Dan Devine	Missouri	172
Wallace Wade	Alabama/Duke	171
Ara Parseghian	Notre Dame	170

*Still actively coaching

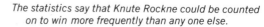

The statistics say that Knute Rockne could be counted on to win more frequently than any one else.

The Big Game

There are so many rivalries, hot and frenetic, that at times it seems there isn't a game listed on a given Saturday that could not be described as a rivalry. Every team has at least one arch-rival, some several. They usually crop up within a conference, frequently because the schools are neighbors. But then there are such pairs as Notre Dame and Southern California or Army and Navy.

Whatever the reason for bitter rivalries, they exist all over the nation's gridirons and they add a certain something to college football. They give students reasons to rage and party and alumni something to savor while preserving common irrationalities.

Harvard and Yale is probably the oldest rivalry in college football lore, that is if you don't count Princeton and Rutgers or Rutgers and Columbia, both of whom began playing each other with special rapacity a few years before Harvard and Yale first met in full football combat in the autumn of 1875.

Army and Navy put on the most picturesque show with their precision-marching Cadets and Midshipmen and all the VIPs from Washington who come for the game. It has been said that the specially-scheduled Saturday morning trains from Washington to Phila-

delphia the day of this illustrious contest carry more scrambled eggs on Army and Navy hat peaks than were served to the invading American forces on D-Day morning. Tradition also has it that the President of the United States attends the game, sitting on the Army side for one half and the Navy side the other. The Commander-in-Chief is supposed to favor neither service academy, but no one believes Dwight D. Eisenhower found a scintilla of pleasure when Navy did something especially well on the field before him. And most observers found John F. Kennedy inordinately quiet and unanimated while he sat his half on the Army side of the field.

Certainly the most extravagant display of alumni riches is evinced in Dallas when Texas and Oklahoma get together each year and the Longhorn and Sooner oil men and ranchers invade with their squadrons of private planes and convoys of limousines. Tailgate parties outside the Cotton Bowl have featured everything from silver bowls of Beluga caviar and magnums of Dom Perignon to down home Tex-Mex chili and barbecued ribs. Probably the most imaginative pranks have come from the fertile minds of the students of Stanford and California.

> **"Football is only a game. Spiritual things are eternal. Nevertheless, Beat Texas!"**
>
> A SIGN OUTSIDE OF THE FIRST BAPTIST CHURCH IN FAYETTEVILLE, ARKANSAS.

We have selected seven especially fervid rivalries to chronicle in some depth here. But there are so many others.

Why, do you ask, have we forgotten these?

Pittsburgh—Penn State
Tennessee—Vanderbilt
Purdue—Indiana
Texas—Texas A&M
Louisiana State—Tulane
Missouri—Kansas
Alabama—Auburn
Michigan—Michigan State
Mississippi—Mississippi State
North Carolina—North Carolina State

Oklahoma—Nebraska
Georgia—Georgia Tech
Washington—Washington State
Clemson—South Carolina
Cornell—Colgate
Texas—Arkansas
Notre Dame—Army
Minnesota—Michigan

Because if we hadn't it would have simply given rise to another list of rivalries of which the same question could be asked. Perhaps college football could be described as a quilt woven of rivalries of many shapes and many faces, one of the reasons it is such a lustrous and vibrant sport.

HARVARD
YALE

TA.D. Jones, one of Yale's more venerable coaches, stood before his team in the Eli dressing room one day in the mid-1920s and said: "Gentlemen, you are about to play football for Yale against Harvard. Never in your lives will you do anything so important."

Years later, at the Yale Bowl on a Saturday afternoon in November of 1983, Harvard and Yale met to play the one-hundredth game in their august Ivy League rivalry. Although it had been many a decade since either team had seriously pursued anything as unscholarly as a national football championship, the event hardly went unnoticed. Approximately 70,000 fans cheered as more than 60 former Harvard and Yale captains were brought onto the field before the game. The eldest was 94-year-old Hamilton Fish of Harvard, two-time All-American tackle (1908–09), who could

also boast of having tackled Jim Thorpe. Harvard won the most ancient alumnus contest by a mere two years over Yale's Henry Ketchum, age 92, center, and another two-time All-American (1911–12). Harvard also went on to win the ensuing game that day, 16–7.

Not surprisingly, no one at the 1983 game had been present at the very first Harvard-Yale contest, which was held more than a century earlier in 1875. A milestone in the history of American football, that original battle was primarily one of concessions because each team played a different form of the game: Harvard's version was based loosely on rugby while Yale's was based on soccer, so the two schools had to resolve their conflicting styles of play.

Two delegates from each school convened at Springfield, Massachusetts, to agree on a series of "concessionary rules." As Harvard's newspaper, the

Auspiciously dressed for the occasion, Harvard students watch an 1887 game from their carriage.

Crimson, would report after the game: "The adopted rules were not fully understood by either team, and the Yale men said that they differed from theirs more than from Harvard's...." Yale had consented to play Harvard's rugby-style rules, and Harvard had agreed to play the game at Yale.

So, on a Friday evening in November 1875, the Harvard team, accompanied by about 150 students, boarded a train to New Haven for the game the following afternoon. On Saturday morning, Yale students obligingly led members of the Harvard team on a tour of New Haven's major sights. The spirit of good-natured camaraderie was even carried over to the game, with rooters for either side applauding good plays, regardless of who made them.

That Saturday was a perfect day for football, slightly overcast with virtually no wind. Approximately 2,000 people crowded into the grandstands at Yale's Hamilton Park for the game, scheduled at 2:30. One of the fascinated fans was Walter Camp, who would attend Yale the following year, and later do so much to establish the modern rules of American football.

Harvard won the toss and Yale kicked off. The players from Cambridge scored the first touchdown six

Pep Talk

Hefty Herman Hickman, Yale's colorful coach from 1948 to 1951, known as the poet laureate of the Great Smokies (he was from Tennessee), was noted for his unique pep talks, which included quoting the classics in stentorian tones. This memorable one from before a Harvard game was preserved by John McCallum in his book *Ivy League Football Since 1872:*

"'Ye call me chief,' he (Hickman) declaimed, 'and ye do well to call me chief. If ye are men, follow me! Strike down your guard, gain the mountain passes, and there do bloody work as did your sires at old Thermopylae!' His voice impassioned now, his features grim with determination. 'Is Sparta dead? Is the old Grecian spirit frozen in your veins, that you do crouch and cower like a belabored hound beneath his master's last? O, comrades, warriors, Thracians! If we must fight, let us fight for ourselves. If we must slaughter, let us slaughter our oppressors! If we must die, let it be under the clear sky, by the bright waters, in noble, honorable battle!'

"Then, having concluded his rendition of *Spartacus to the Gladiators,* he snapped his fingers. 'Whadya say, men,' he growled. 'Let's go, gang. Whadya say, let's go chew up those Harvards.'"

Yale cheerleaders in recent action.

How to Enjoy a Football Game

by Franklin P. Adams

I was now wet, chilly, and virtually void of merriment.

A nastier voice yells, "Get choah winnink cullahs heah."

On the trolley, the conductor climbs up and down my back.

This excerpt from an article which appeared in Liberty Magazine, December 4, 1937, was written by Franklin P. Adams, noted wit, philosopher, and charter member of the Algonquin Round Table.

"You can have your football games. I'm through. Too much trouble, for one thing. And too vicarious. I'm funny that way. I'd rather play my own tenth-rate—oh, all right, eleventh-rate—tennis than watch Budge pass von Cramm at the net. I'd rather play The Battle Cry of Freedom on my harmonica than listen, all dressed up, to Jascha Heifetz play anything in Carnegie Hall. I don't say that I don't like to see Budge or to hear Heifetz; but if it's a choice, I'll do something I participate in.

"That is one of the things the matter with the United States: vicariousness. It's a big subject; it's why people listen to the radio, go to see movies that they may live somebody else's romance, read book reviews instead of books, and go to games that they don't play and never have played. The bigger the crowd and the more they pay for tickets, the more vicarious are the spectators . . .

"The football crowd, audience, or aggregation of spectators is the worst of the whole vicarious lot. It is true that many of the crowd are alumni of the universities twenty-two of whose students are out there jousting. To a boy playing a game I can see that it makes a big difference—too much, I think—whether his team wins or loses. But what difference does it make to an alumnus?

"I wore my good coat, like a fool," says the Little Woman.

The standard of scholarship may be twice as high at Atwater as at Bingham, to swipe a couple of names from George Ade's The College Widow. Bingham beats Atwater year after year. To hear a Bingham alumnus talk, you would think that he personally made all those tackles and runs—an alumnus from fifty to sixty years of age.

"I'm not guessing. I have two brothers-in-law who have been out of Princeton at least thirty-five years. From September to Thanksgiving they have no other thought and no other conversation but football. Take it from their wives, they are at their boringest during the football season. All their talk is last Saturday's game or next Saturday's game. Multiply those two by millions.

"My diagnosis is not that such football fans are just Great Big Boys; they are puerile, they are immature; they are not perennially youthful, they are incurably childish. Do they ever voice their pride, night after night, when or if their college acquires somebody on the faculty? Do they all get together and say, 'All together now: Three short cheers for Einstein!'? . . .

"Bored though you might be by alumni who replay every game, you don't know punishment until you attend a game with somebody who used to play, particularly on one of the teams contending out there on the field. The only thing comparable to it is going to a play with a lad who designed the scenery. He takes all the fun out of it. You enjoy the play and the acting; this fellow tells you that the desk in the left corner is all wrong, and is ruining the play; it is an 1831 item, and the play's period is 1830. 'What an anachronism!' he whispers . . .

"I blame the newspapers as much as the alumni.

"About Tuesday you read the ballyhoo. Harvard, spurred by last Saturday's staggering defeat, has a fighting chance against Yale. Thursday one of the Yale stars has galloping rigor mortis and may be out of the game ten days.

Saturday morning he is on crutches or in a wheel chair, and that afternoon he plays the Game of His Life. The sporting writers, in their forecasts, say that Yale may win; on the other hand, if Harvard, etc. They are the greatest of the However boys.

"Well, by some miracle you have tickets. The papers last night said that all seats had been sold, and that somebody had offered $100 for a pair of the Coveted Pasteboards. Incidentally, I never met anybody who paid more than the printed price of $3.30 or $4.40 for a ticket. Saturday morning is Fair and Warmer, known as Ideal Football Weather for the spectators. You are going from New York to New Haven, and by train—the most favorable conditions. You are ready at ten, and the Little Woman, a prey to Speed Madness, is ready at 10.45. Accoutered with two lap rugs, you board the train at 11.05, and you get seats. The train leaves at 11.20; you settle down to read. Every time you get interested an unpleasantly voiced man comes through the car with 'Buy or sell football tickets.' And another, with a nastier, louder voice yells, 'Get choah winnink cullahs heah.' These lads are nuisances. . . .

"At two the Bowl is reached; at 2.10 we find our Portal, near the goal posts. The game is on; no score yet. But there are two alumni behind us complaining loudly. 'They make me sick,' says one. 'Been out twenty-six years and I get these seats! The longer you're out the worse the seats. I suppose in 1950 they'll give me seats in Bridgeport.' 'Shut up, the play'll all be down here. It's the Harvard goal line this quarter.' This goes on during the first half.

"The game is no good. It ends Harvard 13, Yale 0. But in the third quarter the sun vanishes; it is raining and snowing. 'I wore my good coat, like a fool,' says the Little Woman. 'This'll ruin it.' P.S. It ruined it. The game ended in a concoction half rain, half snow, and a jigger of bitterness, mine about having to get her a new coat or have this one dyed or something, and hers because I didn't tell her to wear the old one. 'You wouldn't have done it.' 'I would.' 'And then you'd have met somebody on the train, and said to me: "Me in that old coat! I felt like a fool."' 'That,' I said "is no coincidence."'

"We arrived home at 7.40, tired, angry, still wet, hungry. 'The cook is out, and no dinner will I get,' she cooed. So we went to a good place where you can get all you can eat and more than you want to drink for forty-five dollars. First thing I knew it was two o'clock of a Sunday morning.

"Football isn't worth the candle to me. This season I'm sleeping of a Saturday morning, having lunch at home, listening to a broadcast of the game I'm most interested in, but lying on a couch near the fireplace, with a stein on the taboret. And at 4.22, when the game is over, there I am, warm and at peace with the universe, no residents of which I have seen for three hours."

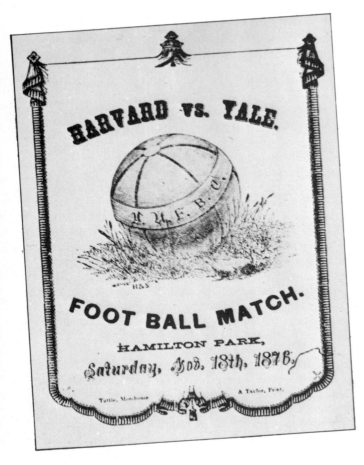

The program cover from the second meeting of these famous rivals.

Football and the Poet

Archibald MacLeish, noted poet, essayist, and dramatist, Librarian of Congress, Boylston Professor at Harvard, and three time recipient of the Pulitzer Prize, played football while a student at Yale. In the following speech, he recalls those days:

"It is historically true that I played football at Yale. It is historically true that I won my freshman numerals. It is even historically true that I won my Y—as an all-purpose, all-position substitute on a series of Yale teams which never beat Harvard. . . .

"I have only one glorious memory of those four years and its setting is not Soldiers' Field in Cambridge but the bar of the long-vanished Tremont Hotel in Boston. We—we being the Yale freshman team of the fall of 1911—had just held the best Harvard freshman team in a generation (Brickley, Bradlee, Hardwick, Collidge, Logan) to a nothing–nothing tie in a downpour of helpful rain and we were relaxing, not without noise, when the coach of that famous Harvard freshman team approached us, looked us over, focused (he had had a drink or two himself) on me and announced in the voice of an indignant beagle sighting a fox that I was, without question, the dirtiest little sonofabitch of a center ever to visit Cambridge, Massachusetts. It was heady praise. But unhappily I didn't deserve that honor either: I was little but not that little."

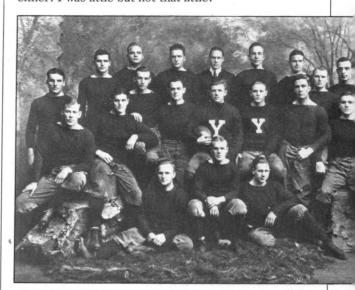

Archibald MacLeish (top row, fourth from right) standing tall on Yale's 1913 football team.

minutes after the game began and kicked a goal a few minutes later. Before the first of the three half-hour periods ended, Harvard kicked a second goal. In the second period, Harvard scored a touchdown after an attempted kick for a goal hit the uprights. According to the rules of the day, a kicked goal was worth more than a touchdown.

When Yale was threatening to score in the third period, one of its players was thrown on the ball, which deflated. The ball was pumped up and put in play again, but Yale's chances for victory had burst. The final score was 4 goals and 4 touchdowns for Harvard, none for Yale.

Until about 1910 or so, what are now known as Ivy League teams, especially Yale, Harvard, and Princeton, dominated college football. Yale and Harvard contests were always well-fought battles, but the overall crown for the Golden Age of the Ivy League, the late 1800s and the first decade of the 20th century, must be handed to Yale. By 1910, after 31 meetings, Yale had triumphed in 23 of the games, Harvard only 5, and 3 ended in ties.

Tailgating in style at the Yale Bowl.

And there were some grand names on the roster in those days. Walter Camp began his remarkable football career as a player at Yale in 1876: he coached the Eli from 1888 through 1892. At end from 1885 through 1888 was Amos Alonzo Stagg. In the Harvard-Yale games of 1888 through 1891, spectators watched the legendary strongman Pudge Heffelfinger bolster the Yale line. Debuting in 1891 was Frank Hinkey, one of the school's all-time great ends, called the "football freak" because at a fragile 150 pounds, with a noticeably anemic pallor, he hardly appeared to be what he was—the most brutal and feared tackler of his time. In the early 1900s, Yale could also claim such other early luminaries as T.A.D. Jones and Ted Coy.

Harvard had its share of stellar lights as well around this time, backs like Charles Daly, Benjamin Dibblee, Percy Wendell, Charlie Brickley, and Eddie Mahan, among others.

Yale's dominance in the rivalry came to an end when Percy Haughton took over the head coaching duties at Harvard in 1908. During his nine-year tenure, Yale won only two of the nine contests. By the mid-1920s, Harvard-Yale matches no longer carried the possibility of propelling either team to a national championship. Over the years, quite a few people destined for prominence in other fields participated in the annual brawls, such as Archibald MacLeish and John Hersey from Yale and Bobby and Ted Kennedy from Harvard, the latter best remembered as having scored Harvard's only touchdown in their 1955 loss to Yale.

End Pete Varney of Harvard snares a pass which, along with a 2-point conversion, enabled the Crimson to tie Yale in 1968.

Kennedy and the Heisman

Robert Kennedy, who played varsity football while at Harvard, was asked to present the Heisman Award to Terry Baker of Oregon State for the 1962 season. Kennedy was happy to make the appearance, though somewhat reluctant to hand over the trophy instead of keeping it for himself. The following is excerpted from his speech:

"It is a singular pleasure to be present at this award of the John W. Heisman Football Trophy. For some of us former aspirants, it is great pleasure just to *see* the trophy.

"When I received the letter from the Heisman Award Committee, I thought for a second that it had been delayed in the post office for 15 years.

"In fact, I would prefer to believe that I am here, not as Attorney General, but rather as a senior who once got the 'short end of the stick' from the Heisman Trophy Selection Committee in 1947.

"Some of you sports enthusiasts may have wondered about the origin of that sports expression 'the short end.' Well, I was the 'short end' at Harvard.

"With respect to the Heisman Awards and the Big Three—Harvard, Yale, and Princeton—the name of the Yale winner started with 'K,' Larry Kelley.

"So, also, the Princeton winner, Dick Kazmaier. *The 'K's' at Harvard are still dying with suspense.*

"This is not the time or the place to cry 'discrimination'. . . . I mean 'foul.'

"But why do the Heisman winners always have to be big guys???

"And from the backfield???

"Why did 26 of the 28 winners have to be backs???

"Why do they have to be regulars all the time???

"It's about time they recognized good, short substitutes!

"And only four of the 28 winners had three syllables in their names.

"The whole thing seems top heavy or something.

"There are two things I keep in mind about the late John Heisman. One: he was enthusiastic about the smaller players.

"He was really teed off when Albie Booth was not chosen All America.

"He once compiled a list of All Americans who weighed less than 150 pounds—I was 147 myself.

"This list included Poe, Pollard, Hinkey, Casey, Daly, Weekes, Maulbetsch, Eckersall, Stevenson, Steffen, Strupper, Stinchcomb, and Stuhldreyer.

"No 'K's' here either. . . and only a few with three syllable names.

"The second thing I keep before me about the great John Heisman. He was courageous enough to *change* his selections, even years later.

"He picked his first all-time All American team in 1920. He changed it drastically in 1932.

"I'm not hinting, and I don't want to cause next year's Selection Committee a lot of trouble. But these things aren't necessarily final.

"All this old watchcharm wants is justice. And I don't mean 'Choo Choo' Justice of North Carolina either.

"I salute Terry Baker and congratulate him and Oregon State University on the national recognition and honor they are accorded here tonight.

"Even though he is a back, a regular, and tall, and rangy, he fully deserves the Heisman Trophy. *This year.*

"But I would like to have a small vicarious share in this honor accorded his fine school. A Kennedy was head football coach at Oregon State a few years back. More precisely, in 1894. Beat the Oregon Webfoots that year 16 to 0. Lost only one game. *We* played only three that year.

"John Heisman was one of the most inventive of the great coaches. He played a great part in the origin of the forward pass, the spinner, and the double pass from center, and the Heisman shift.

"However, with all of that, he never did come up with a top-grade mechanical engineer who is a left-handed passer, a right-handed pitcher, a left-handed writer, and a right-handed bowler.

"In kicking at least, Terry is a left-footer.

"What a United States Marshal he'd make!

"It is said that he can switch as fast and often as his fellow Oregonian, Senator Wayne Morse. I regret the possibilities of this dexterity since Terry's Jefferson High School team in Portland was known as the Jefferson 'Democrats.' "

The Kennedy footballers: John at Choate (left), and Bobby (center) and Ted at Harvard.

The Crimson's *whimsical coverage of 1968 contest against Yale, a true moral victory.*

The most memorable modern installment of the old rivalry came in 1968, when by a somewhat miraculous turn of events, both teams had undefeated seasons going into the big game. That year, Harvard had developed a defensive powerhouse, while Yale, led by quarterback Brian Dowling and halfback Calvin Hill, produced its best offense in many years.

With 42 seconds left to go, the Bulldogs were ahead 29–13. Sportswriters were already wrapping up their stories describing the ruination of the Crimson's heretofore perfect season. But in that 42 seconds, Harvard scored a touchdown, a two-point conversion, and another touchdown just as time expired. Then, with the game clock at zero, Harvard racked up another two-point conversion to tie the score. The *Crimson* captured the miracle finish with its proud headline: "Harvard Beats Yale, 29–29."

SERIES STANDINGS

Yale	Harvard
55 Wins	38 Wins
38 Losses	55 Losses
8 Ties	8 Ties
Best Game: 1957, 54–0	Best Game: 1915, 41–0

Series Scoring

Year	Harvard	Yale	Year	Harvard	Yale
1875	4	0	1933	19	6
1876	0	1	1934	0	14
1878	0	1	1935	7	14
1879	0	0	1936	13	14
1880	0	1	1937	13	6
1881	0	0 *	1938	7	0
1882	0	1	1939	7	20
1883	2	23	1940	28	0
1884	0	48	1941	14	0
1886	4	29	1942	3	7
1887	8	17	1945	0	28
1889	0	6	1946	14	27
1890	12	6	1947	21	31
1891	0	10	1948	20	7
1892	0	6	1949	6	29
1893	0	6	1950	6	14
1894	4	12	1951	21	21
1897	0	0	1952	14	41
1898	17	0	1953	13	0
1899	0	0	1954	13	9
1900	0	28	1955	7	21
1901	22	0	1956	14	42
1902	0	23	1957	0	54
1903	0	16	1958	28	0
1904	0	12	1959	35	6
1905	0	6	1960	6	39
1906	0	6	1961	27	0
1907	0	12	1962	14	6
1908	4	0	1963	6	20
1909	0	8	1964	18	14
1910	0	0	1965	13	0
1911	0	0	1966	17	0
1912	20	0	1967	20	24
1913	15	5	1968	29	29
1914	36	0	1969	0	7
1915	41	0	1970	14	12
1916	3	6	1971	35	16
1919	10	3	1972	17	28
1920	9	0	1973	0	35
1921	10	3	1974	21	16
1922	10	3	1975	10	7
1923	0	13	1976	7	21
1924	6	19	1977	7	24
1925	0	0	1978	28	35
1926	7	12	1979	22	7
1927	0	14	1980	0	14
1928	17	0	1981	0	28
1929	10	6	1982	45	7
1930	13	0	1983	16	7
1931	0	3	1984	27	30
1932	0	19			

*Yale won the 1881 contest because of four Harvard safeties, which were counted only as tie-breakers.

ARMY
NAVY

What remains one of college football's most color-ful rivalries began nearly a century ago. In 1890, the Naval Academy at Annapolis, Maryland, challenged West Point's Military Academy to a game of soccer-style football, with, of course, the bruising body contact that had become an integral part of the American game. The mere fact that Army had no football team at the time was hardly an excuse to ignore the challenge.

Rushing to fill the void, a young cadet named Dennis Michie gathered together some of the best athletes at West Point and gave them a crash course in the sport. Near the end of November, Navy's Midshipmen sailed up the Hudson and marched across the plains at the Point to meet the inexperienced Army team.

While en route, the Middies commandeered a goat that was grazing in a yard and brought it along to the contest to serve as the team mascot, launching a tradition that remains to this day. The Army team, never to be outdone by Navy, soon adopted a mule as their mascot, just before the game of 1899. The creature selected to counter Navy's goat was relieved of its duties hauling an ice wagon; then it was curried, groomed, bedecked in leggings, and, with black and gold streamers fluttering from its ears and tail, brought to the Army sideline. It must have had the desired effect because the Cadets pummeled the rival Middies 17–5 that day.

Not unexpectedly, a more polished Navy trounced the Cadets in that first football encounter in

The Cadets of 1944 move into the stands at Baltimore for the Army-Navy battle. After five consecutive defeats, Army turned it around and sunk the Midshipmen 23–7, and proceeded to do it again every year until 1950.

1890. The final score was 24–0. Enraged by the lopsided defeat, Army issued an immediate challenge to meet again the following year at Annapolis. When the two teams reassembled in 1891, Army, with a year of rigorous practice behind them, defeated Navy by a score of 32–16. The historic rivalry was under way, but not for long.

After the fourth meeting in the series, in 1893, an Army brigadier general and a Navy rear admiral got into a terrific argument over some game detail and challenged each other to a duel. Shortly thereafter, President Grover Cleveland issued an edict banning future games between the two military academies. The ban was observed until 1899, when officials at both academies agreed to renew the series.

Once the rivalry resumed, it continued to grow in popularity and intensity, despite a number of brief hiatuses: in 1909 after the death of an Army player during a game; in 1917 and 1918 because of World War I; and in 1928 and 1929 when Annapolis and West Point disagreed on eligibility requirements for their players.

In the 20th century, the yearly Army-Navy game evolved into a national phenomenon. A number of sports historians have claimed that the series produced football's first ticket scalpers. To accommodate the huge number of spectators seeking tickets for the classic confrontation, the game has been held throughout much of its history in Philadelphia, first at Franklin Field, and now at Veterans Stadium (though the 1983 game was played at the Rose Bowl).

Chris "Red" Cagle was an outstanding runner for Army from 1926 through 1929, a three-time consensus All-American.

Cadets on parade in 1943.

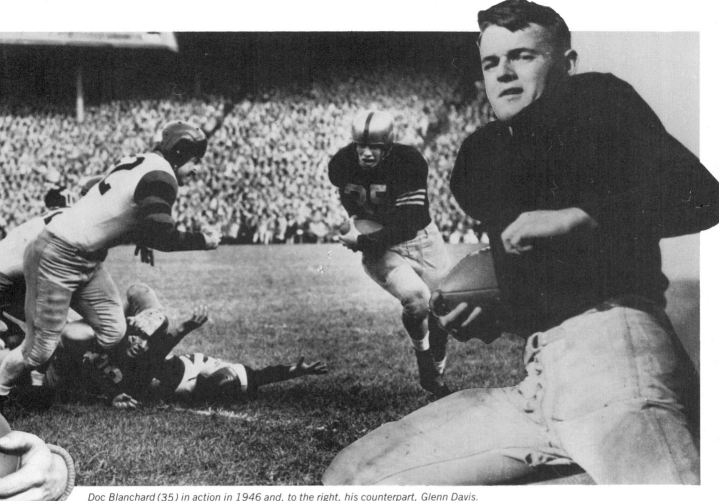

Doc Blanchard (35) in action in 1946 and, to the right, his counterpart, Glenn Davis.

In 1926, the teams helped to dedicate Chicago's Soldier Field. Before a crowd estimated at 110,000, Army, led by All-American Chris "Red" Cagle, and an undefeated Navy team battled to a 21–21 tie in what many consider one of the greatest games of all time. Two decades later, an equally astounding game was played at Philadelphia's Muncipal Stadium.

Going into the final game of 1946, Earl "Red" Blaik's Cadets were undefeated, cursed only by a tie with Notre Dame; in fact that magnificent Army team had not lost in three seasons. They were still in contention with Notre Dame for the national championship, and it was the final game for Army's famous one-two punch, Mr. Inside, Felix "Doc" Blanchard, and Mr. Outside, Glenn Davis.

By contrast, Navy's fortunes had sunk as rapidly as a PT boat hit by a torpedo. Beaten only by Army the previous year, Navy found its course reversed in 1946 when a series of resignations following the end of World War II and serious injuries to no fewer than five running backs had left the team in a state of disrepair.

After winning their first game in 1946, Navy proceeded to lose the next seven. In desperation, the Midshipmen decided to import a new mascot, finding what was reported to be the "smelliest, nastiest goat in all Texas." The eleventh in the great line of goats on the Navy sideline, Billy XI, as he was dubbed, was greeted by the commanding officer at Annapolis and was promptly tethered next to his predecessor, the disreputed Billy X. Then, with an almost divine sign that Navy was down but not out, Billy X responded by

Stop The War

Coach Earl Blaik received this telegram just after the 1944 Army-Navy game, which Army won to cap an undefeated season.

The greatest of all Army teams. We have stopped the war to celebrate your magnificent success.

Douglas MacArthur

The Midshipmen on parade at Annapolis.

kicking the starch out of the upstart replacement and was given a last-minute reprieve.

Billy X and the Middies traveled to Municipal Stadium as 28-point underdogs. President Harry S Truman and 100,000 other fans (the game had been sold out before the start of the season) saw the festivities open with a large group of Army cheerleaders pulling an enormous wooden goat onto the field. To the surprise of all, a trap door opened in the belly of the "Trojan Goat," and Billy X walked down a ramp onto the field. The cheerleaders then pulled off their Army outfits to reveal their Navy uniforms.

The game began as expected, Army on the march almost without resistance. Doc Blanchard surged into the end zone for the Cadets' first touchdown. By halftime, the score was Army 21, Navy 6, and it looked likely to turn into a rout.

But the scenario didn't go as predicted when the two teams reconvened. Navy scored early in the third quarter, but for the second time in the game missed the extra point. Several press box pundits noted that the Army players seemed tired. Army's next drive stalled at its own 35-yard line when Blanchard, who had been plagued by an injured knee all season, failed to gain the half-yard needed on fourth down. A now

inspired Navy drove down to the Army 5-yard line as the third quarter ended.

Moments later, Navy passed for another touchdown, but once again missed the extra point. The score stood at Army 21, Navy 18. The Cadets were exhausted and were unable to sustain a drive of any kind during the fourth quarter. After several exchanges, the Midshipmen drove all the way to Army's 3-yard line, where it was first down with about a minute and a half to play.

Two Navy rushes into a suddenly revived Army line failed to gain an inch. With the crowd roaring and surging from the stands to the sidelines and no time outs remaining, Navy coach Tom Hamilton sent in a substitute with a play, but it took too long to explain in the huddle, and the Middies were penalized 5 yards. On what turned out to be the final play, a Navy back, Lynn Chewning, cut around end and got to the 3-yard line, where he tried to stop the clock. But the spectators had swelled onto the field, and Chewning couldn't get out of bounds. The Middies tried to stop the clock by sending in a substitute, but time had expired. With that eke-out victory, Army maintained its three-year undefeated streak and stretched its lead in the historic rivalry to 24 triumphs against 19 defeats and 3 ties.

A cartoon by Mullin from just before the big Army-Navy game of 1946.

Four-Star Footballers

Suited up on the Army team of 1915, which beat Navy by a score of 14–0, and lettermen in that same year, were three future generals who were destined to leave indelible marks on history: Dwight D. Eisenhower, Omar Bradley, and James Van Fleet.

Future generals Dwight Eisenhower (second row, third from left), James Van Fleet (top row, left), and Omar Bradley (top row, fourth from left).

War of Words

Dan Jenkins, *Sports Illustrated* staffer, wrote about the furtive goings-on at the 1949 Army-Navy game in his book *Saturday's America.*

"Not only did the Cadets whomp Navy 38–0, but they took advantage of some espionage to embarrass the Midshipmen before all of their admirals. An Army officer on duty at Annapolis had learned of a Navy plan to hoist some banners poking fun at Army's 1949 schedule and to parody 'On, Brave Old Army Team,' the West Point fight song. Soon after both student bodies had done their usual pregame march-on, drills and salutes, they took their places across the field from each other and Navy cheerfully sang the parody:

We don't play Notre Dame.
We don't play Tulane.
We just play Davidson
For that's the fearless Army way.

"Then the Midshipmen lofted a huge banner that said: When Do You Drop Navy?

"Navy was mortified when the Army cheering section immediately unrolled a banner that said: Today!

"Thinking this had to be coincidence, or incredible bad luck, the Middies quickly tried again with another of their banners. This one said: Why Not Schedule Vassar?

"And Army countered with a sign that produced one of the biggest laughs Municipal Stadium ever heard. It read: We Already Got Navy."

Pete Dawkins picks up a few yards for Army in 1958. A senior that year, he won the Heisman and Maxwell trophies, then attended Oxford on a Rhodes Scholarship.

Despite the setback of an honor code scandal at West Point in the early 1950s, the Cadets had a few more impressive years. Their 1958 team, featuring Heisman Trophy winner Pete Dawkins, vied for a national championship with an unbeaten season. And after Earl Blaik retired in 1958, Army had several respectable seasons under Tom Cahill.

But Navy also thrived in the late 1950s and early 60s. The 1957 Midshipmen squad, led by All-American candidate quarterback Tom Forrestal, ranked fifth in the nation. In the 1959 Army-Navy game, halfback Joe Bellino became the first Midshipman ever to score three touchdowns in a single game against Army as the Middies won 43–12. The following year Bellino won the Heisman after another Navy 17–12 win over Army. And Roger Staubach, still another Heisman winner, brought Navy to national prominence in the early 1960s, leading them to victories over Army in 1962 and 1963.

The annual Army-Navy game continues to this day, the last of each school's season, still a sellout, still a marvelous spectacle with uniformed Cadets and Midshipmen parading before it, still the mule and the goat, and as always a bitterly contested football game.

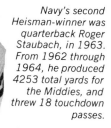

Navy's second Heisman-winner was quarterback Roger Staubach, in 1963. From 1962 through 1964, he produced 4253 total yards for the Middies, and threw 18 touchdown passes.

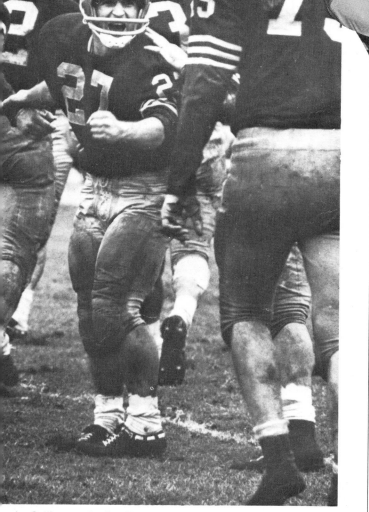

Joe Bellino was the first Navy player to win the Heisman Trophy, in 1960. A fast, tough halfback, he rushed for 1664 yards, and scored 198 points on 31 touchdowns and 12 extra points.

Series Scoring

Year	Army	Navy	Year	Army	Navy
1890	0	24	1943	0	13
1891	32	16	1944	23	7
1892	4	12	1945	32	13
1893	4	6	1946	21	18
1899	17	5	1947	21	0
1900	7	11	1948	21	21
1901	11	5	1949	38	0
1902	22	8	1950	2	14
1903	40	5	1951	7	42
1904	11	0	1952	0	7
1905	6	6	1953	20	7
1906	0	10	1954	20	27
1907	0	6	1955	14	6
1908	6	4	1956	7	7
1910	0	3	1957	0	14
1911	0	3	1958	22	6
1912	0	6	1959	12	43
1913	22	9	1960	12	17
1914	20	0	1961	7	13
1915	14	0	1962	14	34
1916	15	7	1963	15	21
1919	0	6	1964	11	8
1920	0	7	1965	7	7
1921	0	7	1966	20	7
1922	17	14	1967	14	19
1923	0	0	1968	21	14
1924	12	0	1969	27	0
1925	10	3	1970	7	11
1926	21	21	1971	24	23
1927	14	9	1972	23	15
1930	6	0	1973	0	51
1931	17	7	1974	0	19
1932	20	0	1975	6	30
1933	12	7	1976	10	38
1934	0	3	1977	17	14
1935	28	6	1978	0	28
1936	0	7	1979	7	31
1937	6	0	1980	6	33
1938	14	7	1981	3	3
1939	0	10	1982	7	24
1940	0	14	1983	13	42
1941	6	14	1984	28	11
1942	0	14			

SERIES STANDINGS

Army	Navy
38 Wins	40 Wins
40 Losses	38 Losses
7 Ties	7 Ties
Best Game: 1949, 38–0	Best Game: 1973, 51–0

ALABAMA GEORGIA

Alabama and Georgia are rivals because they're neighbors, neighbors that feud over many things; and besides, each state takes its football with an entrenched seriousness. Both schools have other rivalries as well: Alabama-Auburn is a deep-rooted one, so is Georgia-Florida, and then there is Georgia-Georgia Tech and Alabama-Louisiana State. In the South, suffice it to say, rivalries run rampant.

When Alabama's Crimson Tide meets the Bulldogs from Athens, Georgia, there is always something at stake. If it is not a national championship or a conference championship, just the win is important because both teams are among the top 15 winningest college football teams of all time, with Alabama claiming 600 victories and Georgia more than 500.

And they've been at it for a long time. When William L. Dudley organized the Southern Intercollegiate Athletic Association in December 1894, both Alabama and Georgia, along with five other teams, were charter members.

In the beginning, it appeared Georgia would be off to a fine start in the world of intercollegiate football. They lured a young Glenn S. Warner down to Athens to begin his football coaching career in 1895 and paid him a salary of $34 a week. But Warner stayed only two years before heading back north to Cornell.

In the early decades of the 1900s, neither Alabama nor Georgia succeeded in developing powerhouses, but by the 1920s, both teams had begun serious efforts to develop formidable football teams.

Decorated 'Bama fans get into the spirit of things.

Frank Sinkwich (21) bursts through a hole for Georgia, something he excelled at from 1940–42. Fireball Frankie, as the triple-threat back was called, was a two-time consensus All-American.

Alabama signed Wallace Wade as head coach in 1923, and the Tide's fortunes flourished almost immediately. Two years after he took over, his 1925 team (featuring All-American-candidate backs Pooley Hubert and Johnny Mack Brown) went undefeated and untied in 10 games to claim the national championship and the distinction of being the first team from the South to go to the Rose Bowl—where they defeated a tough Washington team, 20–19.

At Georgia in 1923, a young student of Notre Dame's Knute Rockne, Frank Thomas, joined the coaching staff to handle the backfield under head coach Kid Woodruff. Thomas, of course, would later mold his own reputation as a head coach at rival Alabama. But in '23 he helped to turn the Bulldogs into a high-spirited, high-scoring squad that lost only two games all season, to Yale and to Wade's Crimson Tide, which, incidentally, was also dubbed the Red Elephants during that era.

Thomas left Georgia in 1925 for the head coaching job at Chattanooga College, but returned to Georgia as an assistant to his former Notre Dame teammate Harry Mehre, who guided the Bulldogs. In 1931, after Wade announced he was moving from 'Bama to Duke, the powers at Alabama wooed Thomas, and Georgia

was the loser. From 1931 through 1946, Frank Thomas compiled a record at Alabama of 108-20-7, a phenomenal winning percentage of .841, and took the Tide to six bowl games: three for the Roses, one Sugar, one Cotton, and one Orange; and, of course, made life unbearable for his former employer over in Georgia.

Perhaps the finest team Thomas ever tutored at Alabama was the 1934 national champion, which won all 10 games that year with ease, including a 26–6 pounding of Georgia. The team had a marvelous passing tailback in Dixie Howell, in an age when defenses were almost entirely geared to stop the run, and a pair of ends named Don Hutson and Paul Bryant.

In the early 1940s, with Wally Butts at the helm, it was Georgia's turn to stockpile All-Americans. In 1941, they had Frank Sinkwich at tailback, who led the nation in rushing with 1,103 yards and brought the Bulldogs some national attention. But the racehorse back could not get his favored Bulldogs past a determined Alabama that year, and the Tide upset Georgia 27–14. The next year, no matter how inspired the Alabamans were to knock off a Georgia team in the running for a national championship, they could not hold down a team that had bolstered Sinkwich in the backfield with a brand-new All-American named Charlie Trippi. Georgia won that bout 21–10.

In more modern times, the rivalry has been dominated by the great Bear Bryant. The Bear returned to his alma mater at Alabama as head coach in 1958. Perhaps the most famous Alabama-Georgia game during the Bryant epoch occurred in 1962. Its notoriety, however, had much more to do with events off the field than on.

The game marked the first appearance of a young Alabama passing sensation named Joe Namath, who led the Tide to a lopsided 35–0 win over Georgia. But a story in the *Saturday Evening Post* magazine about what allegedly happened before the game sent tremors shuddering through the South and through all of college football. The magazine charged that an insurance worker named George Burnett had overheard a telephone conversation in which Wally Butts, then athletic director of Georgia, and 'Bama's Bear Bryant discussed fixing the game. Butts, the article alleged, described in detail a number of Georgia plays and passed along other pertinent information to Bryant. Both vehemently denied the allegations.

The sensational charges were met with lawsuits and were eventually settled in court to the overwhelming satisfaction of Butts and Bryant. The Bear was awarded $400,000 in damages, and Butts collected about half-a-million dollars. The young star of the game, Joe Namath, eventually got $400,000 for himself too—not by going to court, but simply by signing with the New York Jets in 1965. The two teams did not play each other again until 1972.

In recent years, these rivals have ranked among the nation's best. In 1978 and 1979, Bryant's Alabama teams captured the country's crown, while in the following year the top ranking went to Georgia, with its sensational running back Herschel Walker.

Despite another hiatus from 1978 to 1983, the rivalry still thrives, but that's hardly surprising between next-door neighbors.

SERIES STANDINGS

Alabama	Georgia
31 Wins	21 Wins
21 Losses	31 Losses
4 Ties	4 Ties
Best Games: 1905, 1923, 36–0	Best Game: 1948, 35–0

The man with the famous fragile knees, Joe Namath, ices one down here on the sidelines. Namath quarterbacked Alabama from 1962 through 1964 and his team lost only 3 of 30 games during that stretch. He completed 203 passes for 2714 yards and 25 touchdowns in his college career.

Up and over with Herschel Walker, Georgia's best back since Charlie Trippi and Frank Sinkwich in the early 1940s.

Series Scoring

Year	Alabama	Georgia	Year	Alabama	Georgia
1895	6	30	1942	10	21
1901	0	0	1944	7	14
1902	0	5	1945	28	14
1904	16	5	1946	0	14
1905	36	0	1947	17	7
1907	0	0	1948	0	35
1908	6	6	1949	14	7
1909	14	0	1950	14	7
1910	0	22	1951	16	14
1911	3	11	1952	34	19
1912	9	13	1953	33	12
1913	0	20	1954	0	0
1916	0	3	1955	14	35
1919	6	0	1956	13	16
1920	14	21	1957	14	13
1921	0	22	1958	12	0
1922	10	6	1959	3	17
1923	36	0	1960	21	6
1924	33	0	1961	32	6
1925	27	0	1962	35	0
1926	33	6	1963	32	7
1927	6	20	1964	31	3
1928	19	0	1965	17	18
1929	0	12	1972	25	7
1930	13	0	1973	28	14
1934	26	6	1976	0	21
1935	17	7	1977	18	10
1941	27	14	1984	14	24

TEXAS OKLAHOMA

"It's college football's equivalent of a prison riot—with coeds," wrote *Sports Illustrated*'s Dan Jenkins, describing the annual autumnal madness in Dallas when the Oklahoma Sooners battle the Texas Longhorns. But not all the spectators are as impoverished as the average prison inmate. After all, this is oil country, the land where real-life J.R. Ewings leave their private airplanes at Love Field and their long limos at the gate and make their way to private boxes where they can cheer their alma mater, be it Texas or Oklahoma. "Give a Texas oil man two drinks," Jenkins also wrote, "and he'll bet you every offshore well he's got (and some he hasn't got) that the Longhorns will whip Oklahoma." It takes about the same for an

Oklahoma oilman to wager every dust bowl well he's got that the Sooners will whip Texas.

Texas first played Oklahoma at the turn of the century, and a while later the game became integrated into the Texas state fair festivities. It has become as vital a part of the Texas football scene as chili, chicken-fried steak, and Pearl beer are to the Longhorn diet. There is no home-field advantage because the game is traditionally played at the Cotton Bowl, a stadium that neither Texas nor Oklahoma plays in unless they are invited there for a New Year's Day appearance. Nor is there a crowd advantage. Sooner fans by the thousands flock to Dallas from Norman and other Oklahoma locales to watch the annual brawl, no fewer in number,

gridiron war stands at more than 700. On a more reserved note, the occasion also brings together a cavalcade of affluent alumni who could probably wipe out the national debt if they had a desire to do so. One writer once observed that "there are more lizard-skin cowboy boots at this game than there are lizards in all of Texas."

The classic rivalry also contains a few ironies. Though the game is no longer an intraconference affair, Oklahoma, now a member of the Big Eight, was in fact the Southwest Conference's first champion. During the first 11 years of Bud Wilkinson's reign at Oklahoma, from 1947 through 1957, the Sooners dominated the rivalry, often beating the Texans with key players who had been recruited from the Lone Star State. Wilkinson's Sooners demolished the Texans in 9 of those 11 contests, and once, in 1956, by the embarrassing score of 45–0.

There was some irony on the other side of the fence as well. After Texas posted a humiliating 1–9 record for the 1956 season, predictably a new coach was in demand down in Austin. Following a brief search, the Longhorns found just the savior they needed to reverse the disastrous state of football affairs. His name was Darrell Royal, who in the late 1940s had been an All-American back at none other than Oklahoma. Under this former Sooner, the dominance in the rivalry would shift to Texas. During the seven years that Darrell Royal strode the sideline across the field from Bud Wilkinson (1957–63), his Texas teams won 6 of the encounters, losing only in his first year.

Over the years there have been crucial meetings between these schools. In 1950, for example, the national championship was on the line when the two

devotion, or boisterousness than the Longhorn fans. The action in the stands has sometimes been as bruising as the play on the fields.

The kinetic energy that fills the stadium is all the more remarkable considering the percentage of spectators who must be suffering from the year's biggest hangover. The current record for mass arrests in the yearly revels in downtown Dallas the night before the

Billy Vessels of Oklahoma breaks loose against Texas in the early 1950s. A dazzling breakaway runner, Vessels won the Heisman Trophy in 1952.

teams met. In the fourth quarter, Texas was leading 13–7, punting from their own 11-yard line, but the punter fumbled and the Sooners recovered. Then a pair of All-Americans brought the crucial scores: Billy Vessels slashed off tackle for the touchdown and Jim Weatherall booted the extra point, giving Oklahoma a one-point victory and the national championship.

Another important game was concluded with a taste of irony, the confrontation of 1958. That year, for the first time in nearly half a century, the NCAA rules committee had approved a change in the scoring system. The optional two-point conversion was introduced in an attempt to reduce the number of tie games. Of the coaches who vigorously opposed this change was Darrell Royal of Texas. But that very year, Royal's Longhorns used it to defeat Wilkinson's Sooners by a score of 15–14, and in so doing they not only served Oklahoma their only loss of the season, but

also knocked them out of the running for the national championship.

Even though both the old masters are no longer coaching, the annual battle at the Cotton Bowl in Dallas hasn't mellowed. In fact, one of the most interesting games ever is of quite recent vintage.

It was a dark, rainy Saturday in Dallas when the Sooners visited the Cotton Bowl for the 1984 edition of the rivalry. It was the fifth game of the season for both teams, and they had identical records of 3-0-1, with Texas clinging precariously to a number one ranking.

In the first half of play, the Longhorns took a 10–0 lead on a Todd Dodge touchdown pass and a 40-yard field goal from Jeff Ward. With the playing field soggy and slippery from the rain, the lead appeared to be a most comfortable one.

In the third quarter, however, the Sooners recovered a fumble by Texas tailback Terry Orr and went on

Bobby Bryant heads for the goal line on a reception from quarterback Bobby Lackey to give Texas a come-from-behind 15–14 victory over favored Oklahoma in 1958. The pass is known around Austin as "The Shot that Sank the Sooners."

Series Scoring

Year	Texas	Oklahoma	Year	Texas	Oklahoma
1900	28	2	1946	20	13
1901	12	6	1947	34	14
	11	0	1948	14	20
1902	22	6	1949	14	20
1903	11	5	1950	13	14
1903	6	6	1951	9	7
1904	40	10	1952	20	49
1905	0	2	1953	14	19
1906	10	9	1954	7	14
1907	29	10	1955	0	20
1908	0	50	1956	0	45
1909	30	0	1957	7	21
1910	0	3	1958	15	14
1911	3	6	1959	19	12
1912	6	21	1960	24	0
1913	14	6	1961	28	7
1914	32	7	1962	9	6
1915	13	14	1963	28	7
1916	21	7	1964	28	7
1917	0	14	1965	19	0
1919	7	12	1966	9	18
1922	32	7	1967	9	7
1923	26	14	1968	26	20
1929	21	0	1969	27	17
1930	17	7	1970	41	9
1931	3	0	1971	27	48
1932	17	10	1972	0	27
1933	0	9	1973	13	52
1934	19	0	1974	13	16
1935	12	7	1975	17	24
1936	6	0	1976	6	6
1937	7	7	1977	13	6
1938	0	13	1978	10	31
1939	12	24	1979	16	7
1940	19	16	1980	20	13
1941	40	7	1981	34	14
1942	7	0	1982	22	28
1943	13	7	1983	28	16
1944	20	0	1984	15	15
1945	12	7			

to score a touchdown two plays later. Less than two minutes after that, Oklahoma forced a safety, narrowing the score to 10–9. The inspired Sooners then took the free kick and marched downfield, adding another score on a 24-yard touchdown pass from Danny Bradley. With a lead of 15–10, Oklahoma went for the two-point conversion but failed. Then things began to get a little weird.

With less than six minutes to play in the game, a third-string Texas tailback, freshman Kevin Nelson, scampered 60 yards through the puddles and was not brought down until he reached the Oklahoma 2-yard line. But there the Longhorns stayed for four nightmarish downs, unable to advance an inch against a fortress-like Sooner defense.

When the ball exchanged hands at the 3, Oklahoma found that on three successive downs they couldn't gain an inch. With a call that would endear him forever to second-guessers, Oklahoma coach Barry Switzer decided to take an intentional safety rather than risk a kick from deep in the end zone, because, as he explained later, the Sooners' kicking game had been poor throughout the contest. The safety brought the Longhorns to within three points of the Sooners.

After the free kick, there were two minutes to go, and Texas had the ball at their own 44-yard line. With a precision passing attack, Todd Dodge brought the Longhorns to the Oklahoma 15-yard line with ten seconds remaining in the game. Now it was Texas's turn to gamble. Coach Fred Akers decided they had time for one pass to try for a game-winning touchdown. If it was incomplete, they should still have time for a field goal. But Todd Dodge's pass was tipped and appeared to be intercepted at the sideline by a Sooner defender. Television replays showed that the ball certainly seemed to be caught and controlled before the Oklahoma defender fell out of bounds. But to the consternation of Sooner fans everywhere, the play was ruled an incomplete pass. Texas then lined up and kicked a field goal as time expired, and the game ended in a 15–15 tie. That year, at least, no Texas or Oklahoma oil wells changed hands.

SERIES STANDINGS

Texas	Oklahoma
47 Wins	28 Wins
28 Losses	47 Losses
4 Ties	4 Ties
Best Game: 1941, 40–7	Best Game: 1908, 50–0

NOTRE DAME
USC

The greatest cross-country, or almost cross-country, rivalry in the history of college football has done much to improve the stature of the sport, and, in its earliest contests, brought together two of the game's most legendary coaches, Notre Dame's Knute Rockne and Southern Cal's Howard Jones.

In 1924, the Fighting Irish, under Rockne and with the legendary Four Horsemen, provided the catalyst for the great rivalry by traveling to Pasadena to make their first appearance in the Rose Bowl. Their defeat of Pop Warner's talented Stanford team made Notre Dame the undisputed national champion. When Howard Jones came to Southern Cal in 1925, he brought with him his "beat the best" philosophy. So Southern Cal invited Notre Dame back to the West Coast in 1926, and some of the most exciting moments in intercollegiate football have been provided by the clash of the two teams ever since.

The first two games in the series, 1926 and 1927, were closely fought contests, with Notre Dame winning each by a single point. In 1928, Rockne fielded the only mediocre team he ever had at Notre Dame, his "Minutemen," he called them. "They'll be in the game one minute and the other team will score," the Rock joked. Well, the Trojans scored often enough that year to defeat the Irish for the first time, 27–14. It was part of USC's 9-0-1 season, which earned for Howard Jones's eleven the nickname Thundering Herd.

Notre Dame avenged the loss with a one-point victory the following year, but it was the 1930 game between the two that is remembered by many as one of the great surprises of the series. The Fighting Irish had defeated everyone they encountered that year, but the victories, especially the bruising 7–6 win over Army in the next-to-last game of the season, had taken a toll. Several key players were injured, and powerful

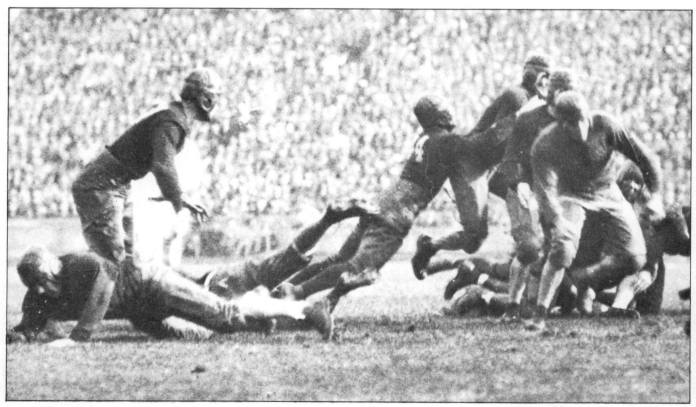

Action from the very first Notre Dame-USC game in 1926, which the Irish won 13–12. The Trojans have the ball here.

Trumpets, priests and prayers have always been part of the Notre Dame retinue.

running back Joe Savoldi had been expelled after it was learned that he was married (which was against Notre Dame rules in those days). On the other hand, the Trojans were completely healthy, and had outscored their nine opponents so far that season by a total of 382–39. The oddsmakers predicted a close game, giving the edge to a healthy USC.

Rockne knew he had to do something to fire up his team. En route to California for the game, the Irish stopped in Tucson, Arizona, where he scheduled a scrimmage. He deemed it a lackluster practice and told his team as much. Then he shook his head, looked at them balefully, and told them that he could not be a part of a team that was so lethargic, could not accompany them to a sure slaughter in Los Angeles. In fact, he said he was quitting as coach and returning to South Bend. His horrified team then begged him to stay, pledging full fervor for when they met USC.

The Rock agreed to stay on and continuously reminded them of their promises until they took the field. It had its effect. Notre Dame held the explosive offense of Southern Cal scoreless, and put 27 points on the scoreboard themselves. It gave them their second undefeated season in a row. "That was the greatest Notre Dame team I've ever seen," Howard Jones said after the game. It was also Rockne's last game. He was killed in a airplane crash before the start of the 1931 season.

Throughout the remainder of the 1930s, Notre Dame searched for another coach as great as Rockne, but didn't find one, and managed only 4 victories against 5 losses and 1 tie with arch-rival Southern Cal.

But the glory that once was Notre Dame's was restored in the 1940s. Frank Leahy, hired as head coach in 1941, finally proved the worthy successor to Rockne. Leahy, who had played for Rockne in 1929 at Notre Dame, led the Irish to two successive triumphs in his first two encounters with the Trojans. Not everyone at the time was thrilled with Notre Dame's revival, nor with the extraordinary zeal Leahy imparted to his players. Said one Trojan player after losing to the Irish, "They'll give you the knee, they'll hold you, they'll clip you, and they'll belt you with an elbow every chance they get. Maybe Leahy doesn't tell them

A Serious Matter

USC takes its rivalry with Notre Dame very seriously. Since 1969, the university has presented the Theodore Gabrielson award to the outstanding USC player in that particular game. Among the award winners: Anthony Davis (1972), Pat Haden (1974), Ricky Bell (1975), Paul McDonald (1978), Chip Banks (1980), and Jeff Simmons (1982).

Happy victors, the Trojan fans celebrate a big win early in their rivalry with Notre Dame.

to do it, but he sure doesn't tell them not to do it."

There may have been some truth to the remark (Leahy's "anything for a win" style of coaching was legendary), but anything a Trojan said about the Fighting Irish during the Leahy years must have been served up with a full bowl of sour grapes. In the 10 games that the Leahy-coached teams played against Southern Cal, Notre Dame won 8, lost only 1, and tied in the other.

One of the most thrilling endings to any game in the rivalry occurred in 1948. Undefeated Notre Dame, in the running for the national championship, met USC in the last game of the season. Trailing by a touchdown with a little more than two minutes remaining, Irish halfback Bill Gay ran the kickoff back 87 yards, to the USC 12-yard line. Leahy planned on a quick touchdown followed by an onsides kick. But it took four plays before Emil Sitko could carry it in for the score—as a result, there was not enough time left for another drive. The tie ruined Notre Dame's perfect season and the national title went to Michigan.

Under John McKay Southern Cal finally turned the tables on Notre Dame. Probably the greatest single joy for USC fans of that era came in 1964 when an unheralded Southern Cal team upset Ara Par-

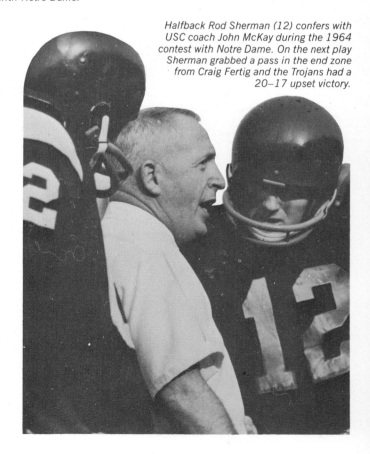

Halfback Rod Sherman (12) confers with USC coach John McKay during the 1964 contest with Notre Dame. On the next play Sherman grabbed a pass in the end zone from Craig Fertig and the Trojans had a 20–17 upset victory.

seghian's bid for an undefeated season and a national championship in the last game of the year.

Notre Dame was an overwhelming favorite to win that game; with consensus All-Americans like quarterback John Huarte and end Jack Snow, the Irish had the nation's number two ranked offense, and they also laid claim to the best defense in the country.

Southern Cal had lost three games and appeared fresh for the slaughter. "I studied the Notre Dame-Stanford film for six hours last night," coach John McKay said, "and I have reached one conclusion: Notre Dame can't be beaten."

A few days later, he added, "I've decided that if we play our very best and make no mistakes whatsoever, we will definitely make a first down." His ploy in the Rockne tradition, to arouse his Trojans to a pitched anger, would ultimately prove successful.

No one was surprised when Notre Dame took a 17–0 lead into the locker room at halftime. But everyone was astounded at the events of Act Two. Southern Cal roared right back into the game as Mike Garrett carried the ball in for a touchdown on the first Trojan drive of the second half. Quarterback Craig Fertig led a second Trojan touchdown march, and suddenly they were a mere 4 points behind the vaunted Irish. Southern Cal's defense was impenetrable, playing its best half of the year. Then they got the ball back in the final minutes, and Fertig passed them down the field. With two minutes to play on fourth down, he rifled a shot to Rod Sherman in the end zone. And that was it; South-

Anthony Davis blasts in for his fourth touchdown of the day in USC's 1974 annihilation of Notre Dame, which included a spectacular comeback. The Trojans, losing to the Irish 24–0 in the second period, rolled off 55 unanswered points. Davis' display included a kickoff runback of 100 yards.

What a Way to Go

In 1931, Notre Dame had gone undefeated in three seasons, a total of 25 wins and 1 tie (in a mudbath at Northwestern). And they were hosting Southern Cal in South Bend where, incredibly, they had lost only one game in 27 years (to Carnegie Tech in 1928).

Knute Rockne was gone by then, and replacing him that year was one of the Rock's former All-American linemen, Hunk Anderson. Howard Jones was at the helm for USC. In the stands were such luminaries as Mayor Jimmy Walker of New York and Mayor Anton Cermak of Chicago, both avid Notre Dame fans. Everyone thought it was to be the conclusion of another undefeated season for the Irish.

It certainly seemed so. With a strong running attack Notre Dame built a 14–0 lead, which they maintained into the fourth quarter. But then the Trojans decided the time had come to change things. Two long marches, engineered

by Orv Mohler, Southern Cal's quarterback, ended in touchdowns, both capped by scoring runs by Gus Shaver. But a missed extra point left Southern Cal a point behind Notre Dame.

Notre Dame, however, had made a big mistake. Earlier in the quarter, before Southern Cal began to move so effectively, Coach Anderson, confident that his team would prevail, had taken most of his regulars out of the game. Now, according to the rules of the day, they could not return during that quarter. The hapless Irish had unintentionally set the stage for their own demise. The reserves could not move the ball, nor could they stop the inspired Trojans. With a minute left, Southern Cal was again within striking distance of the Notre Dame goal. On came Johnny Baker to boot a game-winning 33-yard field goal as Anderson and his first-stringers watched dismally from the Irish sideline.

ern Cal had come up with an amazing rally and beaten top-ranked Notre Dame, which dropped to number three in the national rankings behind undefeated Alabama and Arkansas.

It was a precedent Parseghian would wish had never been set. In an otherwise stellar career of successful coaching, his Notre Dame teams lost to Southern Cal 6 times, managing only 3 wins and 2 ties. But that's the way it is with a rivalry.

In fact, the reversal of momentum between the two schools carried much beyond Parseghian's tenure.

Giles Pellerin (right) with a pair of other USC fans.

Super Fan

The most loyal college football fan in the nation is Giles Pellerin, his devotion to the University of Southern California being unparalleled. Going into the 1984 season, the 77-year-old retired telephone company executive from San Marino, California, had attended 630 *consecutive* Trojan games, at home and away, not missing a single one in 57 years.

Super Fan Pellerin began attending USC games as a sophomore there in 1926. His first game was the home opener that year, when a Howard Jones–led Trojan team trounced Whittier 74–0. Since that time Pellerin has followed the team by plane, train, and automobile, more than 600,000 miles on the road, spending upwards of $60,000 in so doing. Since that first game he has witnessed USC win 431 games, lose 164, and tie 35.

Pellerin has come close to missing a contest or two, especially once in 1949, when he was hospitalized five days before a home game after an emergency operation to remove his appendix. On game day, Giles told the nurses he was going out for a walk on the hospital grounds. Instead he went to the Los Angeles Coliseum and returned to his bed several hours later after USC had beaten Washington 40–28.

After having prevailed for so long, Notre Dame lost 13 games over the next 20 years, tied 2, and won only 5.

And one of those losses was a special disillusionment. It was 1978, and the national championship was on the line. The year before, Notre Dame, coached by Dan Devine, had won the coveted crown. Now Southern Cal, guided by John Robinson, was at the top, only a victory away from taking the title.

The Trojans built a 17–3 lead by the half, and Notre Dame, with its two chief running backs, Vagas Ferguson and Jerome Heavens, out with injuries, seemed doomed. But the Fighting Irish put on a splendid comeback in the fourth quarter. Losing 24–6, quarterback Joe Montana suddenly erupted. First it was a 57-yard bomb to Kris Haines for a touchdown. Then, throwing both long and short, Montana marched the Irish 98 yards for another touchdown, with Pete Buchanan finally carrying it in for the score. Notre Dame again got the ball and moved all the way to the Trojan 2-yard line where, with 48 seconds on the clock, Montana tossed a little bullet to Pete Holohan on a slant-in pattern in the end zone, and the Irish took a 25–24 lead.

There were only 41 seconds left when the Trojans got the ball on their own 30-yard line. Paul McDonald, the Southern Cal quarterback, reacted swiftly and with Montana-like precision. With two passes he moved Southern Cal to Notre Dame's 25-yard line. A handoff to Heisman Trophy candidate Charles White picked up five more yards and positioned the ball in the

A stunned Notre Dame (above) tries to cope with the 27–25 loss in 1978 after USC kicked a field goal in the last two seconds of the game, while the Trojans rejoice (below, left). Notre Dame had scored three touchdowns in the fourth quarter to take the lead before their game collapsed.

center of the field. Southern Cal then stopped the clock with two seconds left, and Frank Jordan came on and coolly booted a 37-yard field goal to give the Trojans a 27–25 victory. *New York Times* columnist Red Smith called it the "gaudiest game in the 50 years of the rivalry."

Series Scoring

Year	Notre Dame	USC	Year	Notre Dame	USC
1926	13	12	1957	40	12
1927	7	6	1958	20	13
1928	14	27	1959	16	6
1929	13	12	1960	17	0
1930	27	0	1961	30	0
1931	14	16	1962	0	25
1932	0	13	1963	17	14
1933	0	19	1964	17	20
1934	14	0	1965	28	7
1935	20	13	1966	51	0
1936	13	13	1967	7	24
1937	13	6	1968	21	21
1938	0	13	1969	14	14
1939	12	20	1970	28	38
1940	10	6	1971	14	28
1941	20	18	1972	23	45
1942	13	0	1973	23	14
1946	26	6	1974	24	55
1947	38	7	1975	17	24
1948	14	14	1976	13	17
1949	32	0	1977	49	19
1950	7	9	1978	25	27
1951	19	12	1979	23	42
1952	9	0	1980	3	20
1953	48	14	1981	7	14
1954	23	17	1982	13	17
1955	20	42	1983	27	6
1956	20	28	1984	19	7

SERIES STANDINGS

Notre Dame	USC
29 Wins	23 Wins
23 Losses	29 Losses
4 Ties	4 Ties
Best Game: 1966, 51–0	Best Game: 1974, 55–24

MICHIGAN OHIO STATE OSU

When Ohio State enjoyed its greatest success in the Big Ten, while Woody Hayes reigned stout and supreme from the early 1950s to his dismissal in 1978, the Buckeyes revered a special goal each year, right up there in importance with winning the national championship and spending New Year's Day in Pasadena. Their sharp-tongued, ill-tempered coach fueled it annually. Many a sportswriter and Big Ten fan had

noticed over the years a peculiar impediment when a certain word came up in interviews or discussions. That word seemed to always twist his tongue into knots and alter his expression to a snarling grimace. The word, of course, was Michigan. And the special goal was simply, Beat Michigan.

There was legitimate cause for Hayes to want to conquer his neighbors to the north. For half a century

Treasured Traditional Trophies

When two rivals go at it on the field, there's usually more at stake than mere victory. To the victor goes the spoils, which often includes some prized old piece of bric-a-brac that has been given trophy status. There are two especially famous trophies, both long on tradition and both from the Big Ten.

The Little Brown Jug goes each year to the winner of the Michigan-Minnesota game. But it should also be noted that North Dakota and South Dakota also play for a Little Brown Jug, Montana and Idaho for a Little Brown Stein, and Gettysburg and Dickinson for a Little Brown Bucket.

The Old Oaken Bucket is the annual prize for the winner of the Indiana-Purdue game. But also battling for an Old Oaken Bucket each year are Albion and Hillsdale and Wayne and Central State. Oaken buckets, however, aren't the only "old"

treasures. Southern Methodist and Texas Christian go after the Old Frying Pan; Bucknell and Temple, the Old Shoe; Morehead State and Eastern Kentucky, the Old Hawg Rifle; Georgetown (Kentucky) and Transylvania, the Old Dinner Bell; Gettysburg and Muhlenberg, the Old Tin Cup; and Brigham Young and Utah State, the Old Wagon Wheel.

A number of schools vie for a Victory Bell each year: UCLA and USC, Duke and North Carolina, Pacific and San Jose, Cincinnati and Miami (Ohio), and Franklin and Hanover.

And Notre Dame plays for a Shillelagh every time they confront either USC, Purdue, or Northwestern.

The following are sundry other treasured trophies, the spoils of specific football combats:

Trophy	Schools
Amos Alonzo Stagg's Bronze Felt Hat	Susquehanna-Lycoming
Axe	Stanford-California
Beer Keg	Kentucky-Tennessee
Bell Clapper	Oklahoma-Oklahoma State
Brass Hat	UCLA-Air Force
Brass Spittoon	Michigan State-Indiana
Buffalo Head	Colorado-Nebraska
Buffalo Nickel	North Dakota-North Dakota State
Cannon	Illinois-Purdue
Captain's Pants (or The Rag)	Louisiana State-Tulane
Church Bell	Nebraska-Missouri
Coal Shuttle	Pittsburgh-Penn State
Copper Bowl	Montana-Montana State
Cowboy Hat	Texas-Oklahoma
Dog Collar	Wichita-Wichita State
Floyd of Rosedale	Iowa-Minnesota
Golden Egg	Mississippi-Mississippi State
Governor's Cup	Florida-Florida State
Illibuck (wooden turtle)	Illinois-Ohio State
Indian Princess	Dartmouth-Cornell
Indian Skull	Wittenberg-Ohio Wesleyan
Indian War Drum	Missouri-Kansas
Japanese Bell (or Enterprise Bell)	Army-Navy

Trophy	Schools
Keg	Syracuse-Colgate
Kit Carson Rifle	Arizona-New Mexico
Little Cannon	Purdue-Illinois
Locomotive Bell	Nevada-Pacific
Megaphone	Notre Dame-Michigan State
O.D.K. Trophy	Alabama-Auburn
Osage War Drum	Kansas-Missouri
Paint Bucket	Memphis State-Arkansas State
Paul Bunyan Axe	Minnesota-Wisconsin
Paul Bunyan Trophy	Michigan-Michigan State
Peace Pact	Kansas-Kansas State
Peace Pipe	Oklahoma-Missouri
Platypus Bowl	Oregon-Oregon State
Rusty Old Cannon	Princeton-Rutgers
Seminole War Canoe	Florida-Miami (Florida)
Shoe	Idaho-Washington State
Silver Goal Posts	Duke-North Carolina
Sitting Bull	South Dakota-North Dakota
Tea Cup	Clemson-South Carolina
Tobacco Bowl	Virginia-VPI
Tomahawk	Northwestern-Illinois
Traveling Saw	West Virginia-Davis & Elkins
Tydings	Maryland-Virginia
We Lost	San Jose State-Fresno State
Wooden Beer Stein	Idaho-Montana
Wooden Goal Post	Colorado-Utah
Yard Stick & Golden Ruler	Michigan-Michigan State

Yost's Little Brown Jug

Notre Dame fans ring their victory bell.

Floyd of Rosedale, coveted object of the Iowa-Minnesota rivalry.

HALF

TIME

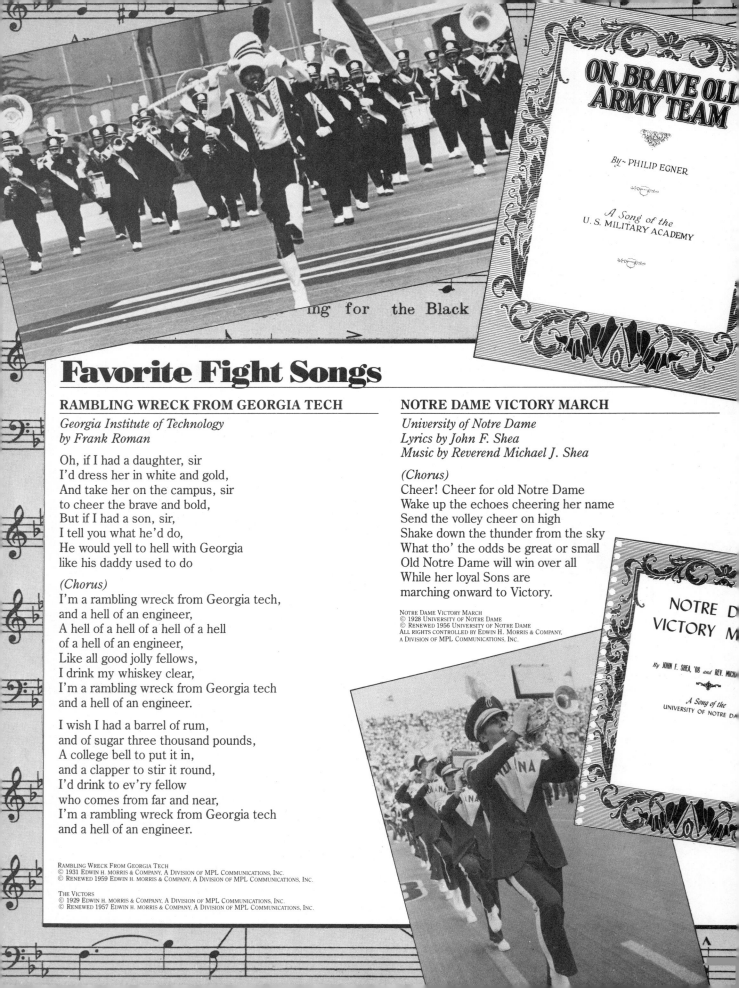

ing for the Black

ON, BRAVE OLD ARMY TEAM

By~ PHILIP EGNER

A Song of the
U. S. MILITARY ACADEMY

Favorite Fight Songs

RAMBLING WRECK FROM GEORGIA TECH

Georgia Institute of Technology
by Frank Roman

Oh, if I had a daughter, sir
I'd dress her in white and gold,
And take her on the campus, sir
to cheer the brave and bold,
But if I had a son, sir,
I tell you what he'd do,
He would yell to hell with Georgia
like his daddy used to do

(Chorus)
I'm a rambling wreck from Georgia tech,
and a hell of an engineer,
A hell of a hell of a hell of a hell
of a hell of an engineer,
Like all good jolly fellows,
I drink my whiskey clear,
I'm a rambling wreck from Georgia tech
and a hell of an engineer.

I wish I had a barrel of rum,
and of sugar three thousand pounds,
A college bell to put it in,
and a clapper to stir it round,
I'd drink to ev'ry fellow
who comes from far and near,
I'm a rambling wreck from Georgia tech
and a hell of an engineer.

NOTRE DAME VICTORY MARCH

University of Notre Dame
Lyrics by John F. Shea
Music by Reverend Michael J. Shea

(Chorus)
Cheer! Cheer for old Notre Dame
Wake up the echoes cheering her name
Send the volley cheer on high
Shake down the thunder from the sky
What tho' the odds be great or small
Old Notre Dame will win over all
While her loyal Sons are
marching onward to Victory.

NOTRE D
VICTORY M

By JOHN F. SHEA, '08 *and* REV. MICH

A Song of the
UNIVERSITY OF NOTRE DA

ON, BRAVE OLD ARMY TEAM

US Military Academy
By Philip Egner

The Army team's the pride and dream
of ev'ry heart in gray.
The Army line you'll ever find
a terror in the fray:
And when the team is fighting
for the Black and Gray and Gold,
We're always near with song and cheer
to "sound off" strong and bold:
The Army team—
Rah! Rah! Rah! Boom!

(Chorus)
On, brave old Army team!
On to the fray.
Fight on to victory
For that's the fearless Army way.

THE VICTORS

University of Michigan
By Louis Elbel

Now for a cheer, they are here triumphant!
Here they come with banners flying,
In stalwart step they're nighing,
With shouts of vict'ry crying,
We hurrah! hurrah!
We greet you now, Hail!
Far we their praises sing
For the glory and the fame they've brought us,
Loud let the bells then ring,
For here they come with banners flying;
Far we their praises sing,
For the glory and the fame they've brought us;
Loud let the bells then ring,
For here they come with banners flying,
Here they come! Hurrah!

(Chorus)
Hail to the victors valiant
Hail to the con-q'ring heroes!
Hail! Hail! to Michigan,
the leaders and best—
Hail to the victors valiant!
Hail to the conq'ring heroes! Hail
Hail to Michigan, The Champions of the West!
We cheer then again, for Michigan!
We cheer with might and main,
We cheer, cheer, cheer,
With might and main we cheer!
Hail to the victors valiant!
Hail to the con-q'ring heroes! Hail!
Hail! to Michigan, the leaders and the best,
Hail! to Michigan, the Champions of the West.

Groucho Marx, shown here in his role as head of Huxley College, helps his brothers and the rest of the school's football team prepare for the epic clash against rival Darwin U. in the 1932 film, *Horse Feathers*.

At The Movies

Father Was a Fullback (1949) and then a football coach, with plenty of problems on the field and at home. Fred MacMurray, shown here on the sidelines, starred in a cast that included Maureen O'Hara, Rudy Vallee, and Natalie Wood.

Former college-football player Ronald Reagan portrays George Gipp, conferring with Pat O'Brien (left) who played the role of Knute Rockne in *Knute Rockne—All American*, the 1940 film that helped immortalize Rock's "win one for the Gipper" speech.

John Derek, shown receiving the jersey, was a college football player with big goals in life in the 1951 film, *Saturday's Hero*. Donna Reed co-starred as his girlfriend.

Harold Lloyd will try anything to win himself a little respect and popularity in *The Freshman* (1925). He's shown here charging for glory in the comic football game finale.

What's in a Nickname?

College football teams must have nicknames, someone decreed back in the previous century, something to define the ferociousness of a team, its speed and agility, its blithe spirit, or perhaps its uniqueness. Yale became the Bulldogs, Princeton the Tigers, Michigan the Wolverines, USC the Trojans, and Notre Dame the Fighting Irish.

When all the Lions, Tigers, Bears, Wildcats, Cowboys, Redskins, Mustangs, Wolf Packs, and Eagles were used up the selections got creative, sometimes strange, sometimes obscure.

Some we take for granted, although their meanings are lost on most of us:

AKRON ZIPS (No relation to zits or zippers.)

KNOX SIWASH (Either an Alaskan breed of dog or a north Pacific Coast Indian, depending on the mood at Knox.)

NORTH CAROLINA TAR HEELS (Those who live in the pine barrens of North Carolina, apparently not careful enough to avoid stepping in the pine tar.)

OKLAHOMA SOONERS (People who occupied homestead land before the authorized time, thus gaining an unfair advantage in choice of location. Texas fans always said Oklahomans were sneaky.)

SOUTHERN ILLINOIS SALUKIS (A breed of dog of the greyhound family, with long ears and silky hair.)

TENNESSEE VOLUNTEERS (Those who enter the military of their own free will.)

VMI KEYDETS (At VMI they don't know how to spell Cadets.)

WAKE FOREST DEMON DEACONS (Like Beastly Bishops or Satanic Seculars maybe?)

WESTERN CAROLINA CATAMOUNTS (Actually a puma or a cougar—cat of the mountain; get it?)

On the other hand, some seem very unlikely when used to describe a fierce football team.

BOSTON U. TERRIERS
AMHERST LORD JEFFS
DELAWARE FIGHTIN' BLUE HENS
FURMAN PALIDANS
OHIO WESLEYAN BATTLING BISHOPS
OREGON DUCKS
PENNSYLVANIA QUAKERS
RICHMOND SPIDERS
SWARTHMORE LITTLE QUAKERS
TEXAS CHRISTIAN HORNED FROGS
TUFTS JUMBOS
VPI GOBBLERS
WILLIAMS EPHMEN
YOUNGSTOWN STATE PENGUINS

Then there are the most common (among major colleges).

TIGERS:
Auburn
Clemson
Grambling
Jackson State
Louisiana State
Memphis State
Missouri
Pacific
Princeton
Tennessee State
Texas Southern

BULLDOGS:
Citadel
Drake
Fresno State

Georgia
Louisiana Tech
Mississippi State
South Carolina State
Yale

WILDCATS:
Arizona
Davidson
Kansas State
Kentucky
New Hampshire
Northwestern
Villanova
Weber State

AND THE SIMPLEST:
Cornell Big Red
Dartmouth Big Green

THE MOST ESOTERIC:
Nebraska Cornhuskers
Purdue Boilermakers

THE MOST POETIC:
Southwestern Louisiana Ragin' Cajuns

THE MOST DIFFICULT TO VISUALIZE:
Hawaii Rainbow Warriors

A Little Out of the Ordinary

★ "Snooks" Dowd of Lehigh, in the game's earlier days, ran 210 yards for a touchdown in a game against Lafayette. He ran the length of the field the wrong way, realized his mistake, circled the goal posts, and raced back the length of the field for a touchdown.

★ In 1900, Kentucky won a football game without running a single offensive play during the contest. In defeating Louisville YMCA, 12–6, Kentucky elected to kick on first down every time it received the ball and scored only on recovered fumbles.

★ Coincidences: In 1966, Augustana (of South Dakota) played Augustana (of Illinois). In addition, both teams were nicknamed the Vikings, both had the same school colors and both had an assistant coach named Kessinger. In case anyone is interested, Augustana of South Dakota won 27–0.

★ In 1897, Georgetown College of Kentucky played its entire schedule against the University of Kentucky (three games).

★ In 1958, Stanford scored two touchdowns and a field goal to California's two touchdowns, but still lost the game. The score 16–15.

★ Marquette lays claim to the longest punt ever. In a 1925 game against Navy at Farragut Field in Annapolis, Maryland, on an exceptionally blustery afternoon, their quarterback Bob Demoling took the snap on his own 20-yard line. He boomed one all the way to Navy's 19, where it bounced, was picked up by the gusting wind, and was carried not just into the end zone but 30 yards beyond it where it plopped into the Chesapeake Bay and was swept out to sea. Total yardage was never precisely determined.

★ Jay Kelley of Santa Clara is credited with perhaps the worst kick ever. In a game back around Prohibition days against highly-favored California, Santa Clara had battled the Golden Bears to a scoreless tie. With only a few minutes remaining, Santa Clara, on fourth down with the ball on Cal's 39-yard line, elected to punt, hoping to strand California deep in its own territory and preserve the tie, a major accomplishment for such a decided underdog. Kelley put his foot to the ball, which sailed almost straight upward, arced a little backwards, landed a yard behind Kelley and then rolled 24 yards the wrong way. California got the ball on Santa Clara's 37 and proceeded to move it in for a touchdown just before time ran out. Kelley was credited with a punt of –25 yards.

★ What's What Publishing company of Omaha, Nebraska, once reported this novel kick: "In the 1926 game between Boston College and Haskell, the spectators were treated to a kick that will probably never be repeated again. Sun Jennings, Haskell's star halfback, who was also the kicker, tried a 50-yard drop kick. The ball soared high in the air and came down directly on the crossbar. It bounced straight up in the air again and fell back on the crossbar to bounce a second time only to again hit the crossbar falling back on the playing field. The ball actually hit the crossbar three times. The game ended in a 21–21 tie."

Scholar Athlete

Johnny Blood McNally, who played for St. Johns of Minnesota and had a very brief stint at Notre Dame in the early 1920s before going on to stardom as a pro, felt his contribution to the Fighting Irish was more academic than athletic. He tells it this way:

"I got in some trouble around St. Patrick's Day, some pretty good celebrating for the saintly Irishman, and then went AWOL. They didn't take to it that well and, as I used to call it, I became a double-dipped dropout at Notre Dame. I'd tried out for football while I was there. Knute Rockne was the coach and they had the Four Horsemen on the varsity that year. I ended up on the freshman team because it was my first year of eligibility there, even though I'd played at St. Johns before. But I didn't do anything on the football field at Notre Dame. I always like to say that my one contribution to Notre Dame football was that I used to write Harry Stuhldreyer's English poetry papers for him."

The Old College Cheer

There's always something special about hearing the old college cheer, shouted out into the crisp autumn air. Here is a selection of some original college football rallying cries, as taken from a turn-of-the-century program.

ALABAMA
Rah, hoo, ree! Universitee! Rah, hoo! Wah, hoo! A.C.U.!

AMHERST
'Rah; 'rah-'rah; 'Rah; 'rah-'rah; Am-h-e-r-s-t!

ANTIOCH
Hobble, gobble! Razzle, dazzle! Zip, Boom, Ah! Antioch! Antioch! Rah! Rah! Rah!

BELOIT
O-Y-Ya-Ya-Ya-B-L-O-I-T!

BROWN
Rah, Rah! Rah, Rah! Rah, Rah! Brown!!

CALIFORNIA
Ha-Ha-Ha-California—U.C. Berk-lee Zip-Boom-ah!

CENTRE
Rackity-cax! Co-ax! Co-ax! (twice) Hurrah! Hurrah! Centre! Centre! Rah! Rah!

COLORADO
Rah, rah, rah! Pike's Peak or Bust! Colorado College! Yell we must!

COLUMBIA
H'ray! h'ray! h'ray! C-O-L-U-M-B-I-A

CORNELL
Cornell! I Yell! Yell! Yell! Cornell!

DARTMOUTH
Wah, woh, wah! wah woh wah! da-didi, Dartmouth! wah who wah!

DICKINSON
Rip-rah-bus-bis—Dickinsoniensis—Tiger!

FRANKLIN AND MARSHALL
Hullabaloo, bala! (twice) Way-up! Way-up! F. and M.! Nevonia!

HARVARD
Rah rah rah! rah rah rah! rah rah rah—Harvard

HEIDELBERG
Killi-killick! Rah, rah, Zik, sik! Ha! Ha! Yi! Hoo! Barn! Zoo! Heidelberg!

ILLINOIS
Rah-hoo-rah, Zip boom ah! Hip-zoo, rah zoo, Jimmy blow your baoo. Ip-sidi-iki, U. of I., Champaign!!

NEBRASKA
U, U, U, N-I-Ver-Ver-Ver-Sit-Y-Oh My!!

NOTRE DAME
Reh! rehl rehl U.N.D., N.D.U.; reh! reh! reh!

OHIO STATE
Wahoo, Wahoo, Rip, Zip, Baz, Zoo, I yell, I yell, for *O.S.U.!*

OHIO WESLEYAN
O-wee-wi-wow! Ala-ka-zu-ki-zow! Ra-zi-zi-zow! Viva! Viva! O.W.U.

PRINCETON
Hooray, Hooray, Hooray, Tiger-Siss-Boom-ah! Princeton

RUTGERS
'Rah! 'rah! 'rah! bow-wow-wow! Rutgers!

STANFORD
Wah, Hoo! Wah Hoo! L.S.J.U.! *Stanford!!*

TEXAS
Hullabaloo! Hoorary, hooray! (twice) Hooray! Hooray! Varsity! Varsity! U.! T.! A.!

VANDERBILT
Vanderbilt, Rah, Rah, Rah! Whiz Boom! Zip-boom, Rah, Rah, Rah!

WASHINGTON AND LEE
Chick-a-go-runk! go-runk! go-runk! ha, ho, hi, ho! Washing-ton and Lee!

WILLIAMS
Rah! Rah! Rah! yums, yams, yums! Will-yums!

YALE
Rah, Rah, Rah! Rah, Rah, Rah! Rah, Rah, Rah! Yale!

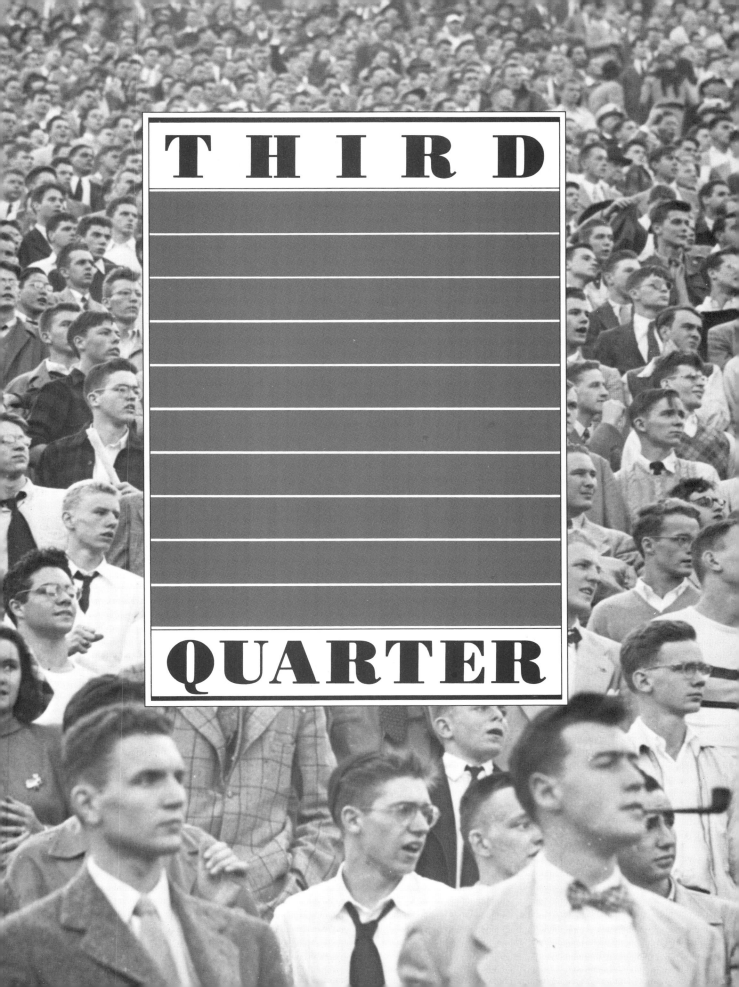

THIRD

QUARTER

The Greatest

Greatness recognized. In November 1925, the Saturday before Thanksgiving, Red Grange, a senior, played his last football game for the University of Illinois, leading them to victory over Ohio State. Then, with hundreds of reporters badgering him on the field and in the locker room as to whether he was going to turn pro or not, he escaped to his hotel. There the lobby was awash with newspaper writers too, so he snuck out of the hotel and, traveling incognito, boarded a train in Columbus for Chicago. Once there he registered in a midtown hotel and awaited word from his manager/agent/partner, C. C. Pyle, who was sitting down with George Halas and Dutch Sternaman, co-owners of the Chicago Bears, in the process of pounding out a contract to make Grange a pro.

While Grange was still a college student, he was already a football legend, spoken of in the same sense of awe as Babe Ruth, Jack Dempsey, Bobby Jones, and Bill Tilden. Now, his next move was the most eagerly anticipated item in sports news.

The entrepreneurial Pyle did, of course, sign Grange up with the Bears and suddenly the then youthful National Football League got a tremendous boost in terms of respectability

> **66My definition of an All-American is a player who has weak opposition and a poet in the press box.99**
>
> BOB ZUPPKE
> ILLINOIS

and economics. (Grange in fact played his first pro game as a Chicago Bear on Thanksgiving Day, five days after his last college game.) Over the next few months, with a special coast to coast football tour, Red Grange managed to earn about $125,000 while picking up an almost equal amount from endorsements and personal appearances, not to mention contracts for three motion pictures—not bad in those days before income taxes.

Today, when greatness is recognized on a college football field it can lead to a pro contract calculated in the millions of dollars. And recognition is almost unlimited. Where Grange had to rely solely on print media to make his name known throughout the country, today's heroes are bolstered by television, which can instantaneously reach tens of millions of people.

Greatness, however, is much more than what it brings in worldly treasures. It is the result of talent, effort, doggedness, concentration, many virtues and qualities threaded through the body of an athlete. Greatness in a team is also the result of a variety of subjective and objective elements, from the wisdom of a coaching staff to the talent and dedication of the players to teamwork and simply getting a

Albie Booth, Yale's super back, known around New Haven as Little Boy Blue.

mildly winded with the score Yale 19, Dartmouth 3.

An undaunted Dartmouth came back, however. Bill McCall took a pitchout from Morton and ran 25 yards for a score. But Yale, even with Albie Booth on the bench, was unstoppable. Filling his little shoes was halfback Bob Lassiter, who raced 53 yards to set up another touchdown and then tossed one to Barres for still another. A 33-point second quarter gave Yale a 23-point lead at the half.

Yale kicked off to start the second half, and Bill

McCall grabbed the ball at his own 8-yard line. He raced with it the length of the field, and suddenly the momentum of the game was irreversibly changed. Dartmouth held Yale, and when the Eli went to punt on fourth down, Dartmouth's Roger Donner broke through and blocked it, picked the ball up on the run, and whisked it in for another Indian touchdown. The score was now 33–24, Yale.

Albie Booth was back in the game for Yale, but Dartmouth was keying on him, and their defense was impregnable. When he couldn't make it on the ground, Booth called for a pass play. He pitched out to Kay Todd, then took off downfield. Todd zeroed in on him and threw the ball, but seemingly from out of nowhere, Dartmouth's Bill McCall cut in front of Booth, snatched the ball away, and sped 60 yards with it to bring the Indians within 3 points of Yale.

The partisan crowd in the Yale Bowl was dismally quiet. Once again, Dartmouth contained Booth and his fellow Bulldogs. And again they marched. With four minutes left and the ball on Yale's 14-yard line, Bill Morton lined up for a field goal. It was perfect, and the score was tied. The Indians then stifled Yale's last attempt to score as time ran out while Booth was attempting a drop kick field goal from the Indians' 20-yard line.

Albie Booth sat on the bench after the game pondering what had happened. After such an illustrious second quarter, how could they have had such a dismal second half, he asked himself. When a sportswriter approached, Booth said, "That's football," shook his head and went on, "crazy game, isn't it."

MINNESOTA NORTHWESTERN 1936

When Minnesota traveled to Evanston, Illinois, in 1936 to face the Northwestern Wildcats, Bernie Bierman's Golden Gophers, reigning national champions from the year before, had not suffered the slings of defeat in 28 games, since 1932.

Grantland Rice had written of Bierman's 1934 Gophers, "Football fans here are no longer discussing whether Minnesota's team is the best in the country

today. They are taking that for granted. What they want to know is this: Shouldn't it be rated the greatest of all time?" Bernie Bierman said of his 1936 squad, "They would class right along with the 1934 team."

The Minnesotans had certified All-Americans in tackle Big Ed Widseth and halfback Andy Uram and a shrewd quarterback named Bud Wilkinson, who would later make the most of his football knowledge as head

Bernie Bierman, head coach at Minnesota from 1932 through 1941, brought the Golden Gophers four national championships and six Big Ten titles.

coach at Oklahoma. They had easily defeated Washington, Nebraska, Michigan, and Purdue, and predictably they were heavy favorites.

Lynn "Pappy" Waldorf's Wildcats, however, had a few things going for them too. They were undefeated and underrated. They had an All-American in guard Steve Reid and near All-Americans in end John Kovatch and halfback Don Heap. And they had Mother Nature, who drenched the field of play and turned it into a quagmire, which helped Northwestern thwart Minnesota's volatile offense.

Despite the slop, Minnesota's Andy Uram broke one in the first quarter, sloshing and sliding 48 yards all the way to Northwestern's 23-yard line. Three plays gained only a few yards, and then Bernie Bierman made a decision he would rue. He went for the first down instead of a field goal, and didn't make it.

Waldorf's Wildcats defied the mud as well in the first period. Don Heap ran for 16 and 26 yards on one drive, and then John Kovatch, on an end-around, picked up 22 more yards. But Northwestern's march fizzled and the remainder of the first half was merely an exchange of possessions.

In the second half, Minnesota dominated, but every time they appeared ready to score something went wrong. A shanked punt, costly penalties, fumbles—Minnesota hardly seemed the team that had rocketed through the four previous seasons without a loss. Still, the Wildcats could not capitalize on the Gophers' misdeeds, and the game went into the final period a scoreless stalemate.

Deep in their own territory, Minnesota halfback Julius Alfonse took a pitchout from Uram, but the slippery ball skittered through his hands. Suddenly bodies with flailing arms and legs piled on top of each other, grabbing for the greased pigskin. When the referee pulled all the players off the pile, he found Northwestern's tackle DeWitt Gibson cradling the ball. The Wildcats took over just 13 yards from the Gophers' goal line.

On the first play reserve fullback Don Geyer hit the line and was smothered by Minnesota defenders. Once again there was a huge pile-up, suggesting another fumble. But as the referee stripped bodies away he did not find a scramble for the ball but instead Big Ed Widseth punching the ball carrier. A flag was thrown—15 yards against Minnesota, 12 of which were walked off—and the ball was placed on the 1-yard line. The Gophers held for two downs, but then fullback Steve Toth charged in for the score. The six points were enough. Northwestern dug in and stopped Minnesota in the mud for the remainder of the game, and the Gophers' illustrious winning streak ended at the final gun.

The Greatest Players

In 1950, the Associated Press conducted a poll of 391 sportswriters and broadcasters to determine the greatest college football player of the first half of the 20th century. The results:

Player	School	No. of Votes
Jim Thorpe	Carlisle	170
Red Grange	Illinois	138
Bronko Nagurski	Minnesota	38
Ernie Nevers	Stanford	7
Sammy Baugh	Texas Christian	7
Don Hutson	Alabama	6
George Gipp	Notre Dame	4
Charlie Trippi	Georgia	3
Willie Heston	Michigan	2
Chic Harley	Ohio State	2
Sid Luckman	Columbia	2
Steve Van Buren	Louisiana State	2
Charley Brickley	Harvard	1
Pete Henry	Washington & Jefferson	1
Bennie Oosterbaan	Michigan	1
Nile Kinnick	Iowa	1
Frankie Albert	Stanford	1
Glenn Dobbs	Tulsa	1
Glenn Davis	Army	1
Doc Blanchard	Army	1
Bulldog Turner	Hardin-Simmons	1
Doak Walker	Southern Methodist	1

PITTSBURGH
FORDHAM
1937

Pitt was the number one ranked team in the nation in 1937. The year before they had barely missed the national title and had demolished Washington in the Rose Bowl. They had just about everybody from that team back, including consensus All-American halfback Marshall Goldberg. Their leader, Jock Sutherland, later acclaimed them the finest team he had fielded in his 20-year college coaching career.

But they also had a nemesis, the Maroon or Rams of Fordham, as they were alternately known, whose line, billed as the Seven Blocks of Granite, was the most formidable defense in college football. In encounters during the two previous seasons, Fordham, coached by former Four Horseman Jimmy Crowley, had held the otherwise explosive-scoring Panthers to consecutive scoreless ties. In fact, during the entire 1936 season, the Maroon had allowed only one touchdown all season.

Two of the Seven Blocks were All-Americans, center Alex Wojciechowicz and tackle Ed Franco; the other five were just a string or two below them on that honor roll. And now with an improved backfield, Crow-ley's eleven from the Bronx had a shot of their own at the national crown.

For both teams, as they confronted each other at the Polo Grounds in 1937 before 53,000 spectators, this was the game of the year, the one in which one team would finally have to lose its claim to the nation's top ranking.

Fordham moved the ball first, reaching the Pitt 40-yard line, where the drive stalled. After the punt, Pitt ripped off 37 yards on four running plays until the Fordham defense shored itself up and held them tight.

At the start of the second quarter, Fordham again set the pace, moving behind the rushing of Angelo Fortunato and Dom Principe. But again Pitt managed to stifle the drive, regaining possession at their own 8-yard line. Shortly thereafter came what appeared to be the break of the game: the Panthers fumbled on their own 23, and Joe Granski recovered for the Rams. Three thrusts at the Pitt line gained only 5 yards, and Fordham's captain, end John Druze missed the field goal attempt.

Pittsburgh got its big chance later in the quarter.

Fordham's line, known as the Seven Blocks of Granite, from the left: Johnny Druze, Al Babartsky, Vince Lombardi, Alex Wojciechowicz, Nat Pierce, Ed Franco, and Leo Pasquin.

High-flying guard Vince Lombardi was a standout member of Fordham's Seven Blocks of Granite in 1936 and 1937.

Halfback Harry Stebbins ran a Fordham punt back 35 yards to the Maroon 40. Then the Panthers ground it out to the Fordham 5. A slick reverse to Marshall Goldberg, and he swept around left end and across the goal line for an apparent touchdown—the first score in three Pitt-Fordham games. But a holding call erased the play. The Ram defense regrouped and held, leaving a scoreless tie at the end of the half.

Further evidence that things were not going Pitt's way came on the first play of the second half, when Stebbins fumbled and Fordham recovered on the Pitt 28. Fordham came up with a fancy reverse, and Principe made it down to the Pitt 10-yard line. But it was now the Panthers' turn to hold. Druze tried an 18-yard field goal this time, but it was partially blocked. Marshall Goldberg picked up the bounding ball in his own end zone and ran it back to the 8, where he was collared by a Fordham player just before breaking into the clear. Two plays later, however, Goldberg fumbled, and Druze recovered, the ball still only eight yards from the Pitt goal line. Principe bulled his way to the 3, and Fordham's rooters were on their feet, chanting "Score, Score, Score." But it was not their destiny. A 15-yard penalty moved them back and a Pittsburgh defense rose to the task. Druze finally tried another field goal, this one from his 30, but it too was wide.

A few minutes later, Pittsburgh had another chance to score when, on fourth down at the Fordham 23, end Bill Daddio tried a field goal, but his was off the mark also. On their next possession Pitt came back again, driving hard, and just when it seemed as though the mighty Fordham defense might be faltering, Alex

Wojciechowicz smashed into Harry Stebbins, dislocated him from the ball, and recovered it for the Rams.

Later in the fourth quarter, Wojie, as most called the Fordham great, again forced a Stebbins fumble, but neither turnover produced any points.

When the final gun went off, there were still two large zeros on the scoreboard. For three years in a row the two fine teams had been unable to score upon each other. The tie would be the only blemish on each team's record at the end of the 1937 season. Pittsburgh (9-0-1) was judged by AP as the best team in the nation because it played a tougher schedule, while Fordham (7-0-1) had to settle for the number three berth, behind the University of California (10-0-1).

ARMY NOTRE DAME 1946

It was surely the game of the year, and many have said it was the college football game of the century. Army, unbeaten and untied in 25 games, had been national champs two years running and was aiming for a third title. Notre Dame, refurbished now that the war was over, was also unbeaten and untied in 1946. The neutral ground for their meeting was New York City's Yankee Stadium, and more than 74,000 fans filled it to overflow. Scalpers were getting as much as $200 a ticket, and more than $500,000 had to be returned to those who had tried to buy tickets through normal channels.

In the stands were such West Point alumni as generals Dwight Eisenhower, Omar Bradley, Jacob Devers, and Maxwell Taylor, as well as Secretary of the Navy James Forrestal, Secretary of War Robert Patterson, and Attorney General Tom Clark. The uniformed Cadets, 2,100 strong, marched in absolute precision before the opening whistle. The Fighting Irish band blared out "Cheer, Cheer for Old Notre Dame," and a staunch band of alumni sent the words to that illustrious fight song into the Bronx skies.

Notre Dame not only had vengeance on their mind—Army had scorched them 59–0 and 48–0 in the

Notre Dame's terrier confronts Army's mule at Yankee stadium before the 1946 battle of the two most powerful teams in college football.

Johnny Lujack was both a great quarterback and one of the game's finest defensive backs as well. A Heisman trophy winner in 1947, he was also a consensus All-American his junior and senior years.

two previous years when many of their players were serving in the armed forces. Coach Frank Leahy was back from duty in the Navy, and he was indeed set upon regaining the Irish's self-esteem. On the other hand, Earl Blaik had his team thirsting for an unprecedented third consecutive national championship.

On the field, Army's dream backfield warmed up. Doc Blanchard was playing at right halfback instead of fullback because Herschel "Ug" Fuson was injured. Glenn Davis was at the other halfback, while junior Rip Rowan filled in at fullback and Arnold Tucker handled the quarterbacking duties. Across the gridiron Notre Dame's gilded backs were loosening up: quarterback Johnny Lujack, halfbacks Terry Brennan and Emil Sitko, and fullback Jim Mello. Sportswriters and spectators alike were predicting a fast-paced, ferocious offensive game, regardless of the fact that both teams had stalwart defenses.

But things do not always turn out as the scribes and fans predict in college football.

Army got the first chance to score early in the opening period. Emil Sitko fumbled the ball on his own 24-yard line, and Army tackle Goble Bryant fell on it. Arnold Tucker hit Glenn Davis for 8 yards to the Notre Dame 16. Blanchard tried three times to get the first down, without success. But on fourth down, Blaik decided to go for it, calling for Blanchard once more. But when he hit the line, the Irish were there, and they stopped him a yard short.

Notre Dame picked up a pair of first downs on the running of Terry Brennan and Sitko, but then had to punt. Army appeared to live up to its reputation on the

Second Thoughts

Terry Brennan, Notre Dame's left halfback in the classic scoreless tie that the Fighting Irish and Army played to in 1946, was the leading ground gainer that day, 69 yards on 14 carries, and had the longest run of the game, a sprint of 22 yards. He remembers the game vividly.

"Thinking back on it, I believe both Blaik and Leahy choked. They both went conservative, ultra-conservative, and that was ridiculous with all the offensive talent on those two teams. We had Johnny Lujack and Emil Sitko in our backfield, they had Blanchard, Davis, and Tucker. In fact, Red Blaik told me much later that he felt they both blew it. They didn't coach for the win, they didn't go for it, neither one, that's what he told me.

"We had the best chance to win it. At one point we were down on their five-yard line. It was third down and

Leahy called for a quarterback sneak. Lujack only got a yard. On fourth down, we went for it. Bill Gompers was in the game at halfback and he tried to get around right end. I still don't understand why we ran the ball at Hank Foldberg, who was the best defensive end they had. We'd gone all the way down the field running to the other side where Barney Poole was the end; he was a slow gumshoe type of a guy and we had been beating him. But we ran right at their best defense and Gompers only got a yard, Foldberg got him.

"They could have won the game at another point. Doc Blanchard broke into the clear, and the only one who had a chance at him was Lujack, who was as great a defensive back as he was a quarterback. Lujack made a helluva one-on-one tackle to bring him down and save the touchdown."

next possession. Blanchard went inside for a first down, and Davis swept outside for another. Davis then took a pitchout from Arnold Tucker and fired to All-American end Barney Poole for another 5 yards. But then Notre Dame's line, peopled with such greats as George Connor, Bill Fischer, Jim Martin, and George Strohmeyer, dug in and stopped the Cadet drive.

In the second quarter, Army had another chance to put some points on the board. From Notre Dame's 46-yard line, Glenn Davis, looking as though he were about to leg one of his patented end runs, suddenly pulled up and tossed a 23-yard pass diagonally across the field, which Blanchard leaped high in the air to grab before tumbling out of bounds. The ball was at the Notre Dame 21-yard line. But again the Irish defense rose to the challenge. This time they not only stopped Army but drove them back to the 37, where the Cadets were forced to punt.

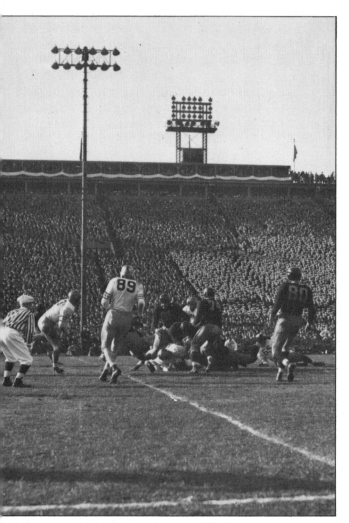

Action on the field during the big game of 1946.

Notre Dame took over on their own 15 and began the longest drive of the game. Substitute halfback Gerry Cowhig burst off tackle and found 20 yards worth of freedom. Lujack hit end Bob Skoglund for another 25 yards. With Leahy platooning backs, the Irish worked their way down to the Army 4-yard line. With fourth down and 2 for a first, Leahy disdained the field goal as Blaik had in the preceding period. The call was for a pitchout to halfback Bill Gompers, but he could only get to the 3-yard line.

Before the half ended, Army had one more shot at taking the lead. Notre Dame bobbled the ball away to Army reserve end Tom Hayes, who dropped on it at the Irish 35. But the Cadets could only muster 2 yards in four plays and turned the ball back to Notre Dame. Everyone in Yankee Stadium was surprised at the scoreless first half, but no one was saying that it was anything but an exciting game.

It was back and forth again in the third quarter. And then it was Army's turn to give Notre Dame the opportunity: a fumble on their own 34, captured by Irish guard John Mastrangelo. But when Lujack rifled a pass over the middle, Arnold Tucker picked it off and raced 32 yards with it. With the ball now on the Army 42, Doc Blanchard broke one for 21 yards, and again Army was threatening. Blanchard and Davis picked up a few more yards, then Tucker drilled one to Hank Foldberg at the 20, and the Cadets had a first down. The crowd from West Point rose to their feet, sensing that their attack had finally found its adrenaline. But the frenzy came to a sudden halt, and the enormous block of Cadets slumped as one back into their seats when Terry Brennan leaped in front of an Army receiver to intercept a pass from Glenn Davis on the Notre Dame 8-yard line.

There was not another scoring threat until the last minute of play. With 48 seconds left, Davis rolled out and threw a long, arcing pass on which Blanchard made a spectacular catch at the 20-yard line, only to be ruled out of bounds. The remaining seconds ticked off the clock, and when it was over neither team had scored, a shock to everyone.

Notre Dame won the battle on paper by outrushing the Cadets 173 yards to 138 and picking up 11 first downs to Army's 9, but Army had had the most chances to post some points, a fact not lost on Notre Dame coach Frank Leahy. "You escaped today," one writer mentioned to him after the game. "I suppose I should be elated over the tie," Leahy said to him. "After all, we didn't lose. But I'm not. There is no jubilation in this dressing room." There wasn't any in Army's either.

Notre Dame huddles for a pep talk in the second quarter of the game against Michigan State, trailing 10–7. Quarterback Terry Hanratty looks on disconsolately, having left the game with an injured shoulder.

Notre Dame's substitute quarterback Coley O'Brien (3), who passed for their only touchdown of the day, gets a pass off under heavy pressure from Phil Hoag (36) and Jeff Richardson (57).

the game. Nick Eddy, their most productive running back, slipped getting off the train in East Lansing and aggravated an already injured shoulder to a degree that would keep him out of the game. Then in the first period of play stalwart center George Goeddeke left the game for good with an injured ankle; shortly after, Hanratty, victim of a savage tackle administered jointly by Bubba Smith and linebacker Charlie Thornhill, suffered a shoulder separation and was also through for the afternoon.

To add to the dismal turn of events, Michigan State marched downfield late in the first quarter and at the beginning of the second, going 73 yards on 10 plays. The score came when fullback Regis Cavender smashed in from the four. Notre Dame could not move the ball substantially in several ensuing possessions. But the Spartans could, at least far enough to enable their barefoot kicker from Hawaii, Dick Kenney, to boot a 47-yard field goal and give MSU a 10–0 lead.

Coley O'Brien, a sophomore, directed the Irish offense in the absence of Hanratty, and he finally got it moving by going to the air. Three completed passes covered 54 yards and gave Notre Dame its first score of the game. The payoff pass was a 34-yarder into the end zone to halfback Bob Gladieux, who was filling in for the injured Eddy.

From that point on, the vaunted Irish defense came back to form. They had allowed only four touchdowns in their preceding eight games and had shut out five of their opponents. Michigan State ran at them and threw into them, but for the remainder of the first half and all of the second, they could not come up with one

legitimate scoring opportunity. The Spartans gained yardage, but mostly in their own territory.

But Notre Dame found no fortune on offense either until the end of the third period, when O'Brien orchestrated a drive that took the Irish from their own 20 to the Spartan 12, where it faltered. Onto the field trotted Joe Azzaro to kick the game-tying field goal.

A big break came Notre Dame's way a little later in the final period when safety Tom Schoen picked off one of Jimmy Raye's passes in Spartan territory and ran it down to the 18. But in three plays they managed to lose 6 yards. Azzaro came back out to attempt a 41-yarder, but it drifted to the right.

With a little more than a minute left, Notre Dame got the ball back again on their own 30-yard line, but fearing a turnover in his own territory, Parseghian chose to run out the clock. The partisan Spartan fans showed their displeasure with a volley of boos, but most unbiased observers agreed it was the prudent thing to do.

Parseghian said in the locker room to reporters, "We'd fought hard to come back and tie it up. After all that, I didn't want to risk giving it to them cheap. You get reckless and it could cost the game. I wasn't going to do a jackass thing like that at this point."

Notre Dame had one more game to play that year, against tough arch-rival USC. They annihilated them 54–0 the following week and as a result of that, and the fact that they had outscored their opponents that season 362–38, they were awarded their first national title since 1949. Duffy Daugherty and his Spartans had to settle for second place.

The National Champions

Since 1936, the NCAA has recognized a national champion based on polls conducted by the two major wire services: Associated Press (AP), which reflects the choice of the nation's football writers, and United Press International (UPI), which polls college football coaches. (Both winners are listed when the two polls did not agree.)

Year	School	Record	Coach	Year	School	Record	Coach
1936	Minnesota	7-1-0	Bernie Bierman	1962	USC	11-0-0	John McKay
1937	Pittsburgh	9-0-1	Jock Sutherland	1963	Texas	11-0-0	Darrell Royal
1938	Texas Christian	11-0-0	Dutch Meyer	1964	Alabama	10-1-0	Paul Bryant
1939	Texas A&M	11-0-0	Homer Norton	1965	Alabama (AP)	9-1-1	Paul Bryant
1940	Minnesota	8-0-0	Bernie Bierman		Michigan State		
1941	Minnesota	8-0-0	Bernie Bierman		(UPI)	10-1-0	Duffy Daugherty
1942	Ohio State	9-1-0	Paul Brown	1966	Notre Dame	9-0-1	Ara Parseghian
1943	Notre Dame	9-1-0	Frank Leahy	1967	USC	10-1-0	John McKay
1944	Army	9-0-0	Earl Blaik	1968	Ohio State	10-0-0	Woody Hayes
1945	Army	9-0-0	Earl Blaik	1969	Texas	11-0-0	Darrell Royal
1946	Notre Dame	8-0-1	Frank Leahy	1970	Nebraska (AP)	11-0-1	Bob Devaney
1947	Notre Dame	9-0-0	Frank Leahy		Texas (UPI)	10-1-0	Darrell Royal
1948	Michigan	9-0-0	Bennie Oosterbaan	1971	Nebraska	13-0-0	Bob Devaney
1949	Notre Dame	10-0-0	Frank Leahy	1972	USC	12-0-0	John McKay
1950	Oklahoma	10-1-0	Bud Wilkinson	1973	Notre Dame		
1951	Tennessee	10-1-0	Bob Neyland		(AP)	11-0-0	Ara Parseghian
1952	Michigan State	9-0-0	Biggie Munn		Alabama (UPI)	11-1-0	Paul Bryant
1953	Maryland	10-1-0	Jim Tatum	1974	Oklahoma (AP)	11-0-0	Barry Switzer
1954	Ohio State				USC (UPI)	10-1-1	John McKay
	(AP)	10-0-0	Woody Hayes	1975	Oklahoma	11-1-0	Barry Switzer
	UCLA (UPI)	9-0-0	Red Sanders	1976	Pittsburgh	12-0-0	Johnny Majors
1955	Oklahoma	11-0-0	Bud Wilkinson	1977	Notre Dame	11-1-0	Dan Devine
1956	Oklahoma	10-0-0	Bud Wilkinson	1978	Alabama (AP)	11-1-0	Paul Bryant
1957	Auburn (AP)	10-0-0	Shug Jordan		USC (UPI)	12-1-0	John Robinson
	Ohio State			1979	Alabama	12-0-0	Paul Bryant
	(UPI)	9-1-0	Woody Hayes	1980	Georgia	12-0-0	Vince Dooley
1958	Louisiana			1981	Clemson	12-0-0	Danny Ford
	State	11-0-0	Paul Dietzel	1982	Penn State	11-1-0	Joe Paterno
1959	Syracuse	11-0-0	Ben Schwartzwalder	1983	Miami		
1960	Minnesota	8-2-0	Murray Warmath		(Florida)	11-1-0	Howard Schnellenberger
1961	Alabama	11-0-0	Paul Bryant	1984	Brigham Young	13-0-0	Lavell Edwards

TEXAS ARKANSAS 1969

The Texas Longhorns in 1969, under Darrell Royal, were an explosive team, dominating the Southwestern Conference. Going into the last game of the season against Arkansas, they were undefeated and in a race with similarly undefeated Penn State for the national championship. In their previous nine games, the Texans had collectively drubbed their opponents 399–88, running up scores such as 69–7 over Texas Christian, 56–14 over Baylor, 56–17 over Navy, and scoring 49 points each in wins over Texas A&M and Texas Tech.

Arkansas, under the tutelage of Frank Broyles, was also undefeated but ranked only seventh by AP and third by UPI. "Everything to win and hardly anything to lose," he told his Razorbacks. By everything he meant a definite shot at the national title, the conference championship, a Cotton Bowl bid, and the opportunity to serve as spoiler to a longtime rival.

Both Texas and Arkansas had only one All-American apiece, the Longhorn tackle Bob McKay and the Razorback center Rodney Brand. But both teams had a number of highly respected ballplayers. Texas halfback Steve Worster, tackle Bobby Wuensch, and defensive end Bill Atessis would receive All-American honors the following year. And they had a fine end in Cotton Speyer and a feared linebacker in Glen Halsell. Arkansas also had several players who were to make All-American ranks: end Chuck Dicus, linebacker Cliff Powell, and running back Bill Burnett.

There were more than 44,000 fans, a capacity crowd, at Razorback Stadium in Fayetteville, Arkansas, including President Richard Nixon, to witness, as one writer put it, "the most important battle in the southwest since the Alamo."

Texas took the opening kickoff, but on their second play from scrimmage they fumbled and Arkansas recovered on the Texas 22-yard line. The Razorbacks belted their way to the 1, where Bill Burnett slashed through for the early score. The Longhorns, used to scoring almost at will, having averaged 44 points a game that season, were thwarted every time they had the ball in the first three quarters.

Arkansas also capitalized on another Texas fumble in the third quarter. Behind the passing of quarterback Bill Montgomery, and some grind-it-out rushing, the Razorbacks moved the ball down to the Longhorns'

29-yard line. From there, Montgomery dropped back and laid one in the arms of Chuck Dicus, his favorite receiver, for another touchdown.

But if the first three quarters belonged to Arkansas, the final period turned out to be totally Texas. It began on the opening play of that quarter. With the Longhorn running game shut down, quarterback James Street went to the air, or at least tried to, but when he could not find a receiver he took off out of the pocket and zigzagged his way 42 yards for a touchdown.

Coach Darrell Royal decided to eschew the kick for conversion. "We felt that was the time for a two-point conversion," he explained later. "If we missed it, we still could have gone for two again and gotten a tie. But if we had kicked after the first touchdown and gone for two after the second, then the pressure is really on us." It proved a fortuitous decision. Street carried to his left on an option, then sliced in for the two points.

Late in the period, Street had the Texans on the move again. But at their own 43 the drive stalled. It was fourth down, a little more than 2 for the first, and just less than five minutes to play. Royal sent in the play, and seeing the formation, the Arkansas punt returner hustled up to join the defense. Texas was going for it. They lined up tight, and Arkansas dug in, expecting the run. Street took the snap, faked a handoff, raced back, and let fly a long one toward the sideline where tight end Randy Peschel was a step or two ahead of the Arkansas defenders. It was right on the mark, and Peschel carried it all the way to the Razorback 13. Texas then moved the ball to the 2, and Jim Bertelsen burst through from there to bring the game to a 14–14 tie. Texas placekicker Happy Feller came on and drilled the go-ahead point.

Arkansas bounced back, but now in desperation. Montgomery passed them from his own 20 all the way to the Texas 39, and there was over a minute left. The partisan crowd was in uproar, screaming for the Razorbacks to pull it out. And for a moment it looked as though they just might do it. Montgomery faded back, spotted Dicus streaking toward the goal line, and rifled the ball to him, but as the end reached for it Texas defensive back Tom Campbell snatched the ball, and with it any hope of victory for the Razorbacks.

Frank Broyles said afterwards, "I'm proud, we played a winning game. We lost on the scoreboard, lost really on just that one play," referring to the surprise fourth-down bomb by Street. Regarding the same play, Darrell Royal added, "Every now and then you just have to suck it up and pick a number. You don't use logic and reason, you just play a hunch. I never considered punting."

Darrell Royal shouts some instructions form the Texas sideline. When he retired in 1976, his record stood at 184 victories, 60 losses and 5 ties.

NEBRASKA OKLAHOMA 1971

A pair of All-Americans, both juniors, flanker Johnny Rodgers of Nebraska (left) and running back Greg Pruitt of Oklahoma.

Millions of Thanksgiving turkey dinners were rescheduled or postponed in 1971 so that college football fans could watch the national telecast of the battle of the unbeatens, Nebraska and Oklahoma. The number one ranked Cornhuskers had been ranked first by AP the year before, and coach Bob Devaney had guided them through a perfect season in '71. Second-ranked Oklahoma, under Chuck Fairbanks, had their eyes on removing Nebraska from the race, and the Sooners had the advantages of the home field and the raucous, all-supporting fans who filled the stadium.

Both teams were loaded with All-American–quality players. Nebraska was led by the quarterbacking of Jerry Tagge, the running of Jeff Kinney, and the running and pass catching of future Heisman Trophy winner Johnny Rodgers. They also had Outland Award winner Larry Jacobson at defensive tackle and All-American Willie Harper at defensive end. Oklahoma was paced by a dazzling runner, Greg Pruitt, a consensus All-American in center Tom Brahaney, an outstanding quarterback in Jack Mildren, and two fine defensive linemen, Derland Moore and Raymond Hamilton.

The game started out with a bang. The Sooners, shortly after receiving the opening kickoff, had to punt, and Johnny Rodgers took it at his own 28-yard line, cut up the middle, weaved his way through defenders, and

Jeff Kinney carried much of the rushing load for the Cornhuskers in 1971, and scored four touchdowns in Nebraska's 35–31 triumph over Oklahoma that year.

carried the ball 72 yards before depositing it in the end zone. Then a truculent Nebraska defense, rated the finest in the nation that year, geared itself to stop Oklahoma's formidable wishbone offense.

But they were not going to be able to do that this Thanksgiving Day. They did manage to bottle up the usually electrifying Greg Pruitt, but they could not stem all the Oklahoma options. Jack Mildren brought the Sooners right back with a 70-yard march, although they had to settle for a field goal.

Now back came Nebraska, as Jerry Tagge led the Cornhusker drive of 54 yards, crowned when Kinney bucked in from the 1-yard line.

Then came Oklahoma again. Mildren engineered an 80-yard invasion this time, carrying it in himself from the 3-yard line. Late in the second quarter, he moved the Sooners 78 yards for still another touchdown, this one by tossing a 24-yard pass to wide receiver Jon Harrison with five seconds left. By intermission, Oklahoma had already chalked up 311 total yards and a 17–14 lead.

Nebraska, however, took control in the third period. Jeff Kinney was close to unstoppable on the ground, and Tagge was effective in the air when he had to be. In fact, Kinney gained 154 yards rushing in the second half alone. He gave the lead back to the Cornhuskers with a 3-yard plunge and then widened the margin by bulling in from the 1. With the score now in Nebraska's favor, 28–17, the momentum changed again.

Oklahoma knocked off chunks of yardage, 75 in all, and reached the Nebraska 3, where Mildren ran it in for his second touchdown of the day. It was a dogged battle in the fourth quarter, but Oklahoma was still on

the rise. Mildren again was the focal point of a major drive, this one 69 yards, and he capped it with a 16-yard touchdown pass, again to Harrison, and the lead passed to the Sooners, 31–28. Nebraskans could not remember when a team had scored so many points against their tremendous defense, which had given up an average of just over eight points a game that year.

This game, the Cornhuskers now knew, would have to be won by their offense. There were about six minutes left when they launched a fateful drive from their 26-yard line. Relying on Kinney carrying the ball, it took 12 plays with many tight situations. On third down and 1 at their own 35-yard line, Kinney broke for a 17-yard gain. Then on another third and 8 at the Oklahoma 46, Tagge was forced out of the pocket, scrambled wildly, then shot one to Johnny Rodgers, who was practically on the ground and sandwiched between two Oklahoma defenders, but he held onto it, and the drive was kept alive. Nebraska continued to battle their way downfield to the 2, and Kinney exploded into the end zone for his fourth touchdown.

With that Nebraska won it, 35–31, one of the great offensive games in college football annals. Nine touchdowns were scored, and a grand total of 829 yards gained by the two teams. Even in defeat Sooner coach Chuck Fairbanks saw it as "a classic game, the greatest one I've ever been involved in." Bob Devaney had no arguments about that.

The Longest Winning Streaks

School	Wins	Years
Oklahoma	47	1953–57
Washington	39	1908–14
Yale	37	1890–93
Yale	37	1887–89
Toledo	35	1969–71
Pennsylvania	34	1894–96
Oklahoma	31	1948–50
Pittsburgh	31	1914–18
Pennsylvania	31	1896–98
Texas	30	1968–70
Michigan	29	1901–03
Alabama	28	1978–80
Oklahoma	28	1973–75
Michigan State	28	1950–53
Nebraska	27	1901–04
Cornell	26	1921–24
Michigan	26	1903–05
Michigan	25	1946–49
Army	25	1944–46
USC	25	1931–33

ALABAMA
USC
1978

It was the third game of the season, and Alabama held the number-one ranking in the nation, while USC languished in seventh place. The year before, the Trojans' 15-game winning streak was decisively terminated in Los Angeles by Bear Bryant's visiting Alabamans. A turnabout would be poetic justice, or something to that effect, as John Robinson told his players.

The 1978 meeting of the two teams was held at Legion Field in Birmingham, Alabama, before more than 77,000 avid 'Bama fans and a national television audience. The Crimson Tide was listed as a 14-point favorite. But perhaps the oddsmakers were not taking into account how volatile USC tailback Charles White, inheritor of that position from such earlier Trojan luminaries as Mike Garrett, O. J. Simpson, Anthony Davis, and Ricky Bell, could be on a given occasion. Or what a fine passer left-handed quarterback Paul McDonald could be when John Robinson wanted to mix things up.

McDonald explained the Trojan game plan: "We'd throw on second down, run on third and long, and screw 'em up with motion. Sometimes I'd call two or three plays in the huddle and then choose one when we got to the line." Coach Robinson described it with a shrug as "a wheeling-dealing offense that could self-destruct at any minute if we start making mistakes."

It didn't destroy itself, however, but it did dismantle favored Alabama. Throughout the first half, USC controlled the line of scrimmage and the momentum of the game. They led off with a beautifully executed drive down the field, mostly on carries by Charles White, but it fell flat on the Tide's 2-yard line when White got separated from the football. On the Trojans' next possession, however, White made everyone forget the miscue when he followed his blockers around right end, suddenly broke by them and the defenders, and raced 40 yards for a touchdown.

The usually productive Alabama offense, which averaged almost 29 points a game that season, spearheaded by running back Major Ogilvie and quarterback Jeff Rutledge, was unable to put more than an occasional dent in the USC defense during either of the first two periods of play. The thousands of 'Bama fans

Charles White, Heisman honoree of 1979, was a unanimous All-American for Southern Cal in both 1978 and 1979. He averaged 127.2 yards a game and the 5598 yards he gained in three seasons is second only to Tony Dorsett's NCAA record of 6082.

were forced to spend most of their time watching the USC offense at work. For almost nine minutes in the second quarter, in fact, USC put together a plodding 23-play drive, which eventually resulted in a field goal. The score at intermission was 10–0.

Bryant roused his Alabamans during the break, and in the third quarter the Tide got on the scoreboard when Ogilvie wove his way through the USC defense for 41 yards and a touchdown.

It failed to daunt Southern Cal. Back they came with White running wild, six yards on one carry, four on the next, picking up needed first downs one after the other. At the Tide's 6-yard line, with the defense keying on White, McDonald went to the air, a little shot over the line of scrimmage to flanker Kevin Williams, who carried it in; the score was now USC 17, Alabama 7.

Later, in the fourth quarter, McDonald again found Williams, this time a 40-yard touchdown play. As time wore down, 'Bama got on the board once more with a 41-yard touchdown pass from Jeff Rutledge to Barry Krauss. Although they had several more possessions they were never back in the game, with Southern Cal leading at the end, 24–14. The game was all USC, 417 total yards gained, with 199 of those accounted for by Charles White's rushing.

Bear Bryant faced the sportswriters after the game, held up his thumb and forefinger about an inch apart, and said, "We been at it six weeks and we ain't improved this much. You don't win championships if you don't improve." A gleeful John Robinson said, "We're not number one. I'm voting us number six. But you're going to be a great team, I sense it. We're not number one now... but in January, who knows."

Alabama did improve, however, and did not lose another game in 1978. USC did lose another, to Arizona State. Ironically, at the end of the season the wire service polls put once-defeated Alabama at the number one spot, with once-defeated USC ranked number two.

USC
STANFORD
1979

In mid-October 1979, USC had easily won their first five games, ensconced at the top of both the AP and UPI polls. Now, on homecoming weekend at the neighborhood Los Angeles Coliseum, they were facing Stanford, a team that had already lost two games. The Trojans were 22-point favorites.

And USC got 21 of those 22 points in the first half, blithely entertaining the students, alumni, and other loyal Angelenos with neatly executed drives spangled by some exciting runs. All-American and Heisman Trophy winner-to-be Charles White scored two Trojan touchdowns, one on an 8-yard power sweep and the other on a 1-yard plunge. The third score was on a dazzling 15-yard run by White's heir apparent, sophomore Marcus Allen. USC led 21–0 when the teams left for the locker room, and White had already amassed 169 yards rushing.

But then something happened. The Cardinal from Palo Alto suddenly came alive. Later, Rod Dowhower, one of Stanford's coaches, shook his head and said, "I can't explain it. I guess we called some plays they

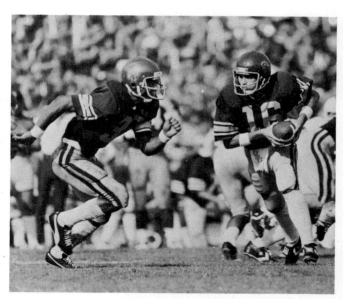

Quarterback Paul McDonald (16) hands off to star fullback Charles White (33) who paced USC early in the game against Stanford. After a brilliant first half, the USC offense was shut down, as Stanford came back to tie the game.

Ken Margerum, Stanford's adhesive-handed wide receiver, looks for one of many pass receptions here in 1979. He was a consensus All-American that year and again in 1980.

didn't expect. We threw long on fourth and five, converted a lot of third- and fourth-down plays."

That they did, and it was all under the masterful manipulation of Cardinal quarterback Turk Schonert. Stanford took the opening kickoff of the second half and started from their 20. Switching to a passing game (and completing three of his first four) as well as running at the gaps, Schonert moved his team to the Trojan 19-yard line, then passed to Mike Dotterer for Stanford's first touchdown.

And the Cardinal defense suddenly became a stone wall to White and Allen and a chasing, grabbing menace to quarterback Paul McDonald. In the fourth quarter, a jarring Stanford tackle caused White to fumble, a costly turnover. Schonert took quick advantage of it by marching the Cardinal 52 yards, then throwing his second touchdown pass of the game, this one to wide receiver Ken Margerum.

Stanford continued to shut down USC's renowned attack (they had averaged almost 36 points in

five games that year). Schonert was soon back at it. From his own 13-yard line he started, and before long a disillusioned homecoming crowd watched as the Turk rolled out, faked a pass, found a hole, and raced in for the touchdown from the Trojan 10-yard line. The extra point tied the game at 21 apiece with four and a half minutes left.

A little less than four minutes later, with 38 seconds on the clock, Stanford had a remote chance to win it, but a fourth-down, 53-yard field goal fell short. A desperate USC frantically moved the ball and, with three seconds left, lined up for a 39-yard field goal, but the snap was juggled and the kick was blocked.

The stalemate proved disastrous to USC at season's end. Their record stood at 11-0-1, including a Rose Bowl victory over Ohio State, but the Stanford blemish left them just short of Alabama's perfect record. And for the second year in a row, John Robinson's Trojans ran second in the national rankings to Bear Bryant's Crimson Tide.

 # PENN STATE NEBRASKA 1982

The way Nebraska came into this game should probably have spread a plague of worry through University Park, Pennsylvania. A week earlier, the Cornhuskers and their incendiary offense had set an NCAA record by amassing 883 total yards in the 68–0 humiliation they dealt to New Mexico State. The week before that they had decimated Big Ten title contender Iowa by a score of 42–7.

Tom Osborne's Nebraskans had two fabulous running backs in Mike Rozier and Roger Craig and a quarterback named Turner Gill who could throw from the pocket or on the run, execute the option, and run the ball with equal aplomb. All that behind a first-rate offensive line, keyed by two-time Outland Award winner Dave Rimington.

They were ranked second in the nation when they came to play Penn State. But the Nittany Lions were hardly laggards, with Heisman candidate Curt Warner and Jon Williams running the ball and Todd Blackledge throwing it. They had already beaten Temple, Mary-

land, and Rutgers.

Predictably Nebraska was the pregame favorite, but they did not play like it in the first half. Penn State's defense controlled the line of scrimmage, consistently stopping Rozier and Craig, who was playing with an injured leg. And late in the first quarter, State's Blackledge iced an 84-yard drive, the highlight of which was a 43-yard pass to Curt Warner, with a 14-yard touchdown pass to tight end Kirk Bowman, who only recently had been converted from an offensive guard and had acquired the ignoble nickname "Stonehands."

In the second period, Paterno tried out his ground game and found Nebraska could not stop Warner, who broke one for 31 yards and then burst in from the 2, giving the Lions a 14–0 advantage.

Nebraska finally got on the board with less than a minute to go in the half, as Gill threw a 30-yard touchdown pass to wide receiver Irving Fryar.

But the second half began much like the first, with Penn State in control. Blackledge boosted the

Mike Rozier, a two-time All-American running back (1982–83) for Nebraska, won the Heisman Trophy in 1983. During three seasons with the Cornhuskers, he averaged 136.6 yards per game and 7.16 per carry, the latter on NCAA record.

score to 21–7 with a pass to flanker Kenny Jackson. That, however, was the end of Nittany dominance.

It was now Turner Gill's turn to shine. Coming right back, he directed the Huskers downfield, finally tossing to Rozier for a score and bringing Nebraska within a touchdown. A field goal in the fourth quarter cut the Lions' lead to 4.

Then Nebraska held. They got the ball back late in the quarter at their own 20-yard line. Passing with deadly precision, two key third-down conversions among them, Gill advanced the Cornhuskers all the way to the Penn State 1, where he dove in with the ball to give Nebraska its first and only lead of the game.

The lead was short-lived thanks to Todd Black-

ledge's masterful performance in the remaining one minute and 18 seconds of the game. Penn State should have had the ball on their own 20 after the kickoff, but an unnecessary roughness call against Nebraska gave it to them at the 35. Blackledge first flipped one to halfback Skeeter Nichols, a screen pass that picked up 16 yards. Two plays later he hit Jackson at the sideline for another 16.

A running play lost a yard, and then Blackledge's magic appeared to vanish itself as he threw two incompletions. It was fourth and 11 yards to go at the Cornhusker 34. There were 28 seconds on the clock. Paterno sent in word to go for the first down. His freshman kicker, Massimo Manca, had failed on three field goal tries earlier in the game, and Paterno had little faith in a 51-yard attempt.

Blackledge dropped back coolly, spotted Kenny Jackson buttonhooking just past the first-down marker, and drilled it to him. One the next play, Blackledge faced a ferocious rush and had to scramble, but he managed to pick up 6 yards and call a time-out. With 13 seconds now left in the game, Blackledge stayed in the pocket and found tight end Mike McCloskey on the sideline at the 2-yard line. It was close, but the referee ruled he was in bounds when he caught the ball. Seven seconds now. Two passes maybe, or one run. State came to the line of scrimmage with two tight ends, bunched up. Blackledge faded back and, under heavy pressure and waiting what seemed like infinity, finally glimpsed "Stonehands" Bowman at the back of the end zone. Throwing off balance, Blackledge's pass was low, but the former lineman made a spectacular shoestring catch and black-and-white-striped arms snapped toward the sky, signaling a touchdown. With the conversion, the final score was Penn State 28, Nebraska 21, but as Joe Paterno observed, "There was enough glory out there for both teams."

The Perfect Teams

This rare group of teams managed to go to an entire season without losing or being scored upon.

Year	School	Record
1888	Yale	13-0
1891	Yale	13-0
1892	Yale	13-0
1898	Kentucky	7-0
1900	Tulane	5-0
1901	Michigan	10-0
1902	Arizona	5-0
1906	Washington St.	6-0
1907	Oregon St.	6-0
1909	Colorado	6-0
	Yale	10-0
1910	Illinois	7-0
	Pittsburgh	9-0
1911	Utah State	5-0
1917	Texas A & M	8-0
1919	Texas A & M	10-0
1932	Colgate	9-0
1938	Duke	9-0
1939	Tennessee	10-0

BOSTON COLLEGE
MIAMI (Florida)
1984

This game, specially arranged for national television and staged at the Orange Bowl on Thanksgiving weekend 1984, was appropriately billed as the "Battle of the Quarterbacks." The meeting of Mutt and Jeff perhaps—Doug Flutie, the five-foot-nine-and-three-quarter-inch quarterback of Boston College, was going against his counterpart from Miami, six-foot-five-inch Bernie Kosar.

Seldom, if ever, in the annals of college football have two passers as spectacular as these taken the field during the same sixty minutes and fared so well. It was a game that was all offense; more precisely, aerial warfare. When it was over, Flutie and Kosar had thrown the ball 84 times for a total of 919 yards. Total offensive yardage for the day was 1,282 yards, surprisingly not an NCAA record (Arizona State and Stanford had racked up 1,436 in 1981). A total of 92 points was

scored. And the winner was decided on the momentous last play of the game.

Flutie, a senior who clinched the Heisman Trophy with this performance, completed his first 11 passes in a row, guiding the Boston College Eagles to a 14–0 lead in the first quarter over the team that, the year before, had snagged the national championship.

Kosar, undismayed, came out in the second quarter and tossed 11 consecutive completions, guiding the team to three touchdowns to put the Hurricanes right back into the ball game. But Flutie was far from idle, and his passing and some strong Eagle rushes enabled BC to post another two touchdowns. The score at the half: Boston College 28, Miami 21.

At the start of the second half, Kosar launched a drive from Miami's own 4-yard line that stormed the length of the field, ending when fullback Melvin Brat-

Doug Flutie, Boston College's mercurial quarterback with the unfailing arm, scrambles here. Flutie ended his college career having completed 677 passes for 10,579 yards, an NCAA record.

ton smashed in from the 2 for the touchdown, with the conversion evening the score.

Each team kicked a field goal later in the period. Then BC booted another to give them a 34–31 edge in the fourth quarter. Miami, however, bounced right back with, surprise of surprises, a breakaway 52-yard

Grantland Rice's All-Time Team

Just before the first half of the 20th century ended, Grantland Rice, who had been selecting All-America teams since the demise of Walter Camp almost 25 years earlier, was asked to publish his "all-time" team. Who were the absolute greatest players at their positions, from the time the game emerged in the Ivy League in the late 1800s up to 1950?

Rice complied, saying, "This side of a house full of ghosts, nothing could be more mythical, but I'll give it a whirl." Some prefatory remarks:

"Who were the best men [backs] I have looked at . . . Jim Thorpe, Red Grange, Bronko Nagurski, Ernie Nevers, Ken Strong, Benny Friedman, Steve Van Buren, Cliff Battles, Dutch Clark, Bill Dudley, Norm Standlee, and such great passing quarterbacks as Sammy Baugh, John Lujack, Sid Luckman, Otto Graham, and Frankie Albert . . . with Bobby Layne coming up in a hurry and Bob Waterfield in close consideration."

Rice explained that all these players went on to play professional football, and therefore enhanced their football reputations. He added that it would be interesting to select an all-time backfield of players who played only in college. His selection:

Position	Player	School
QB	Walter Eckersall	Chicago
HB	George Gipp	Notre Dame
HB	Clint Frank	Yale
FB	Eddie Mahan	Harvard

He gave special mention also to Elmer Oliphant of Army, Ted Coy of Yale, Willie Heston of Michigan, George Pfann of Cornell, and Albie Booth of Yale.

But none of the college-only backs made his all-time college team. Those players who did, with their school and year of graduation:

Position	Player	School	Year
E	Don Hutson	Alabama	1935
E	Bennie Oosterbaan	Michigan	1928
T	Joe Stydahar	West Virginia	1935
T	Fats Henry	Washington & Jefferson	1920
G	Pudge Heffelfinger	Yale	1892
G	Herman Hickman	Tennessee	1932
C	Germany Schultz	Michigan	1906
QB	Sammy Baugh	Texas Christian	1937
HB	Red Grange	Illinois	1925
HB	Jim Thorpe	Carlisle	1915
FB	Bronko Nagurski	Minnesota	1930

Ten Great Things About College Football

As written by Beano Cook, anchor man for Saturday afternoon telecasts of college football games, and it's hard to quarrel with his highlights. "There are certain things people should do before they die," Cook notes. "They should make out a will and make sure they see the following:

1. The dotting of the i at Ohio State.

It's like seeing 'Casablanca.' You could see it 1,000 times but it still excites you. You know he's going to say, 'We'll always have Paris' and that the i is going to be dotted. But it still sends a chill up your spine.

A couple of years ago they invited former band members back to Ohio State for an Oldtimers Day. They had two bands on the field at the same time and two guys dotting the i at the same time. It had to be one of the greatest moments in college football.

I'd rather dot the i before I die than be president. I think that's a greater honor.

2. Hearing the Victory March at Notre Dame.

When the Victory March starts and the team comes out of the tunnel, it's kind of like hearing the National Anthem when you're in a foreign country. It does something to you. That is, of course, as long as your team isn't the one playing Notre Dame. If you happen to be the visiting team, it's no fun.

Did you know the Victory March is the fourth most famous song in America? The National Anthem is No. 1, although nobody knows the words to the second verse. Then there's 'God Bless America,' 'White Christmas' and the 'Victory March.' You have to have Kate Smith singing 'God Bless America,' Bing Crosby singing 'White Christmas' and you have to be at Notre Dame to appreciate the Victory March.

3. Walking through the woods at the University of North Carolina.

There's a wonderful stadium there in a gulley, surrounded by woods. The guy who gave the land for the stadium did so under the stipulation that the trees never be cut down. I hope some lawyer doesn't find a loophole, because it's a beautiful place to visit in October. You're walking through the same woods that Thomas Wolfe and Charles Kuralt walked through. That's what makes it exciting.

4. An autumn afternoon at West Point.

The thing about pro football is that all the stadiums look the same now. One Stefanie Powers is great, but if every one looked like her, we would get bored. What makes college football different is its different settings, like at West Point, when the corps marches in. Even if you were just a private in the Army and had to pull KP as I did, it's still a great scene.

5. The Yale Band.

They're very disorganized, but it doesn't matter. And what makes their fight song, 'Bulldog, Bulldog,' so extra special is that it was written by Cole Porter.

6. A night game at LSU.

Most tailgate parties start a few hours before the game. At LSU, they start Thursday afternoon.

7. The Florida-Georgia game.

This is one of the great spectacles in sport, the World's Largest Outdoor Cocktail Party.

I like it better than the Texas-Oklahoma game because there are too many rich people at that game. The Florida-Georgia game has more real fans. There might be more hard drinking at a Texas-Oklahoma game—more bourbon—but there's more real drinking by the average guy at Florida-Georgia.

8. Nebraska fans.

I think Nebraska fans are as fair as anybody, and I like it when everybody is in red.

They keep telling me that all those farmers out there are broke. The price of hogs is down, bacon is down, and they're getting one cent to every 80 bushels of wheat. But when that team goes to Hawaii, as it seems to do every four years, 15,000 fans go along with them. How can they be broke?

9. The Trojan Horse at USC.

I don't like the Los Angeles Coliseum particularly, but that horse is great. When he charges around that track, it's the greatest performance since the '32 Olympics.

The USC cheerleaders, who incidentally might be just a little bit too pretty, are OK, but it's the horse that makes it special at USC.

10. The Michigan-Ohio State game.

This to me is the greatest rivalry in all sports. Maybe the North Central states are declining in industry, but this rivalry never will decline.

Army-Navy is a close second for me, because you know most of the players involved will graduate.

Rivalries are what college football has over pro football. In pro football, the rivalries change. Pittsburgh-Oakland was a stiff rivalry for a couple of years, especially after the Immaculate Reception. But if the Steelers and Raiders play next year, it'll be a good game, but you know it won't be Michigan-Ohio State."

That halftime show-stopper, dotting the i at Ohio State, one of Beamo Cook's ten favorite things about college football.

touchdown run by Bratton, giving Miami its first lead of the game, 38–34.

Flutie went right to work, starting at BC's 18-yard line. With just under four minutes remaining, he had driven the Eagles to the Hurricanes' 1-yard line. Fullback Steve Strachan vaulted over the Miami defense and plopped into the end zone to regain the lead for Boston College, 41–38.

There were two and a half minutes remaining when the Hurricanes, after the kickoff, were stranded on their own 10. It was third and a distant 19 yards for the first down. Kosar dropped back, but BC rushers converged on him at the Miami goal line. He scrambled, somehow got free, and tossed a little floater to Darryl Oliver, who raced 20 yards for the first down. With that catalyst and later a fourth-and-one conversion, Kosar moved the Hurricanes to the Eagle 1-yard line. Melvin Bratton got the call again and burst in for his fourth touchdown of the game. It was now Miami 45, Boston College 41.

There were only 28 seconds on the clock when Miami kicked off, but there was no movement in the aisles of the Orange Bowl, as the more than 30,000 wildly entertained fans stood together to see what might happen next. And they were rewarded.

Using up 22 precious seconds, Flutie got the Eagles out to their own 48-yard line. With six seconds left, he called in the huddle for a "Flood Tip," a desperation play, a Hail Mary pass. Three wide receivers lined up to the right, their mission to race like hell down the field, get in the end zone, and, in the maelstrom, to catch the ball.

Flutie took the snap and dropped back. There was only a two-man rush, but one of them got through. The diminutive quarterback sidestepped him and rolled out to his right. He was all the way back at his own 37-yard line and still under pressure when he set himself and hurled the ball toward Miami's end zone. The ball traveled 64 yards in the air, just over the hands of three Miami defenders who leaped in unison, banged into each other, but did not touch the ball. And just behind them was Flutie's roommate, wide receiver Gerard Phelan, who caught the ball just before falling to the turf. For the twelfth time that afternoon, the referee reached for the sky to signal a touchdown.

It was, as reported in *The New York Times*, "the last spectacular play of a spectacular game." Or, as described in *Sports Illustrated*, "one wildly wonderful play, punctuating a wildly wonderful game."

The final score was 47–45, and Boston College was triumphant in one of the most pyrotechnical games in college football history. As for the aerial warfare: Flutie had thrown 34 completions in 46 attempts for 472 yards, while Kosar completed 25 of 38 passes for 447 yards, but it is that one desperate pass for which the game will always be remembered.

The Heisman Trophy

In 1935, the Downtown Athletic Club of New York decided to institute an annual award for the most outstanding college football player in the United States. A trophy was designed, the now-familiar bronze figure of a ball carrier with a menacing stiff-arm, and it was agreed that the first would be awarded after the conclusion of that football season.

In October of the following year, the club's director of athletics, John W. Heisman, who was also one of the greatest early innovators and coaches of the game of football, died.

Members of the club felt it only appropriate to rename their award the Heisman Memorial Trophy.

Over the years, it has traditionally been awarded to a back, most often a running back, with only two exceptions—ends Larry Kelley of Yale of 1936, and Leon Hart of Notre Dame in 1949. Today the winner is selected by a poll of sportswriters and sportscasters, and it remains college football's ultimate symbol of excellence.

Year	Winner	Position	School	Runners-up
1935	Jay Berwanger	HB	Chicago	Monk Meyer (Army) Bill Shakespeare (Notre Dame)
1936	Larry Kelley	E	Yale	Sam Francis (Nebraska) Ray Buivid (Marquette)
1937	Clint Frank	HB	Yale	Byron "Whizzer" White (Colorado) Marshall Goldberg (Pittsburgh)
1938	Davey O'Brien	QB	TCU	Marshall Goldberg (Pittsburgh) Sid Luckman (Columbia)
1939	Nile Kinnick	HB	Iowa	Tom Harmon (Michigan) Paul Christman (Missouri)
1940	Tom Harmon	HB	Michigan	John Kimbrough (Texas A&M) George Franck (Minnesota)
1941	Bruce Smith	HB	Minnesota	Angelo Bertelli (Notre Dame) Frankie Albert (Stanford)
1942	Frank Sinkwich	HB	Georgia	Paul Governali (Columbia) Clint Castleberry (Georgia Tech)
1943	Angelo Bertelli	QB	Notre Dame	Bob Odell (Pennsylvania) Otto Graham (Northwestern)
1944	Les Horvath	QB	Ohio State	Glenn Davis (Army) Doc Blanchard (Army)
1945	Doc Blanchard	FB	Army	Glenn Davis (Army) Bob Fenimore (Oklahoma A&M)
1946	Glenn Davis	HB	Army	Charlie Trippi (Georgia) Johnny Lujack (Notre Dame)
1947	Johnny Lujack	QB	Notre Dame	Bob Chappius (Michigan) Doak Walker (SMU)
1948	Doak Walker	HB	SMU	Charlie Justice (North Carolina) Chuck Bednarik (Pennsylvania)
1949	Leon Hart	E	Notre Dame	Charlie Justice (North Carolina) Doak Walker (SMU)
1950	Vic Janowicz	HB	Ohio State	Kyle Rote (SMU) Reds Bagnell (Pennsylvania)
1951	Dick Kazmaier	HB	Princeton	Hank Lauricella (Tennessee) Babe Parilli (Kentucky)
1952	Billy Vessels	HB	Oklahoma	Jack Scarbath (Maryland) Paul Giel (Minnesota)
1953	Johnny Lattner	HB	Notre Dame	Paul Giel (Minnesota) Paul Cameron (UCLA)
1954	Alan Ameche	FB	Wisconsin	Kurt Burris (Oklahoma) Howard Cassady (Ohio State)
1955	Howard Cassady	HB	Ohio State	Jim Swink (TCU) George Welsh (Navy)
1956	Paul Hornung	QB	Notre Dame	Johnny Majors (Tennessee) Tommy McDonald (Oklahoma)
1957	John David Crow	HB	Texas A&M	Alex Karras (Iowa) Walt Kowalczyk (Michigan State)
1958	Pete Dawkins	HB	Army	Randy Duncan (Iowa) Billy Cannon (LSU)

Year	Winner	Position	School	Runners-up
1959	Billy Cannon	HB	LSU	Richie Lucas (Penn State) / Don Meredith (SMU)
1960	Joe Bellino	HB	Navy	Tom Brown (Minnesota) / Jake Gibbs (Mississippi)
1961	Ernie Davis	HB	Syracuse	Bob Ferguson (Ohio State) / Jimmy Saxton (Texas)
1962	Terry Baker	QB	Oregon State	Jerry Stovall (LSU) / Bob Bell (Minnesota)
1963	Roger Staubach	QB	Navy	Billy Lothridge (Georgia Tech) / Sherman Lewis (Michigan State)
1964	John Huarte	QB	Notre Dame	Jerry Rhome (Tulsa) / Dick Butkus (Illinois)
1965	Mike Garrett	HB	USC	Howard Twilley (Tulsa) / Jim Grabowski (Illinois)
1966	Steve Spurrier	QB	Florida	Bob Griese (Purdue) / Nick Eddy (Notre Dame)
1967	Gary Beban	QB	UCLA	O. J. Simpson (USC) / Leroy Keyes (Purdue)
1968	O. J. Simpson	HB	USC	Leroy Keyes (Purdue) / Terry Hanratty (Notre Dame)
1969	Steve Owens	HB	Oklahoma	Mike Phipps (Purdue) / Rex Kern (Ohio State)
1970	Jim Plunkett	QB	Stanford	Joe Theismann (Notre Dame) / Archie Manning (Mississippi)
1971	Pat Sullivan	QB	Auburn	Ed Marinaro (Cornell) / Greg Pruitt (Oklahoma)
1972	Johnny Rodgers	FL	Nebraska	Greg Pruitt (Oklahoma) / Rich Glover (Nebraska)
1973	John Cappelletti	HB	Penn State	John Hicks (Ohio State) / Roosevelt Leaks (Texas)
1974	Archie Griffin	HB	Ohio State	Anthony Davis (USC) / Joe Washington (Oklahoma)
1975	Archie Griffin	HB	Ohio State	Chuck Muncie (California) / Ricky Bell (USC)
1976	Tony Dorsett	HB	Pittsburgh	Ricky Bell (USC) / Rob Lytle (Michigan)
1977	Earl Campbell	HB	Texas	Terry Miller (Oklahoma State) / Ken MacAfee (Notre Dame)
1978	Billy Sims	HB	Oklahoma	Chuck Fusina (Penn State) / Rick Leach (Michigan)
1979	Charles White	HB	USC	Billy Sims (Oklahoma) / Marc Wilson (Brigham Young)
1980	George Rogers	HB	South Carolina	Hugh Green (Pittsburgh) / Herschel Walker (Georgia)
1981	Marcus Allen	HB	USC	Herschel Walker (Georgia) / Jim McMahon (Brigham Young)
1982	Herschel Walker	HB	Georgia	John Elway (Stanford) / Eric Dickerson (SMU)
1983	Mike Rozier	HB	Nebraska	Steve Young (Brigham Young) / Doug Flutie (Boston College)
1984	Doug Flutie	QB	Boston College	Keith Byars (Ohio State) / Robbie Bosco (Brigham Young)

UNDERCLASSMEN WHO HAVE WON THE HEISMAN (ALL JUNIORS)

Player	School	Year	Player	School	Year
Doc Blanchard	Army	1945	Archie Griffin	Ohio State	1974
Doak Walker	SMU	1948	Billy Sims	Oklahoma	1978
Vic Janowicz	Ohio State	1950	Herschel Walker	Georgia	1982
Roger Staubach	Navy	1963			

The Greatest Teams of the 20th Century

The 1900s

Michigan, 1901. All of Fielding Yost's Wolverine teams in the early 1900s were great. From 1901 to 1905, they lost only 1 game, and tied another, while winning 55. The 1901 squad outscored its opponents 550–0 (Buffalo fell to them 128–0 and their closest game was a 21–0 win over Ohio State). They played in the first Rose Bowl and decimated Stanford 49–0. Willie Heston was only a freshman that year but he was already spectacular, and Neil Snow, who played both end and fullback was a consensus All-American. As good as Stagg's 1905 Chicago team, spearheaded by Walter Eckersall, was, they would have been conquered by Yost's 1901 Michiganers.

The first real passing combo: end Knute Rockne (left) and quarterback Gus Dorais of Notre Dame.

SCHOOL	RECORD	COACH	NOTABLE PLAYERS	
Michigan				
1901	11-0-0	Fielding Yost	Willie Heston ('01)	HB
1902	11-0-0		Boss Weeks	QB
			Tug Wilson	G
			Dan McGugin	G
			Neil Snow ('01)	E, FB
			Al Herrinstein	HB
			Ev Sweeley	E
Chicago				
1905	9-0-0	Amos A. Stagg	Walter Eckersall	QB
			Mark Catlin	E
			Hugo Bezdek	FB
			Fred Walker	HB
Yale				
1907	9-0-1	Samuel Morse	Tad Jones	QB
			Clarence Alcott	E
			Ted Coy	HB
			Horatio Biglow	T
Yale				
1909	10-0-0	Howard Jones	Ted Coy	HB
			John Kilpatrick	E
			Henry Hobbs	T
			Hamlin Andruss	G
			Carroll Cooney	C
			Steve Philbin	HB

Walter Eckersall of Chicago.

The 1910s

Notre Dame, 1919. Knute Rockne used to lapse into euphoric descriptions of the 1913 Notre Dame team, the one on which he and back Gus Dorais startled the football world with the forward pass. But the team he coached in 1919 to a perfect season was certainly the best of that decade. George Gipp was a junior, fast becoming one of the most famous names in the game. With Dutch Bergman, the other halfback, and Pete Bahan at quarterback, they vanquished their opponents 229–47 that year.

SCHOOL	RECORD	COACH	NOTABLE PLAYERS	
Carlisle				
1911	11-1-0	Pop Warner	Jim Thorpe	HB
1912	12-1-1		Joe Guyon ('12)	HB
Harvard				
1912	9-0-0	Percy Haughton	Charley Brickley	HB
			Sam Felton	E
			Stan Pennock	G
			Percy Wendell	HB
Notre Dame				
1913	7-0-0	Jesse Harper	Gus Dorais	QB
			Ray Eichenlaub	FB
			Knute Rockne	E
			Joe Pliska	HB
Georgia Tech				
1917	9-0-0	John Heisman	Joe Guyon	HB
			Ev Strupper	HB
			Judy Harlan	QB
			Bill Fincher	T
			Six Carpenter	T
Notre Dame				
1919	9-0-0	Knute Rockne	George Gipp	HB
			Hunk Anderson	G
			John Mohardt	FB
			Eddie Anderson	E

fractured bones in both ankles during the regular season and was not playing at full strength.

More than 53,000 people crowded into the Rose Bowl to watch the two powerhouses. Rockne started his second string, a ploy he often used, in order to wear down his opponent before putting in his lustrous first-stringers. The subs could not contain Nevers and Stanford, however, and after the Indians marched steadily down the field, Rockne pulled them and got down to business.

But it took a while. After a fumble by Crowley, Stanford halfback Murray Cuddeback kicked a 17-yard field goal, the lone score in the first quarter. After that, however, it was almost all Notre Dame. Elmer Layden bucked in for a touchdown in the second quarter, and a few minutes later he snatched a pass Ernie Nevers threw into the flat and raced with it 78 yards for another Irish touchdown. Layden repeated the feat in the fourth quarter, this time for a 70-yard touchdown.

Stanford gave Rockne's blessed Irish another touchdown in the third quarter when safety Fred Solomon fumbled a Notre Dame punt, and Ed Hunsinger picked it up and toted it 20 yards for a score. Nevers said after the game, "They lived up to their reputation." And Rockne said, "The Four Horsemen have the right to ride with the gridiron great."

SCORING

Notre Dame	0	13	7	7—27
Stanford	3	0	7	0—10

Notre Dame:	Touchdowns—Layden (3), Hunsinger; PAT—Crowley (3).
Stanford:	Touchdown—Shipkey; Field goal—Cuddeback; PAT—Cuddeback.

1926
Alabama 20
Washington 19

Both Alabama and Washington had certified superstar backs in 1926. The Crimson Tide boasted Johnny Mack Brown, who later would become a movie star in dozens of westerns, and Washington had George "Wildcat" Wilson.

Alabama, coached by the famed Wallace Wade, was undefeated going into the Rose Bowl and notorious for its niggardly defense. On the other hand, Washington was an explosive offensive team that had scored 450 points during the regular season. And, at least in the first half, it appeared offense would prevail.

Rockne and Warner

After Notre Dame and the Four Horsemen defeated Stanford 27–10 in the Rose Bowl on January 1, 1925, Stanford's coach, Pop Warner, fumed about the outcome because his team had outgained Knute Rockne's triumphant eleven and toted up more first downs. In an interview after the game, Warner stormed about, then said that a new scoring system should be instituted immediately, in which a team would get point credits for its first downs and yardage gained.

When victorious coach Rockne was asked if he had a comment on Warner's proposal, he said: "Sure, but I'll not say it until they start giving baseball victories to the teams that have the most men left on base."

Wildcat Wilson was uncontrollable, running, passing, and intercepting 'Bama passes. The Huskies racked up two touchdowns, but they couldn't convert the extra points, which would prove to be their downfall.

Washington's 12–0 halftime lead seemed comfortable, but Wilson was hurt and on the sidelines. Alabama took quick advantage of it, scoring 3 touchdowns in the first seven minutes of the third quarter. Quarterback Pooley Hubert, after carrying the ball on every play of the drive, snuck in from the 1 for the first score. Then Johnny Mack Brown streaked down the

Johnny Mack Brown as a football player for Alabama below and duded up as a Cowboy, a role he performed in countless westerns during the 1930s and 40s.

Wrong-Way Riegels

In the most infamous run in college football annals, Roy Riegels, California's lineman and center, scooped up a Georgia Tech fumble in the 1929 Rose Bowl game and began running laterally across the field (you could run with a fumble in those days), turned the corner, and streaked off toward the goal line. Only it was his own goal he was racing towards. More than 66,000 fans sat dumbfounded as Riegels ran the 80 yards the wrong way with his teammate Benny Lom in desperate pursuit. Riegels made it into the end zone but Lom pulled him back out to the one-yard line before Georgia Tech tacklers brought him to the turf. On the ensuing play, California tried to punt out of danger (Riegels centered the ball) but it was blocked and the ball bounced out of the end zone. The two-point safety proved to be the margin of victory at day's end, the final score Georgia Tech 8, California 7.

field and without losing a step gathered in a long, lofty pass from Grant Gillis, a picture-perfect 59-yard touchdown play. On Alabama's next possession, Hubert found Brown on Washington's 3-yard line, delivered the ball to him, and then watched as Brown, double-teamed, smashed his way into the end zone. Wilson came back into the game for the Huskies and led them to another touchdown but couldn't get them any closer than the one-point margin by which they finally lost.

SCORING

Alabama	0	0	20	0—20
Washington	6	6	0	7—19
Alabama:	Touchdowns—Hubert, Brown (2); PAT—Buckler (2).			
Washington	Touchdowns—Patton, Cole, Guttormsen; PAT—Cook.			

1935
Alabama 29
Stanford 13

Frank Thomas was coach of Alabama when they made their fourth appearance in the Rose Bowl. And at each end of his offensive line, he had two men who were destined to become football legends, each in a different way: Don Hutson, the greatest pass-catcher of his time, and Paul Bryant, who would gain his fame as a coach. Besides that, 'Bama also had one of the best tailbacks anywhere in Dixie Howell, who Grantland Rice called the "human howitzer" because of his powerful pinpoint passing.

The Crimson Tide, sporting a 10-0 record and ranked number one in the nation, was a favorite, but in the first quarter they barely resembled a national champ. Stanford totally dominated the quarter, and

'Bama was held to a measly four yards during the entire period. But then Howell and Hutson came alive, and Alabama erupted with 22 points in the second quarter, and the almost 85,000 spectators were treated to one of the finest offensive displays ever.

Dixie Howell ended the day with a total of 160 yards passing and another 111 rushing (67 of which were earned on a dazzling touchdown run). But sitting up in the stands, Curly Lambeau, coach of the Green Bay Packers, was more impressed with the fleet-footed end who seemed to be able to catch anything thrown within ten feet of him, and made a silent vow that he was going to put Don Hutson in a Packer uniform the next year.

SCORING

Alabama	0	22	0	7—29
Stanford	7	0	6	0—13

Alabama: Touchdowns—Howell (2), Hutson (2); Field goal—Smith; PAT—Smith (2).
Stanford: Touchdowns—Grayson, Van Dellen; PAT—Moscrip.

Action from the 1935 Rose Bowl game. That's Alabama's Don Hutson at far right.

1949
Northwestern 20
California 14

California and its coach, Lynn "Pappy" Waldorf, really wanted to play Michigan, the nation's top-ranked team, in the Rose Bowl. But the Wolverines had been

there the year before and under the terms of the agreement between the Pacific Coast Conference and the Big Ten, they could not appear in successive games. So Northwestern, the second place team, came instead.

The Golden Bears from Berkeley, with their All-American back Jackie Jensen, were the decided favorites, but Waldorf, who had coached at Northwestern earlier in his career, was wary of the Wildcats. His concern was justified in the first quarter when halfback Frank Aschenbrenner shot through the California defense on a 73-yard touchdown jaunt. Not to be outdone, however, Jackie Jensen on the first play from scrimmage after the kickoff raced 67 yards to enable California to tie the game.

In the second quarter, Northwestern fullback Art Murakowski bucked in from the 1, only to fumble the ball in the end zone, but field judge Jay Berwanger (who was the first Heisman Trophy winner in 1935) ruled that he had crossed the goal before the fumble and let the touchdown stand.

Jackie Jensen left the game in the third quarter with an injury and never returned, but California still moved the ball and finally regained the lead, 14–13. But then, with a Frank Merriwell ending, Northwestern pulled it out. There was less than three minutes to

The Fiery Red

Mel Hein, who after his college football career forged another with the New York Giants, where he was named the All-Pro center an unprecedented eight consecutive times, got to the Rose Bowl in 1931, the last time Washington State appeared in the classic. He tells about the experience:

"Our coach, a fine man, Babe Hollingberry, was somewhat of a showman and he was superstitious. In the showman role he bought a lot of new uniforms for our appearance in the Rose Bowl—bright crimson red. The headgear was red, the shoes were red, the stockings were red, everything was red. I think it scared us more than Alabama because we didn't play too good a ball game. They walloped us 24–0. They simply had a better team than we had.

"The superstitious part of Babe Hollingberry came out when we got back to Pullman, the city where Washington State's campus was located, after the game. No one ever saw those uniforms again, and the story was that Babe had a big bonfire and burned them all. He didn't want any of his teams ever to wear those uniforms again."

play in the game, and the Wildcats had the ball on the Golden Bears' 43-yard line, second down and 8 yards to go for a first down. Northwestern came out of the huddle, lined up in their typical T formation, with quarterback Don Burson behind the center calling signals. Suddenly halfback Frank Aschenbrenner went into motion to the right, and Burson shifted over a man. The snap went directly to halfback Ed Tunnicliff, who charged toward the slot at right tackle, then veered off to follow Aschenbrenner's interference around right end. Cal was totally taken in, not a defender in touching distance of Tunnicliff, who raced down the sideline for the game-winning touchdown.

SCORING

Northwestern	7	6	0	7—20
California	7	0	7	0—14

Northwestern: Touchdowns—Aschenbrenner, Murakowski, Tunnicliff; PAT—Farrar (2).
California: Touchdowns—Jensen, Swaner; PAT—Cullom (2).

1956
Michigan State 17
UCLA 14

Duffy Daugherty's Michigan State eleven was ranked second in the nation at the end of the 1955 season, only undefeated Oklahoma having fared better. And UCLA was number four. Their meeting in Pasadena produced one of the most chaotic endings in Rose Bowl history.

The Spartans were quarterbacked by consensus All-American Earl Morrall, but he had a tough time getting going. His first pass of the game was intercepted deep in his own territory, and a few plays later, UCLA turned it into the game's first score.

Morrall redeemed himself in the following period of play, leading an 80-yard march down the field and icing it with a 13-yard touchdown pass to halfback Clarence Peaks. The game remained tied at 7 into the fourth quarter, but then Peaks took a pitchout from Morrall, pulled up, and heaved a long pass to end John Lewis, who shook off a tackler and carried the ball into

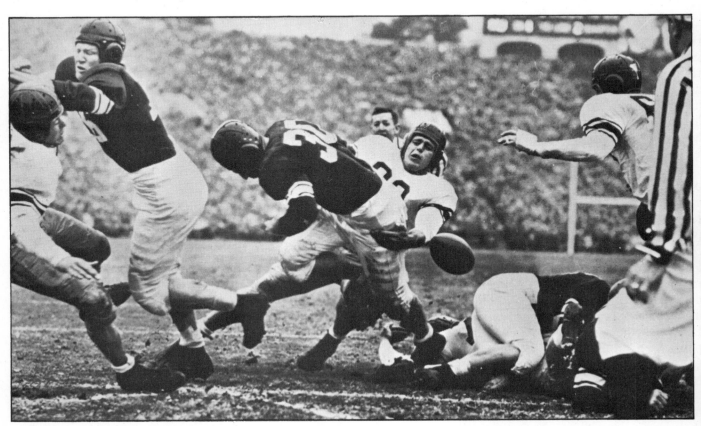

Northwestern's Art Murakowski fumbles as he crosses the goal line in the 1949 Rose Bowl classic against California. There is little doubt about the fumble, but the referee ruled he had possession as he crossed into the end zone, awarding Northwestern the touchdown that later proved to be their margin of victory.

UCLA puts an extra point on the board against Michigan State, but it was State's kicking that won the contest for them in the closing seconds of the game.

the end zone for a 67-yard touchdown.

Then it was UCLA quarterback Ronnie Knox's turn, engineering his own march, which culminated when substitute fullback Doug Peters bucked in from the 1. But Morrall moved the Spartans again, and it appeared the game was Michigan State's when, with just over a minute and a half left, kicker Gerry Planutis lined up for a try from the UCLA 22. But he missed and the Bruins took possession of the ball. That's when the chaos started.

On the first play of their possession, UCLA was penalized 15 yards for coaching from the sideline, called when an assistant coach shouted to Knox to pass the ball. Then, from the 5, Knox faded back to pass and threw the ball away under a heavy Michigan State rush, but UCLA was penalized again, this time for having an ineligible receiver downfield. The ball was moved back to UCLA's 1-yard line. "Punt it out of danger" was the Bruin decision at this point. Seemingly determined to force a win on Michigan State, UCLA got off a short punt and then drew a 15-yard penalty when UCLA's Hardeman Cureton bumped into Clarence Peaks, who had signaled for a fair catch. Michigan State ended up on the UCLA 19-yard line.

Michigan State, seemingly as reluctant as UCLA to win, fumbled the ball twice, recovered both times, then incurred a 10-yard penalty for illegal use of the hands, and used up all their time-outs. But finally they worked their way back to the UCLA 19, and with only

seconds left Daugherty pulled off a desperate but decisive move. He sent a substitute in, drawing a five-yard delay-of-game penalty, which stopped the clock, enabling his team to line up for a field goal try. But it wasn't regular placekicker Planutis, who had missed three attempts in the game, standing behind the holder—instead it was end Dave Kaiser, who boomed the ball 41 yards straight through the uprights for a last-second victory.

SCORING

Michigan State	0	7	0	10	—17
UCLA	7	0	0	7	—14

Michigan State: Touchdowns—Peaks, Lewis; Field goal—Kaiser; PAT—Planutis (2).
UCLA: Touchdowns—Davenport, Peters; PAT—Decker (2).

1963
USC   42
Wisconsin 37

This particular Rose Bowl game matched number one USC, undefeated in 11 games, and number two Wisconsin, and the result was a display of passing pyrotechnics unprecedented in the bowl's history.

Led by All-American candidate quarterback Pete

Ben Wilson (49) picks up some yardage for USC, just a part of the powerful offense that gave the Trojans a 42–37 victory.

Beathard, USC was a decided favorite, and they played like one as they transformed a 21–7 halftime lead into a 42–14 desecration by the fourth quarter. Beathard was unstoppable, setting two Rose Bowl records with 401 yards gained passing and 4 touchdown passes, completing 33 of 48.

Many of the more than 100,000 fans had already left the scene of the crime when suddenly Wisconsin erupted, and USC was very nearly overwhelmed. A pair of touchdowns, one on a run by Badger halfback Lou Holland and another on a pass from Ron VanderKelen to halfback Gary Kroner made the score 42–28. A safety gave Wisconsin another two points and possession of the ball. Again VanderKelen moved the Badgers, capping the drive with another touchdown pass, this time to end Pat Richter, and the score was now 42–37 with a little over a minute to play. But an onside kick failed, and time finally ran out on Wisconsin in what was almost the greatest bowl game rally ever.

SCORING

USC	7	14	14	7—42
Wisconsin	7	0	7	23—37

USC: Touchdowns—Bedsole (2), Butcher, Wilson, Heller, Hill; PAT—Lupo (6).

Wisconsin: Touchdowns—Kurek, VanderKelen, Holland, Korner, Richter; PAT—Korner (5); Safety.

1972
Stanford 13
Michigan 12

Stanford and Michigan had met in the Rose Bowl once before, 70 years earlier in the very first contest

for the roses. The Cardinal of Stanford had waited a long time to avenge that original 49–0 shellacking.

Stanford had been to the classic the year before, drubbing a favored Ohio State team, 27–17, behind the passing of Heisman Trophy winner Jim Plunkett. Plunkett was gone by New Year's Day, 1972, but in his place was Don Bunce, who would rise to the occasion. Michigan had been undefeated, winning 11 games and the Big Ten title, and was favored to beat Stanford.

The Wolverines had led 3–0 at the half and 10–3 at the start of the fourth quarter. Then Johnny Ralston, Stanford's adventuresome coach, took a gamble that paid off. With fourth and 10 on his own 33-yard line, he had his Indians fake a punt as Jackie Brown swept around right end for 31 yards. Moments later, the same swift back cut off tackle and broke free—24 yards and a touchdown.

Michigan got within range of a field goal, but the 46-yard try fell short, and into the hands of safety Jim Ferguson, who tried to run it back, only to be tackled in the end zone for a safety.

Losing by two points, Stanford had the ball on their own 22-yard line with one minute and 48 seconds left. Now it was Don Bunce's moment to glimmer under the California sun. He threw for 13 to tight end Bill Scott, picked up 16 and then another 12 on tosses to flanker John Winesberry, plus 11 more when he hit split end Miles Moore, and 14 on a strike to fullback Reggie Sanderson. Suddenly Stanford stood on the Michigan 14-yard line with 14 seconds to go, and on came Rod Garcia to boot the game-winning field goal, giving Stanford both long-awaited revenge and back-to-back Rose Bowl victories.

Two-time Heisman Trophy winner Archie Griffin (45), shown to the right, picks up a few yards for Ohio State in the 1975 Rose Bowl. The Trojans held him to a mere 76 yards that afternoon.

A kind of USC family: wide receiver John McKay, Jr. (left), his dad, coach John McKay, and quarterback Pat Haden.

1975
USC 18
Ohio State 17

The confrontation between the Buckeyes of Ohio State and the Trojans of Southern California brought together two of the best running backs in college football, both consensus All-Americans: Heisman Trophy winner Archie Griffin and Anthony Davis, runner-up for that award. But the Trojans would hold Griffin to a mere 76 yards, the first time in 23 games that he had not collected over 100 yards rushing, and Davis had to leave the game injured in the second period after gaining 71 yards for the Trojans.

The two highly-ranked teams were at their defensive best in the first half. The Bruins got a field goal in the first quarter but lost the lead in the next period when Buckeye fullback Champ Henson bulled in from the 2. There was not another score until the fourth quarter.

Pat Haden, USC's All-American candidate quarterback and a Rhodes Scholar, regained the lead for his Trojans when he found tight end Jim Obradovich in the end zone. But Ohio State came right back in one of Woody Hayes' patented plodding drives, which climaxed when quarterback Cornelius Greene carried it in from the 3. The Buckeyes got the ball again and increased their lead to 17–10 with a field goal by Tom Skladany.

But then it was time for some frenetic last-minute action by Southern Cal. Pat Haden guided the Trojans down the field 83 yards, the most important play a 38-yard touchdown pass to wide receiver John McKay, the son and namesake of Southern Cal's coach. A kicked extra point would tie it, but coach McKay would have none of that. "We didn't come to play for a tie," he said later. So Pat Haden took the snap, rolled to his right, and rifled one to Shelton Diggs in the end zone for a two-point conversion and a one-point lead. In the last seconds of the game, Skladany tried for a record 62-yard field goal for Ohio State, but it fell short. An unhappy Woody Hayes said after the game: "We got beaten by a better team. One point better."

Rose Bowl Results

Year	Schools	Score	Coaches	Outstanding Players
1902	Michigan Stanford	49 0	Fielding Yost Charles Fickert	Neil Snow
1916	Washington State Brown	14 0	Bill Dietz Eddie Robinson	Carl Dietz
1917	Oregon Pennsylvania	14 0	Hugo Bezdek Bob Folwell	John Beckett
1918	Mare Island Camp Lewis	19 7	Hugo Bezdek W. L. Stanton	Hollis Huntington
1919	Great Lakes Mare Island	17 0	C. J. McReavy Lone Star Dietz	George Halas
1920	Harvard Oregon	7 6	Robert Fisher Ellery Huntington	Eddie Casey
1921	California Ohio State	28 0	Andy Smith J. W. Wilce	Brick Muller
1922	California Washington & Jefferson	0 0	Andy Smith Earle Neale	Russ Stein
1923	USC Penn State	14 3	Elmer Henderson Hugo Bezdek	Leo Calland
1924	Washington Navy	14 14	Enoch Bagshaw Bob Folwell	Ira McKee
1925	Notre Dame Stanford	27 10	Knute Rockne Glenn Warner	Elmer Layden Ernie Nevers
1926	Alabama Washington	20 19	Wallace Wade Enoch Bagshaw	Johnny Mack Brown
1927	Alabama Stanford	7 7	Wallace Wade Glenn Warner	Fred Pickhard
1928	Stanford Pittsburgh	7 6	Glenn Warner Jock Sutherland	Cliff Hoffman
1929	Georgia Tech California	8 7	Bill Alexander Nibs Price	Benny Lom
1930	USC Pittsburgh	47 14	Howard Jones Jock Sutherland	Russ Saunders
1931	Alabama Washington State	24 0	Wallace Wade Babe Hollingberry	John Campbell
1932	USC Tulane	21 12	Howard Jones Bernie Bierman	Ernie Pinckert
1933	USC Pittsburgh	35 0	Howard Jones Jock Sutherland	Homer Griffith
1934	Columbia Stanford	7 0	Lou Little Claude Thornhill	Cliff Montgomery
1935	Alabama Stanford	29 13	Frank Thomas Claude Thornhill	Dixie Howell
1936	Stanford SMU	7 0	Claude Thornhill Madison Bell	Jim Moscrip, Keith Topping
1937	Pittsburgh Washington	21 0	Jock Sutherland James Phelan	Bill Daddio
1938	California Alabama	13 0	Leonard Allison Frank Thomas	Vic Bottari
1939	USC Duke	7 3	Howard Jones Wallace Wade	Doyle Nave, Al Krueger
1940	USC Tennessee	14 0	Howard Jones Bob Neyland	Ambrose Schindler
1941	Stanford Nebraska	21 13	Clark Shaughnessy L. M. Jones	Pete Kmetovic
1942	Oregon State Duke	20 16	Alonzo Stiner Wallace Wade	Don Duran

Year	Schools	Score	Coaches	Outstanding Players
1943	Georgia	9	Wally Butts	Charlie Trippi
	UCLA	0	Ed Horrell	
1944	USC	29	Jeff Cravath	Norman Verry
	Washington	0	Ralph Welch	
1945	USC	25	Jeff Cravath	Jim Hardy
	Tennessee	0	J. H. Barnhill	
1946	Alabama	34	Frank Thomas	Harry Gilmer
	USC	14	Jeff Cravath	
1947	Illinois	45	Ray Eliot	Buddy Young, Julie Rykovich
	UCLA	14	Bert LaBrucherie	
1948	Michigan	49	Fritz Crisler	Bob Chappius
	USC	0	Jeff Cravath	
1949	Northwestern	20	Bob Voights	Frank Aschenbrenner
	California	14	Lynn Waldorf	
1950	Ohio State	17	Wes Fesler	Fred Morrison
	California	14	Lynn Waldorf	
1951	Michigan	14	Bennie Oosterbaan	Don Dufek
	California	6	Lynn Waldorf	
1952	Illinois	40	Ray Eliot	Bill Tate
	Stanford	7	Chuck Taylor	
1953	USC	7	Jess Hill	Rudy Bukich
	Wisconsin	0	Ivan Williamson	
1954	Michigan State	28	Biggie Munn	Billy Wells
	UCLA	20	Henry Sanders	
1955	Ohio State	20	Woody Hayes	Dave Leggett
	USC	7	Jess Hill	
1956	Michigan State	17	Duffy Daugherty	Walt Kowalczyk
	UCLA	14	Henry Sanders	
1957	Iowa	35	Forest Evashevski	Ken Ploen
	Oregon State	19	Tommy Prothro	
1958	Ohio State	10	Woody Hayes	
	Oregon	7	Len Casanova	Jack Crabtree
1959	Iowa	38	Forest Evashevski	Bob Jeter
	California	12	Pete Elliott	
1960	Washington	44	Jim Owens	Bob Schloredt, George Fleming
	Wisconsin	8	Milt Bruhn	
1961	Washington	17	Jim Owens	Bob Schloredt
	Minnesota	7	Murray Warmath	
1962	Minnesota	21	Murray Warmath	Sandy Stephens
	UCLA	3	Bill Barnes	
1963	USC	42	John McKay	Pete Beathard
	Wisconsin	37	Milt Bruhn	Ron VanderKelen
1964	Illinois	17	Pete Elliott	Jim Grabowski
	Washington	7	Jim Owens	
1965	Michigan	34	Chalmers Elliott	Mel Anthony
	Oregon State	7	Tommy Prothro	
1966	UCLA	14	Tommy Prothro	Bob Stiles
	Michigan State	12	Duffy Daugherty	
1967	Purdue	14	Jack Mollenkopf	John Charles
	USC	13	John McKay	
1968	USC	14	John McKay	O. J. Simpson
	Indiana	3	Johnny Pont	
1969	Ohio State	27	Woody Hayes	Rex Kern
	USC	16	John McKay	
1970	USC	10	John McKay	Bobby Chandler
	Michigan	3	Bo Schembechler	

Rose Bowl Results

Year	Schools	Score	Coaches	Outstanding Players
1971	Stanford	27	John Ralston	Jim Plunkett
	Ohio State	17	Woody Hayes	
1972	Stanford	13	John Ralston	Don Bunce
	Michigan	12	Bo Schembechler	
1973	USC	42	John McKay	Sam Cunningham
	Ohio State	17	Woody Hayes	
1974	Ohio State	42	Woody Hayes	Cornelius Greene
	USC	21	John McKay	
1975	USC	18	John McKay	Pat Haden, John McKay
	Ohio State	17	Woody Hayes	
1976	UCLA	23	Dick Vermeil	John Sciarra
	Ohio State	10	Woody Hayes	
1977	USC	14	John Robinson	Vince Evans
	Michigan	6	Bo Schembechler	
1978	Washington	27	Don James	Warren Moon
	Michigan	20	Bo Schembechler	
1979	USC	17	John Robinson	Charles White
	Michigan	10	Bo Schembechler	Rick Leach
1980	USC	17	John Robinson	Charles White
	Ohio State	16	Earle Bruce	
1981	Michigan	23	Bo Schembechler	Butch Woolfolk
	Washington	6	Don James	
1982	Washington	28	Don James	Jacque Robinson
	Iowa	0	Hayden Fry	
1983	UCLA	24	Terry Donahue	Tom Ramsey and Don Rogers
	Michigan	14	Bo Schembechler	
1984	UCLA	45	Terry Donahue	Rick Neuheisel
	Illinois	9	Mike White	
1985	USC	20	Ted Tollner	Tim Green and Jack Del Rio
	Ohio State	17	Earle Bruce	

1938 Orange Bowl Queen Barbara Syche.

THE ORANGE BOWL

If sunny southern California could have a New Year's Day football spectacle, why couldn't sunny southern Florida? So speculated a group of businessmen and civic officials in the early 1930s. They had no trouble selling the idea in tourist-happy Miami.

It was 1933, and the pageant that emerged was called the Palm Festival. To be featured was a football game that would pit the University of Miami, just then getting started in intercollegiate athletics, against any respectable team it could entice to come down there. New York's Manhattan College agreed.

The game was actually played on January 2, at a local field by the name of Moore Park, and 3,500 showed up for it. Manhattan was favored but perhaps could not get used to the January warmth and was unable to score. Miami's one touchdown was enough. Next year Duquesne came down from Pittsburgh and demolished Miami, 33–7.

In 1935, the Palm Festival became the Orange Bowl Festival. A new charter was drawn up, and the first official Orange Bowl game was played on the site of what is today the Orange Bowl Stadium. In 1935, however, it was merely a small field with wooden bleachers that accommodated just over 5,000 spectators that New Year's Day when Bucknell, from Lewisburg, Pennsylvania, clashed with the Miami Hurricanes. And once again it was not Miami's day, as they were wiped out 26–0.

Over the years, the Orange Bowl festival has included such other sporting events as a regatta, tennis and golf tournaments, and, of course, a parade. It also became the first major bowl to stage a game at night, when more than 80,000 fans clustered under the lights to watch Nebraska beat Louisiana State 17–12 on New Year's eve, 1971.

This imaginative float, lit up for the night, was part of the 1978 Orange Bowl festivities.

Games Worth Remembering 1944

Louisiana State 19
Texas A&M 14

Steve Van Buren, one of the best running backs in the nation in 1943, almost single-handedly won this game for LSU. It was also one of the more unusual bowl games in that the war had depleted the college football ranks, so 17- and even 16-year-olds were escalated to the college level. One writer referred to this game as the "Teenage Bowl."

The Texas Aggies had beaten Louisiana State during the regular season and were favored. The Aggies displayed a strong passing attack, but Van Buren set the tone of the game in the first period, running the ball in from the 11 for one touchdown and tossing a pass for another. Then in the third quarter, he ripped off a dazzling 63-yard run, and that proved to be the winning margin.

SCORING				
Louisiana State	12	0	7	0—19
Texas A&M	7	0	7	0—14
Louisiana State:	Touchdowns—Van Buren (2), Goode; PAT—Van Buren.			
Texas A&M:	Touchdowns—Burditt, Settegast; PAT—Turner (2).			

LSU's fabled running back Steve Van Buren (17) takes off on one of his two touchdown runs in the 1944 Orange Bowl.

1949
Texas 41
Georgia 28

Georgia was a weighty favorite, undefeated in the regular season and led by running back Joe Geri. Texas had lost three games during the regular season and tied another; the only name of consequence on the roster would not become well-known in football until a number of years later, and then it would be as a coach—Tom Landry, the Texas quarterback.

The game was entertaining, with the lead changing hands five times during the four quarters until Texas tacked on two touchdowns at the end, giving the final score a more lopsided appearance than the game warranted.

The longest run of the day was the first touchdown, a 71-yard jaunt by Georgia's Al Bodine with an

Tom Landry (above) quarterbacked Texas to a 41–28 win over Georgia in 1949, but his real football fame wouldn't come until he took on the coaching chores for the Dallas Cowboys.

intercepted pass. And the 69 points scored still stands as a record Orange Bowl high, matched only by Oklahoma's 48–21 victory over Duke in 1958.

SCORING

Texas	13	7	7	14—41
Georgia	7	7	7	7—28

Texas: Touchdowns—Borneman, Landry, Samuels, Procter, Clay (2); PAT—Clay (5).
Georgia: Touchdowns—Bodine, Geri (2), Walston; PAT—Geri (4).

1956
Oklahoma 20
Maryland 6

Bud Wilkinson's Sooners had treated Oklahoma fans to 29 consecutive victories by the time they arrived at the Orange Bowl on the first day of 1956. They were an easy choice for the number one berth at the end of the regular season. But Maryland had gone undefeated that season as well. Not only that, coach Jim Tatum and a lot of others around Maryland remembered the humiliation two years earlier when the Terrapins came to the Orange Bowl as undefeated national champs, only to be upset by Oklahoma.

Maryland played a determined first half, their defense shutting down the running of All-American Tommy McDonald and the rest of the famed Oklahoma offense as well. On top of that, they held the lead with a touchdown from end Ed Vereb. "The sweet spoils of revenge are but a half away," one broadcaster noted.

But they were much farther away than that, as Oklahoma proved quickly in the second half. On their first possession the Sooners drove down the field, and finally Tommy McDonald raced around end to score. On their next possession, Oklahoma marched down field again, this time with quarterback Jay O'Neal carrying it in for a 14–6 lead. The final blow came in the last quarter when Carl Dodd snatched a Maryland pass and raced 82 yards for the game's final score.

SCORING

Oklahoma	0	0	14	6—20
Maryland	0	6	0	0—6

Oklahoma: Touchdowns—McDonald, O'Neal, Dodd; PAT—Prince (2).
Maryland: Touchdown—Vereb.

Lineback Tommy Nobis on the sidelines for Texas, one of the Longhorns' defensive stars in their 21–17 victory over Alabama.

1965

Texas 21
Alabama 17

Texas had been to the Orange Bowl only once (1949) prior to 1965, obviously much more accustomed to the Cotton Bowl, which they had already won six times. Alabama, on the other hand, was much more at home in the Sugar Bowl, which they had won two of the preceding three years.

Bear Bryant's Crimson Tide, quarterbacked by All-American Joe Namath, were ranked number one when they arrived in Miami, after a perfect season. Texas had lost only to unbeaten Arkansas.

In the first quarter, Texas had the ball on their own 21-yard line when halfback Ernie Koy broke loose

and sprinted 79 yards for a touchdown, at the time the longest run from scrimmage in Orange Bowl history. A few minutes later, and just into the second quarter, Longhorn quarterback Jim Judson hit streaking split end George Sauer on a 69-yard touchdown pass. A shocked Alabama fumbled not too many minutes later, and Ernie Koy carried the ball in for the Longhorns' third touchdown of the half.

After the intermission, Alabama fought back with a touchdown and a field goal to make a game of it. Their chance to win came in the fourth quarter, a onetime shot; inches from the goal line, on fourth down, a pained, gimpy Joe Namath tried to sneak it in and was turned back by an inspired Texas defense.

SCORING

Texas	7	14	0	0—21
Alabama	0	7	7	3—17

Texas:	Touchdowns—Koy (2), Sauer; PAT—Conway (3).
Alabama:	Touchdowns—Trimble, Perkins; Field goal—Ray; PAT—Ray (2).

Joe Namath, the college game's premier quarterback, could not get his Alabama team by Texas in the 1965 Orange Bowl.

1968

Oklahoma 26
Tennessee 24

Tennessee rated a little higher than Oklahoma at the close of the 1967 regular season, both trailing USC, which nestled in the top spot. A national championship was not riding on the game, but it promised to be the best of the bowl match-ups that year.

Oklahoma was now under the tutelage of Chuck Fairbanks, and they had a bull of a fullback in Steve Owens. They also were aiming for a higher ranking, perhaps even a number one, if USC through some twist of fate might fall to Indiana in the Rose Bowl.

The Sooners came out on a roll, racking up 19 points in the first half and holding the Volunteers from Tennessee scoreless. But then Tennessee came alive in the third quarter, and a pair of touchdowns put them right back in the game, as they trailed by a mere 5 points. In the fourth quarter, Tennessee added another 10 points, but Oklahoma, leading all the way, got 7 when defensive back Bob Stephenson picked off a Volunteer pass and ran it back for a touchdown.

Tennessee fought all the way, moving the ball as the clock worked against them. But finally, with 14 seconds remaining and behind by 2 points, they got within field goal range. There was hardly a sound in the Orange Bowl as Karl Kremser put his foot to the pigskin, but when the 43-yard attempt veered off the Oklahoma partisans erupted. There was no national championship for the Sooners, however, who remained in the shadow of USC, a team also victorious that New Year's Day.

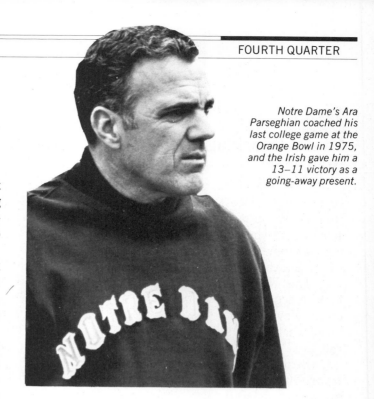

Notre Dame's Ara Parseghian coached his last college game at the Orange Bowl in 1975, and the Irish gave him a 13–11 victory as a going-away present.

be a spoiler to number one ranked Alabama. It was Ara Parseghian's last game as Notre Dame's head coach, and he wanted to leave on a higher note than the 55–24 trimming his Irish had taken from Southern Cal's Trojans in the last game of the regular season.

Across the field was Bear Bryant's team, eager to solidify its claim to the national title, and reverse the diabolical trend of their bowl appearances—they had lost 7 in a row.

But it was not to be. The star-crossed Crimson Tide were as lackluster as they had been in any of the preceding bowl games. Notre Dame got off to a fast start, and fullback Wayne Bullock put them on the board when he bulled his way into the 'Bama end zone in the first quarter. In the next period, Mark McLane ran another one in from the 9, a missed extra point leaving the score at 13–0.

That was enough. The Irish gave up a field goal, and in the fourth quarter a touchdown when Richard Todd unleashed a long one to Russ Schamun. Alabama threatened in the closing minutes, getting close to field goal range, but then their bowl demons took over as Todd was intercepted. Ara Parseghian left Notre Dame just as he had come in 11 years earlier, with a win.

SCORING

Oklahoma	7	12	0	7—26
Tennessee	0	0	14	10—24

Oklahoma:	Touchdowns—Warmack, Hinton, Owens, Stephenson; PAT—Vachon (2).
Tennessee:	Touchdowns—Glover, Fulton, Warren; Field goal—Kremser; PAT—Kremser (3).

1975

Notre Dame 13
Alabama   11

Notre Dame was the reigning national champion, but they had lost two games during the 1974 season. There was no chance for a repeat title, but they could

SCORING

Notre Dame	7	6	0	0—13
Alabama	0	3	0	8—11

Notre Dame:	Touchdowns—Bullock, McLane; PAT—Reeve.
Alabama:	Touchdown—Schamun; Field goal—Ridgway; PAT—Pugh (2 points).

1984

Miami (Florida) 31
Nebraska   30

The Miami Hurricanes had not won an Orange Bowl contest since 1946, when they barely edged out Holy Cross; in fact, they had not been to the classic since 1951, when they lost to Clemson by a point. But this was to be their year, and they unseated undefeated Nebraska, the nation's top-ranked team.

The Nebraska Cornhuskers were an 11-point favorite according to the bookmakers, to which Miami coach Howard Schnellenberger said, "I doubt they know what a bunch of alley cats Nebraska is about to run into."

Besides a confident coach Miami had quarterback Bernie Kosar, a drop-back passer with the finesse of a pro, and a defense that was obsessed with stopping All-American running back, Mike Rozier.

The Hurricanes lived up to their nickname in the first quarter. Kosar passed them down the field, then threw a short one to tight end Glenn Dennison for the score. A field goal and another strike to Dennison made the score 17–0 at the end of the period.

In the second quarter, it was Nebraska's turn. The Cornhuskers, who had averaged 52 points a game during the regular season, came back and put 10 on the board. Then a minute into the second half, they

tied it. But Kosar went back to the air to set up first one touchdown and then another, and Miami took a 31–17 lead into the fourth quarter.

Nebraska fought back gamely, driving 76 yards to narrow the lead to 7 points. There were just under two minutes left in the game when the Cornhuskers got the ball back, and again they marched. At Miami's 24-yard line, fourth and 8, coach Tom Osborne called for a pitchout to Jeff Smith, who had replaced Mike Rozier after he injured his foot. Smith not only passed the first-down marker but made it all the way in for the score.

One point would tie it, and that would be enough to maintain Nebraska's grip on the national championship. A two-point conversion would win the game. Osborne, subscribing to the dictum that a true champion only plays to win, went for the 2, a roll-out pass that defensive back Kenny Calhoun batted away to give Miami its first national championship.

SCORING

Miami (Florida)	17	0	14	0—31
Nebraska	0	10	7	13—30

Miami (Florida): Touchdowns—Dennison (2), Highsmith (2); Field goal—Davis; PAT—Davis (4).

Nebraska: Touchdowns—Steinkuhler, Gill, Smith (2); Field goal—Livingston; PAT—Livingston (3).

Nebraska lines up for a pass, but it was Miami's quarterback Bernie Kosar who dominated in the air that day.

Orange Bowl Results

Year	Schools	Score	Coaches	Outstanding Players
1935	Bucknell	26	Hooks Mylin	—
	Miami (Florida)	0	Tom McCann	
1936	Catholic U.	20	A. J. Bergman	—
	Mississippi	19	Ed Walker	
1937	Duquesne	13	Jack Smith	—
	Mississippi State	12	Ralph Sasse	
1938	Auburn	6	Jack Meagher	—
	Michigan State	0	Charlie Bachman	
1939	Tennessee	17	Bob Neyland	—
	Oklahoma	0	Tom Stidham	
1940	Georgia Tech	21	W. A. Alexander	—
	Missouri	7	Don Faurot	
1941	Mississippi State	14	Allyn McKeen	—
	Georgetown	7	Jack Haggerty	
1942	Georgia	40	Wally Butts	—
	Texas Christian	26	Leo Meyer	
1943	Alabama	37	Frank Thomas	—
	Boston College	21	Dennis Myers	
1944	Louisiana State	19	Bernie Moore	—
	Texas A&M	14	Homer Norton	
1945	Tulsa	26	Henry Frnka	—
	Georgia Tech	12	W. A. Alexander	
1946	Miami (Florida)	13	Jack Harding	—
	Holy Cross	6	John DaGrosa	
1947	Rice	8	Jess Neely	—
	Tennessee	0	Bob Neyland	
1948	Georgia Tech	20	Bobby Dodd	—
	Kansas	14	George Sauer	
1949	Texas	41	Blair Cherry	—
	Georgia	28	Wally Butts	
1950	Santa Clara	21	Len Casanova	—
	Kentucky	13	Paul Bryant	
1951	Clemson	15	Frank Howard	—
	Miami (Florida)	14	Andy Gustafson	
1952	Georgia Tech	17	Bobby Dodd	—
	Baylor	14	George Sauer	
1953	Alabama	61	Red Drew	—
	Syracuse	6	Ben Schwartzwalder	
1954	Oklahoma	7	Bud Wilkinson	—
	Maryland	0	Jim Tatum	
1955	Duke	34	Bill Murray	—
	Nebraska	7	Bill Glassford	
1956	Oklahoma	20	Bud Wilkinson	—
	Maryland	6	Jim Tatum	
1957	Colorado	27	Dallas Ward	—
	Clemson	21	Frank Howard	
1958	Oklahoma	48	Bud Wilkinson	—
	Duke	21	Bill Murray	
1959	Oklahoma	21	Bud Wilkinson	—
	Syracuse	6	Ben Schwartzwalder	
1960	Georgia	14	Wally Butts	—
	Missouri	0	Dan Devine	
1961	Missouri	21	Dan Devine	—
	Navy	14	Wayne Hardin	
1962	Louisiana State	25	Paul Dietzel	—
	Colorado	7	Sonny Grandelius	

Year	Schools	Score	Coaches	Outstanding Players
1963	Alabama	17	Paul Bryant	—
	Oklahoma	0	Bud Wilkinson	
1964	Nebraska	13	Bob Devaney	—
	Auburn	7	Shug Jordan	
1965	Texas	21	Darrell Royal	
	Alabama	17	Paul Bryant	Joe Namath
1966	Alabama	39	Paul Bryant	Steve Sloan
	Nebraska	28	Bob Devaney	
1967	Florida	27	Ray Graves	Larry Smith
	Georgia Tech	12	Bobby Dodd	
1968	Oklahoma	26	Chuck Fairbanks	Bob Warmack
	Tennessee	24	Doug Dickey	
1969	Penn State	15	Joe Paterno	
	Kansas	14	Pepper Rodgers	Donnie Shanklin
1970	Penn State	10	Joe Paterno	Chuck Burkhart, Mike Reid
	Missouri	3	Dan Devine	
1971	Nebraska	17	Bob Devaney	Jerry Tagge, Willie Harper
	Louisiana State	12	Charles McClendon	
1972	Nebraska	38	Bob Devaney	Jerry Tagge, Rich Glover
	Alabama	6	Paul Bryant	
1973	Nebraska	40	Bob Devaney	Johnny Rodgers, Rich Glover
	Notre Dame	6	Ara Parseghian	
1974	Penn State	16	Joe Paterno	Tom Shulman, Randy Crowder
	Louisiana State	9	Charles McClendon	
1975	Notre Dame	13	Ara Parseghian	Wayne Bullock, Leroy Cook
	Alabama	11	Paul Bryant	
1976	Oklahoma	14	Barry Switzer	Steve Davis, Lee Roy Selmon
	Michigan	6	Bo Schembechler	
1977	Ohio State	27	Woody Hayes	Rod Gerald, Tom Cousineau
	Colorado	10	Bill Mallory	
1978	Arkansas	31	Lew Holtz	Roland Sales, Reggie Freeman
	Oklahoma	6	Barry Switzer	
1979	Oklahoma	31	Barry Switzer	Billy Sims, Reggie Kinlan
	Nebraska	24	Tom Osborne	
1980	Oklahoma	24	Barry Switzer	J. C. Watts, Bud Hebert
	Florida State	7	Bobby Bowden	
1981	Oklahoma	18	Barry Switzer	J. C. Watts
	Florida State	17	Bobby Bowden	Jarvis Cowsey
1982	Clemson	22	Danny Ford	Homer Jordan, Jeff Davis
	Nebraska	15	Tom Osborne	
1983	Nebraska	21	Tom Osborne	Turner Gill, Dave Rimington
	Louisiana State	20	Jerry Stovall	
1984	Miami (Florida)	31	Howard Schnellenberger	Jack Hernandez, Bernie Kosar
	Nebraska	30	Tom Osborne	
1985	Washington	28	Don James	Ron Holmes, Jacque Robinson
	Oklahoma	17	Barry Switzer	

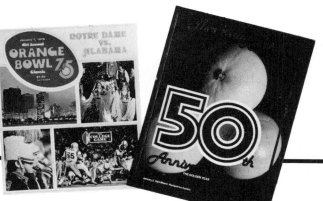

THE SUGAR BOWL

It took almost eight years for the Sugar Bowl to become a reality, from its inception in 1927 in the minds of Colonel James M. Thompson, publisher of the *New Orleans Item,* and one of his sports columnists, Fred Digby, until the first kickoff of the classic on January 1, 1935.

The two members of the New Orleans journalism community campaigned lustily for a football game to rival the Rose Bowl. Digby actually wanted the game to be the highlight of a midwinter sports carnival, one that would include a variety of athletic competitions. New Orleans was the ideal site for such a pageant, they argued: the climate was pleasant, the city was a

Tulane Stadium in New Orleans, Louisiana, home of the Sugar Bowl until 1976, when the classic was moved to the Louisiana Superdome.

The contingent from Texas Christian looks on from the bench in the 1939 Sugar Bowl.

Fans line up for tickets to the 1939 game between TCU and Carnegie Tech (the Horned Frogs won it 15–7), which was played on January 2 that year because New Year's Day fell on a Sunday.

popular winter tourist haunt, the residents of the area were avowed football fans, it would focus positive, healthy publicity on the city. And would it be successful? Look at the Rose Bowl, Digby pointed out—by 1927 it was drawing close to 60,000 spectators.

The city and factions within it, however, did not leap on the Thompson/Digby bandwagon. Instead they listened and hedged and postponed action on the project. But finally in 1934 enough support was inspired, and a Mid-Winter Sports Association was founded, a charter was drawn up, and plans for a New Year's Day college football game were laid.

It was agreed to enter into the charter that the game would be a "nonprofit civic enterprise" and any and all proceeds would be distributed to charitable and educational institutions in the area. The site of the game was to be Tulane Stadium, with a seating/ standing capacity in 1935 of about 24,000.

Fred Digby's dream had come to life, and it was only appropriate that he name his prodigy. He came up with Sugar Bowl not merely because the state was then the leading sugar producer in the United States but also because the site of Tulane Stadium was a former sugar plantation.

A crowd of 22,026 showed up for the first Sugar Bowl game, which featured Tulane and Temple, and the largely partisan crowd was entertained by a Tulane win, 20–14. It was an exciting game. Temple, coached by the immortal Pop Warner, jumped out to a 14–0 lead, but saw it washed away in the second half by Tulane's relentless Green Wave. The play of the day

was tallied by Tulane's Monk Simons when he ran back a Temple kickoff 85 yards for a touchdown.

From that first game until the 1975 contest, all Sugar Bowl games were played in Tulane Stadium (long since known as the Sugar Bowl), which was sequentially enlarged over the years until it could accommodate about 81,000 spectators. In 1976, the game was moved to the $163 million Louisiana Superdome, its home ever since.

Charlie O'Rourke breaks loose on what proved to be the game-winning touchdown for Boston College in their 19–13 defeat of Tennessee in the 1941 Sugar Bowl.

Games Worth Remembering

1945

Duke   29
Alabama 26

The Sugar Bowl crowd of some 72,000 that year caught a glimpse of budding greatness when Alabama's 18-year-old freshman quarterback Harry Gilmer took the field. Gilmer, who would make the jump pass famous and in 1946 went on to lead the Crimson Tide to an undefeated season and a Rose Bowl victory, completed all eight of his pass attempts against Duke and nearly won the game in the last seconds.

But the Duke Blue Devils were a tenacious bunch. They were down 12–7 at the end of the first quarter and 19–13 at halftime. Their game was running the ball, and they did it well. To take the lead in the third quarter, they marched 64 yards on ten consecutive carries by fullback Tom Davis.

Alabama turned it around in the fourth quarter when Hugh Morrow intercepted a Duke pass and raced 75 yards with it for a touchdown. With the Crimson Tide ahead 26–20 and three minutes remaining, Alabama, on their own 1-yard line, made what turned out to be a terrible decision: an intentional safety, which ceded 2 points but gave them a free kick, on which they hoped to send the ball deep into Duke territory. Only the kick wasn't very good, leaving the ball on Alabama's 40-yard line. Duke rattled off two 20-yard runs and a touchdown; the score was now 29–26 in favor of the Blue Devils.

Still, with Gilmer guiding them, Alabama had a chance, and everyone in Tulane Stadium knew it. Gilmer got the Tide out to their own 42-yard line. Then, with time for only one more play, he faded back, eluded several Duke tacklers, spotted end Ralph Jones downfield. Gilmer lofted a long pass that dropped into Jones' hands at the 25-yard line, but the lone trailing Duke defender lunged and got ahold of Jones' jersey, hung on, and wrestled him to the ground.

SCORING				
Duke	7	6	7	9—29
Alabama	12	7	0	7—26
Duke:	Touchdowns—Clark (2), Davis (2); PAT—Raether (3); Safety.			
Alabama:	Touchdowns—Hodges (2), Jones, Morrow; PAT—Morrow (2).			

Harry Gilmer, carrying the ball for Alabama here, had a great day as a freshman in the 1945 Sugar Bowl game (8 for 8 passing, including a touchdown), but the Crimson Tide still fell to Duke, 29–26.

1947

Georgia   20
North Carolina 10

The game was billed as the battle of the halfbacks, appropriately enough, considering that Charlie Trippi was at right half for Georgia and Charlie "Choo Choo" Justice was North Carolina's left half. Both were legitimate All-Americans in a year gilded with running backs of such esteem as Doc Blanchard and Glenn Davis of Army, Doak Walker of Southern Methodist, Clyde "Smackover" Scott of Arkansas, Buddy Young of Illinois, Bob Chappius of Michigan, and Emil Sitko of Notre Dame.

Georgia was favored, undefeated in the regular season and ranked only behind the magnificent Army and Notre Dame teams. But during the first half, there was scant evidence of the quality of the Georgia eleven, nor was there any dazzle from the two premier halfbacks. The score at intermission was North Carolina 7, Georgia 0.

The Bulldogs must have gotten a bit of inspiration from coach Wally Butts before coming back on the field because they played a much better game in the second half. A concerted drive resulted in one touchdown, and a 67-yard pass play from Trippi to end Dan Edwards in the third quarter gave them the lead, which they would not relinquish.

Both heralded backs played superb football in the second half: Trippi was the force that brought Georgia victory while Justice, with feats such as a 49-yard kickoff return and pinpoint passing, kept the Tar Heels in the game.

SCORING

Georgia	0	0	13	7—20
North Carolina	0	7	3	0—10

Georgia:	Touchdowns—Rauch (2), Edwards; PAT—Jernigan (2).
North Carolina:	Touchdown—Pupa; Field goal—Cox; PAT—Cox.

1951
Kentucky 13
Oklahoma 7

By the end of the 1950 season Bud Wilkinson's Sooners had run their amazing winning streak to 31 games, at the time the longest streak in modern football history. Bear Bryant's Kentucky team had lost only to Tennessee, who in turn had lost only to a much weaker Mississippi State team. While number one ranked Oklahoma had already taken the national championship for the year, Kentucky hoped to stake a claim as the nation's best team with a New Year's Day win.

Charlie Trippi lofts a jump pass in the 1947 Sugar Bowl, leading Georgia to a 20–10 triumph over North Carolina. Trippi rushed for 77 yards and passed for another 64 that day.

Babe Parilli (10) eludes an Oklahoma tackler in the 1951 Sugar Bowl, and helps Kentucky to a 13–7 victory over the Sooners.

It was a star-studded cast. Favored Oklahoma had halfback Billy Vessels, fullback Buck McPhail, and tackle Jim Weatherall; Kentucky could boast quarterback Babe Parilli and tackles Bob Gain and Walt Yowarsky, all All-American caliber.

But Oklahoma was star-crossed that day. In the opening period quarterback Claude Arnold fumbled on his own 25, and Walt Yowarsky came up with the ball for Kentucky. On the next play, Babe Parilli passed to halfback Shorty Jamerson for the game's first score.

Kentucky's defense was awesome that day as well. Oklahoma got virtually nowhere throughout the first three quarters; in all they had seven fumbles, five of which the Kentuckians recovered.

Parilli passed the Wildcats to the Oklahoma 1-yard line in the second period, and then handed off to Jamerson for the score. That was enough. Kentucky gave up a touchdown in the fourth quarter, earned principally on the rushing of Billy Vessels, paydirt coming when Vessels tossed a pass to halfback Merrill Green. That was all for the Sooners, a far cry from their usual five- to six-touchdown performance.

With characteristic class, Wilkinson said after the game, "We knew it had to come sometime. When it did we wanted it to come from a team we had respect for. I can state sincerely that we lost to a great team, a great school, a great coach, and a great state."

SCORING

Kentucky	7	6	0	0—13
Oklahoma	0	0	0	7— 7

Kentucky Touchdowns—Jamerson (2); PAT—Gain.
Oklahoma Touchdown—Green; PAT—Weatherall.

1959
Louisiana State 7
Clemson　　　　　0

LSU was a unanimous choice as the best team in the United States in 1958. In its backfield were such luminaries as halfback Billy Cannon, who would win the Heisman Trophy the next year, halfback Johnny Robinson, and quarterback Warren Rabb; roving its sideline was coach of the year Paul Dietzel. In addition, LSU used a three-platoon system capable of wearing down the strongest of opponents. And twice-beaten Clemson fell short of that category. As a result, some oddsmakers were favoring the Tigers from Baton Rouge by as much as 17 points.

But for all that, there was only a single score in the entire game, and that was hardly earned. Clemson shut down the running attack of Cannon and Robinson and harassed Rabb throughout the game. The Tigers played their best game of the year, but they made one fatal mistake. In the third quarter, Clemson was forced to punt from their own 20, but the snap was bad and LSU tackle Duane Leopard broke through to fall on the ball on Clemson's 11-yard line. In two plays LSU could only advance the ball to the 9, but then Cannon took a pitchout on an end-around option and passed to Mickey Mangham in the end zone.

SCORING

Louisiana State	0	0	7	0—7
Clemson	0	0	0	0—0

Louisiana State:　Touchdown—Mangham; PAT—Cannon.

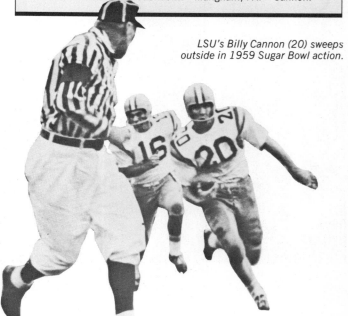

LSU's Billy Cannon (20) sweeps outside in 1959 Sugar Bowl action.

1966

Missouri 20
Florida 18

Neither Missouri nor Florida was ranked in the top five when the 1965 season came to a close, but the two teams put on the best display of football in any of the major bowls on New Year's Day, 1966.

Missouri, under coach Dan Devine, appeared to have an easy win with a 20–0 lead going into the fourth quarter. Florida could not stop Missouri's hard-charging running game, especially Charlie Brown, who picked up 120 yards on 22 carries. But Florida had Steve Spurrier at quarterback, an All-American candidate who the next year would become only the sixth quarterback to win the Heisman Trophy. And in the fourth quarter he put on as dazzling a display as was ever performed in any closing quarter of any bowl game.

Florida's Steve Spurrier hurls one of his record-setting passes in the 1966 Sugar classic. He set five records that day when he completed 27 of 45 passes for 352 yards and gained a total of 344 yards passing and rushing on 52 plays. But Florida still lost to Missouri, 20–18.

He rallied a disheartened Florida offense, marched them down the field, and tossed a touchdown pass to put them on the scoreboard, but a two-point conversion try failed. He goaded the defense from the sideline to stop Missouri, and they did. Back on the field, again Spurrier moved the Gators, passing flawlessly, finally carrying the ball in for another touchdown. With the score 20–12, there was little choice but to go for a two-point conversion, but again it didn't work. Florida's defense held, however, and soon Spurrier was passing them down the field again, culminating with a touchdown toss. A two-pointer would tie it, but for the third consecutive time, the attempt failed. Finally, time ran out on the charging Spurrier and his fellow Floridians.

After the final gun, Spurrier had five Sugar Bowl records in his portfolio: completed passes, 27; attempted passes, 45; yards gained passing, 352; yards gained passing and rushing, 344; most plays passing and rushing, 52, but not the mark he sought the most—victory.

SCORING

| Missouri | 0 | 17 | 3 | 0—20 |
| Florida | 0 | 0 | 0 | 18—18 |

Missouri: Touchdowns—Brown, Denny; Field goal—Bates (2); PAT—Bates (2).
Florida: Touchdowns—Harper, Spurrier, Casey.

1973
Notre Dame 24
Alabama   23

The national championship was on the line when Ara Parseghian's Fighting Irish took to the astroturf at Tulane Stadium to do battle with Bear Bryant's Crimson Tide. Both teams had gone through the regular season undefeated, although Alabama claimed the number one ranking.

No Fighting Irish team had gone undefeated since 1949. It was the kind of situation Parseghian loved, the ultimate opportunity to stir his players to greatness.

Alabama was a slight favorite, but that was soon discounted as quarterback Tom Clements, with pinpoint passing, marched Notre Dame down the field, then gave the football to fullback Wayne Bullock at the 1 to blast in with the game's first score. The Irish failed to make the conversion. The Tide came back in the second period when Wilbur Jackson crossed the Notre Dame goal line, and the successful conversion

gave Alabama a 1-point lead. But Notre Dame was explosive. Al Hunter grabbed the Alabama kickoff on his 7-yard line and scampered for a bowl record 93-yard touchdown return. A two-point conversion gave Notre Dame a 14–7 lead, which was narrowed before the half by an Alabama field goal.

Alabama regained the lead in the third quarter, slogging out a concerted drive that had begun on their own 70-yard line, on which they finally scored. 'Bama then held, got the ball back, but fumbled, and the Irish recovered just 12 yards shy of the Tide's goal line. That distance was erased on the first play from scrimmage when Earl Penick lugged the ball in to give Notre Dame a 21–17 lead. But to illustrate to Parseghian's chagrin that Notre Dame was not faultless, they turned over a fumble in the fourth quarter. 'Bama quickly converted it into a touchdown of their own, giving them a lead of 23–21, but they missed the extra point. This would prove fatal to Bear Bryant's Alabamans. Bob Thomas kicked a 19-yard field goal to regain the lead for the Irish and then an inspired Notre Dame defense held for the victory. With that narrow victory, Notre Dame wrested the national title from Alabama.

SCORING

| Notre Dame | 6 | 8 | 7 | 3—24 |
| Alabama | 0 | 10 | 7 | 6—23 |

Notre Dame: Touchdowns—Bullock, Hunter, Pennock; Field goal—Thomas; PAT—Thomas, Dmmerle (2 points).
Alabama: Touchdowns—Jackson (2), Todd; Field goal—Davis; PAT—Davis (2).

1979
Alabama   14
Penn State 7

Penn State, under Joe Paterno, came to the Sugar Bowl with the expressed intention of ensuring their claim to the national championship. The Nittany Lions brought with them a 19-game winning streak and the number one ranking. But Bear Bryant's second-ranked Alabama team was thirsting for a win that would give them the national title.

Penn State had Heisman Trophy runner-up Chuck Fusina at quarterback and a powerful fullback in Matt Suhey, as well as All-American linemen Keith Dorney and Bruce Clark. Alabama was quarterbacked by Jeff Rutledge and had a most accomplished running back in Tony Nathan.

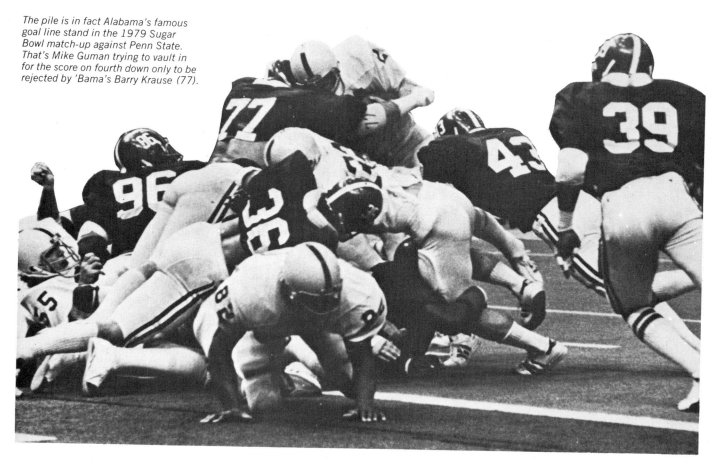

The pile is in fact Alabama's famous goal line stand in the 1979 Sugar Bowl match-up against Penn State. That's Mike Guman trying to vault in for the score on fourth down only to be rejected by 'Bama's Barry Krause (77).

The game, heralded as only the fifth major bowl match-up in history between the nation's top-ranked teams, promised to be an explosive one, with two fine offenses and such high stakes. But it was defense that ruled as neither team scored in the first quarter. Late in the second period, the Crimson Tide got a drive going. The nation's number one ranked defense could not stop 'Bama's running attack, which moved the ball 80 yards, including a 30-yard gainer on a sweep by Tony Nathan. The climax came when Rutledge hit split end Bruce Bolton in the end zone.

In the third quarter, Penn State intercepted Rutledge and moved the ball to 'Bama's 17-yard line, where Chuck Fusina rifled a pass to Scott Fitzkee for the score. But with time running out in the period, Lou Ikner took a Penn punt and slithered through for 62 yards and another touchdown for the Crimson Tide.

Penn State had its chance in the fourth quarter when it moved the ball to the Alabama 1-yard line. Three rushes at the stalwart Alabama defense were fruitless, and it finally came down to fourth and inches. Mike Guman tried to vault over the Alabama line but was hurled back; that was the last chance for a disheartened and disillusioned Penn State team, and gone

with it was the crown Paterno wanted so much. After the game he shrugged it off: "Alabama has as much right to a national championship as anyone; I think they beat an awfully good team today."

SCORING

Alabama	0	7	7	0—14
Penn State	0	0	7	0— 7

Alabama: Touchdowns—Bolton, Ikner; PAT—McElroy (2).
Penn State: Touchdown—Fitzkee; PAT—Bahr.

1981
Georgia   17
Notre Dame 10

It was said that the Georgia Bulldogs of 1980 were the luckiest team ever to win a national championship: lucky to have been ranked number one at the end of the regular season when they hadn't played a team that finished in the top 20; lucky to have escaped

Joe Paterno exhorting his Nittany Lions in their 1983 defeat.

with wins in at least three regular season games; and lucky to have come out on top in the Sugar Bowl.

Their luck in the Sugar Bowl bordered on the miraculous. They won the game by a touchdown, but Notre Dame outgained them, 138 yards to 7, in the air, and 190 yards to 127 on the ground. And the interesting thing about Georgia's rushing total was that freshman sensation Herschel Walker ran for 150 yards, while his running mates totaled 23 yards *in losses*.

Notre Dame took the lead in the first quarter when Harry Oliver booted a 50-yard field goal, but from then on it was nothing but a litany of blunders for the Irish. First there was a blocked field goal that Georgia shortly converted into a field goal of its own. Then when the Bulldogs kicked off, the two Notre Dame returners were confused as to who was going to catch the ball and run it back, so neither did. The ball bounced around near the 1-yard line, where Georgia's Steve Kelly dove on it. A few moments later Herschel Walker vaulted into the end zone. Another Notre Dame fumble at their own 20 was recovered by the Bulldogs, and a few plays later, Walker skirted the end for still another Georgia score and a 17–3 halftime lead. In the second half, Notre Dame managed a touchdown, but was plagued by several interceptions and a missed field goal from the 13.

It was Dan Devine's last game as head coach of

the Fighting Irish, only his sixteenth loss against 53 victories at Notre Dame; for Georgia it was their first national championship.

SCORING

Georgia	10	7	0	0—17
Notre Dame	3	0	7	0—10

Georgia: Touchdowns—Walker (2); Field goal—Robinson; PAT—Robinson (2).
Notre Dame: Touchdown—Carter; Field goal—Oliver; PAT—Oliver.

1983
Penn State 27
Georgia 23

The Sugar Bowl in 1983 was again the site where the nation's two top-ranked teams met to decide the championship. Georgia, behind the running of Heisman award winner Herschel Walker, was number one at season's end, and Penn State, with a defense so deceptive and difficult to adjust to that it had earned the nickname "Magic," was just a notch beneath.

Penn State came out throwing, as quarterback Todd Blackledge passed his way to the Georgia 2, where top running back Curt Warner carried it in for the first score of the game. The Nittany Lions could virtually do nothing wrong in the first half. Kevin Baugh returned punts for 66, 24, and 10 yards; Black-ledge completed 9 of 16 passes for 160 yards; Warner ran for another touchdown; and Nick Gancitano kicked 2 field goals. Georgia, which managed a field goal earlier, finally scored a touchdown with five seconds left in the half, when John Lastinger lobbed one to flanker Herman Archie in the end zone. Even with that they were still trailing 20–10.

The momentum shifted at the start of the second half as Lastinger engineered a 60-yard drive that ended when Herschel Walker blasted in from the 1-yard line. Penn State's passing game was shut down by a fiery Georgia defense, and Curt Warner was severely hampered by leg cramps.

But when everything seemed to be falling apart, Joe Paterno sent in a little surprise from the sideline:

first a play-action fake to Warner, then Blackledge dropped back in the pocket and heaved a 47-yard pass into the end zone, where it was caught by a diving Gregg Garrity.

Georgia came back with a touchdown in the fourth quarter, but an inspired Magic defense otherwise shut down the Bulldogs, giving Paterno and Penn State their long-sought national championship.

SCORING

Penn State	7	13	0	7—27
Georgia	3	7	7	6—23

Penn State:	Touchdowns—Warner (2), Garrity; Field goals—Gancitano (2); PAT—Gancitano (3).
Georgia:	Touchdowns—Archie, Walker, Kay; Field goal—Manca; PAT—Manca (2).

Joe Paterno, finally victorious, as Penn State beat Georgia 27–23.

Sugar Bowl Results

Year	Schools	Score	Coaches	Outstanding Players
1935	Tulane	20	Ted Cox	—
	Temple	14	Pop Warner	
1936	Texas Christian	3	Leo Meyer	—
	Louisiana State	2	Bernie Moore	
1937	Santa Clara	21	Buck Shaw	—
	Louisiana State	14	Bernie Moore	
1938	Santa Clara	6	Buck Shaw	—
	Louisiana State	0	Bernie Moore	
1939	Texas Christian	15	Dutch Meyer	—
	Carnegie Tech	7	Bill Kern	
1940	Texas A & M	14	Homer Norton	—
	Tulane	13	Red Dawson	
1941	Boston College	19	Frank Leahy	—
	Tennessee	13	Bob Neyland	
1942	Fordham	2	Jim Crowley	—
	Missouri	0	Don Faurot	
1943	Tennessee	14	J. H. Barnhill	—
	Tulsa	7	Henry Frnka	
1944	Georgia Tech	20	W. A. Alexander	—
	Tulsa	18	Henry Frnka	
1945	Duke	29	Eddie Cameron	—
	Alabama	26	Frank Thomas	
1946	Oklahoma A & M	33	Jim Lookabaugh	—
	St. Mary's	13	Jim Phelan	
1947	Georgia	20	Wally Butts	—
	North Carolina	10	Carl Snavely	
1948	Texas	27	Blair Cherry	Bobby Layne
	Alabama	7	Red Drew	
1949	Oklahoma	14	Bud Wilkinson	Jack Mitchell
	North Carolina	6	Carl Snavely	
1950	Oklahoma	35	Bud Wilkinson	Leon Heath
	Louisiana State	0	Gaynell Tinsley	
1951	Kentucky	13	Paul Bryant	Walt Yowarsky
	Oklahoma	7	Bud Wilkinson	
1952	Maryland	28	Jim Tatum	Ed Modzelewski
	Tennessee	13	Bob Neyland	
1953	Georgia Tech	24	Bobby Dodd	Leon Hardeman
	Mississippi	7	John Vaught	
1954	Georgia Tech	42	Bobby Dodd	Pepper Rodgers
	West Virginia	19	Art Lewis	
1955	Navy	21	Eddie Erdelatz	Joe Gattuso
	Mississippi	0	John Vaught	
1956	Georgia Tech	7	Bobby Dodd	Franklin Brooks
	Pittsburgh	0	John Michelosen	
1957	Baylor	13	Sam Boyd	Del Shofner
	Tennessee	7	Bowden Wyatt	
1958	Mississippi	39	John Vaught	Ray Brown
	Texas	7	Darrell Royal	
1959	Louisiana State	7	Paul Dietzel	Billy Cannon
	Clemson	0	Frank Howard	
1960	Mississippi	21	John Vaught	Bobby Franklin
	Louisiana State	0	Paul Dietzel	
1961	Mississippi	14	John Vaught	Jake Gibbs
	Rice	6	Jess Neely	
1962	Alabama	10	Paul Bryant	Mike Fracchia
	Arkansas	3	Frank Broyles	

Year	Schools	Score	Coaches	Outstanding Players
1963	Mississippi	17	John Vaught	Glynn Griffing
	Arkansas	13	Frank Broyles	
1964	Alabama	12	Paul Bryant	Tim Davis
	Mississippi	7	John Vaught	
1965	Louisiana State	13	Charles McClendon	Doug Moreau
	Syracuse	10	Ben Schwartzwalder	
1966	Missouri	20	Dan Devine	Steve Spurrier
	Florida	18	Ray Graves	
1967	Alabama	34	Paul Bryant	Kenny Stabler
	Nebraska	7	Bob Devaney	
1968	Louisiana State	20	Charles McClendon	Glenn Smith
	Wyoming	13	Lloyd Eaton	
1969	Arkansas	16	Frank Broyles	Chuck Dicus
	Georgia	2	Vince Dooley	
1970	Mississippi	27	John Vaught	Archie Manning
	Arkansas	22	Frank Broyles	
1971	Tennessee	34	Bill Battle	Bobby Scott
	Air Force	13	Ben Martin	
1972	Oklahoma	40	Chuck Fairbanks	Jack Mildren
	Auburn	22	Ralph Jordan	
1973	Oklahoma	14	Chuck Fairbanks	Tinker Owens
	Penn State	0	Joe Paterno	
1974	Notre Dame	24	Ara Parseghian	Tom Clements
	Alabama	23	Paul Bryant	
1975	Nebraska	13	Tom Osborne	Tony Davis
	Florida	10	Doug Dickey	
1976	Alabama	13	Paul Bryant	Richard Todd
	Penn State	6	Joe Paterno	
1977	Pittsburgh	27	Johnny Majors	Matt Cavanaugh
	Georgia	3	Vince Dooley	
1978	Alabama	35	Paul Bryant	Jeff Rutledge
	Ohio State	6	Woody Hayes	
1979	Alabama	14	Paul Bryant	Barry Krauss
	Penn State	7	Joe Paterno	
1980	Alabama	24	Paul Bryant	Major Ogilvie
	Arkansas	9	Lew Holtz	
1981	Georgia	17	Vince Dooley	Herschel Walker
	Notre Dame	10	Dan Devine	
1982	Pittsburgh	24	Jackie Sherrill	Dan Marino
	Georgia	20	Vince Dooley	
1983	Penn State	27	Joe Paterno	Todd Blackledge
	Georgia	23	Vince Dooley	
1984	Auburn	9	Pat Dye	Bo Jackson
	Michigan	7	Bo Schembechler	
1985	Nebraska	28	Tom Osborne	Craig Sundberg
	LSU	10	Bill Arnsparger	

THE COTTON BOWL

UNIVERSITY OF MISSOURI vs. TEXAS UNIVERSITY

Annual **COTTON BOWL**
NEW YEAR'S DAY
CLASSIC

1946

DALLAS, TEXAS

25c

J Curtis Sanford, a Texas oil magnate, was in Los Angeles one New Year's Day in the mid-1930s and went to Pasadena to take in the Rose Bowl festivities and game. He also heard talk that day about the two other cities that had just started similar New Year's Day pageants; Miami with its Orange Bowl, and New Orleans with the Sugar Bowl. Why not stage one in Dallas, his own hometown? He found the idea so appealing that he decided to finance it himself.

And so was born the Cotton Bowl in Dallas in 1937. It was not a blossoming success at the outset, even though it showcased Texas Christian's marvelous Sammy Baugh in his last college game. In fact, the benevolent Mr. Sanford lost several thousand dollars.

Marquette came all the way down from Milwaukee to face the Horned Frogs in a stadium on the Texas state fairgrounds in Dallas, but only about 17,000 fans showed up. Those who did were treated to a Sammy Baugh touchdown pass to L. D. Meyer, who proved to be the game's most glittering star. Meyer ran for another touchdown and kicked a field goal and an extra point to account for all 16 of the Horned Frogs points. The final score was 16–6.

During the first four years of the Cotton Bowl, J. Curtis Sanford remained the *pater familias*, advancing money, promoting the event, and guiding its administration. He turned all his responsibilities over to a newly formed Cotton Bowl Athletic Association in 1940, which was instituted as an agency of the Southwest Conference. Two years later, it was agreed that the winner of that conference would automatically be invited to play in the Cotton Bowl.

The Cotton Bowl in Dallas, Texas.

Byron "Whizzer" White tosses one for Colorado in the 1938 Cotton Bowl. He threw one touchdown pass and intercepted a Rice pass to score another that day, but Colorado lost 28–14.

Games Worth Remembering
1938

Rice   28
Colorado 14

Colorado College (now the University of Colorado) had gone undefeated through the 1937 season, but skeptics noted that they had not played any team of renown, and therefore would provide little competition for Southwest Conference champion Rice, which had played and defeated a number of nationally ranked teams.

What Colorado had, however, was a triple threat back named Byron "Whizzer" White, who had earned All-American honors and a Rhodes scholarship. With White running and passing, Colorado moved down the field with relative ease in the first quarter. At Rice's 8-yard line, he dropped back and threw to halfback Joe Antonio for the game's initial score. When Rice got the ball, White anticipated a pass and picked it off, sprinting 47 yards to give Colorado a 14–0 edge.

But Rice was, in fact, a much stronger team, and in the second period the Owls asserted themselves. What got them going was sophomore quarterback

Ernie Lain, who came off the bench and passed Rice to victory. In the second quarter, Lain threw for two touchdowns and ran another in himself, then passed for still another in the third period. In the meantime, Rice's defense thwarted Whizzer White, and with him the entire Colorado offense.

SCORING				
Rice	0	21	7	0—28
Colorado	14	0	0	0—14
Rice:	Touchdowns—Schuehle, Lain, Cordill, Steen; PAT—Vestal (4).			
Colorado:	Touchdowns—Antonio, White; PAT—White (2).			

1946

Texas   40
Missouri 27

If ever there was a one-man show in a bowl game, it was Texas quarterback Bobby Layne's curtain raising performance in the 1946 Cotton Bowl game. He had a role in every one of the Longhorns' 40 points that day.

Dick Moegle, streaking along the sideline for Rice in the 1954 Cotton Bowl, is about to be tackled by Alabama fullback Tommy Lewis (42). The only problem was that Lewis was not in the game at the time, but just decided to come off the bench and stop Moegle. Rice was awarded a touchdown by the officials and went on to pummel the Crimson Tide 28–6.

The blond-haired All-American started the day with a 48-yard touchdown pass to halfback Joe Baumgardner. Then he proceeded to score four touchdowns himself, three by running and one on a pass reception, plus a fifth on a throw to Rex Baumgardner. In between, he kicked four extra points for the Longhorns. At day's end he had completed 11 of 12 passes, mostly to All-American end Hub Bechtol, and engineered 466 total yards.

Layne's 4 touchdowns, 28 points scored, 4 conversions, and completion percentage of .917 all became long-standing Cotton Bowl records. And the 67 points scored in the game was the highest total in a Cotton Bowl contest up until 1985, when Boston College beat Houston 45–28.

SCORING

Texas	14	7	6	13—40
Missouri	7	7	0	13—27

Texas:	Touchdowns—Baumgardner (2), Layne (4); PAT—Layne (4).
Missouri:	Touchdowns—Oakes, Dellastatious, Bonnett, Hopkins; PAT—Kekeris (3).

1949
Southern Methodist 21
Oregon   13

There was a plentiful supply of present and future All-Americans on hand for the 1949 Cotton Bowl classic. Southern Methodist had Doak Walker and Kyle Rote in the backfield, while Norm Van Brocklin quarterbacked Oregon.

The Mustangs of Southern Methodist, whose campus was only a few miles from the Cotton Bowl, were the favorites both with the oddsmakers and the 69,000 fans who packed the recently enlarged stadium. They had reason to be happy from the opening kickoff, which SMU received and then, behind Doak Walker's guidance, took down the length of the field, where Walker carried it in from the 1-yard line.

Oregon had no trouble gaining yards in the first half, but they could not score points. And they fell behind further at the start of the second half when Kyle Rote broke loose on a 36-yard touchdown jaunt. SMU scored again in the final period to provide the winning margin, overcoming Norm Van Brocklin's two touchdown strikes in the same period.

SCORING

| SMU | 7 | 0 | 7 | 7—21 |
| Oregon | 0 | 0 | 0 | 13—13 |

| SMU: | Touchdowns—Walker, Rote, Roberts; PAT—Walker (2), Ethridge. |
| Oregon: | Touchdowns—Wilkins, Sanders; PAT—Daniels. |

1957

Texas Christian 28
Syracuse   27

Texas Christian had not won a Cotton Bowl game since the very first one back in 1937. And Syracuse had made only one appearance in a major bowl game, and that was its 61–6 humiliation at the hands of Alabama in the 1953 Orange Bowl.

In 1957, the TCU Horned Frogs had All-American Jim Swink at halfback, and the Syracuse Orangemen had All-American Jim Brown to carry the

Jim Swink, carrying the ball here, scored what turned out to be the game-winning touchdown as TCU snuck by Syracuse 28–27 in 1957.

Jim Brown (44) ran for three touchdowns against Texas Christian in 1957 at the Cotton Bowl but Syracuse lost to the Horned Frogs by a point.

ball for them. The game was touted as a battle between the dazzling open-field running of Swink and the enormous power of Brown. Both lived up to their reputations that day, especially Brown. With Syracuse trailing by a touchdown in the second quarter, he blasted in twice for touchdowns and kicked two extra points to keep the Orangemen in the game. The Horned Frogs scored again, and the teams went to their dressing rooms at a 14–14 deadlock.

TCU took the lead in the third period when quarterback Chuck Curtis swept left end for a touchdown, but Brown tied it up on another run in the final quarter. Then Swink got into the scoring column to give the Frogs a 28–21 lead. Brown pounded out yardage and then decoyed the Texas Christian defense to let Chuck Zimmerman loft a 27-yard touchdown pass to halfback Jim Ridlon.

There was only a little over a minute when Brown lined up for the game-tying conversion. But a substitute end by the name of Chico Mendoza became the New Year's Day hero when he broke into the backfield to slap away Brown's kick and give Texas Christian a long-awaited Cotton Bowl triumph.

SCORING

| TCU | 7 | 7 | 7 | 7—28 |
| Syracuse | 0 | 14 | 0 | 13—27 |

| TCU: | Touchdowns—Nikkell, Shofner, Curtis, Swink; PAT—Pollard (4). |
| Syracuse: | Touchdowns—Brown (3), Ridlon; PAT—Brown (3). |

Ara Parseghian (left) and Darrell Royal shake hands after Texas defeated Notre Dame 21–17 in the 1970 Cotton Bowl.

1970

Texas   21
Notre Dame 17

Texas was number one in the nation going into the Cotton Bowl, with a record of 10-0. (Only Penn State, similarly undefeated, threatened their crown.) Notre Dame, under Ara Parseghian, prided itself as a spoiler, and the Fighting Irish were at a bowl game for the first time since the Four Horsemen ran over Ernie Nevers and Stanford at the Rose Bowl 45 years earlier.

Texas fans, including former President Lyndon B. Johnson, thronged the Cotton Bowl to see their team clinch the national title. Coach Darrell Royal's Texas team had decimated Tennessee in the Cotton Bowl the year before, and from that squad remained quarterback James Street and running back Ted Koy (whose older brother Ernie had led Texas to an Orange Bowl triumph in 1965). The Longhorns also had halfback Jim Bertelsen and All-American fullback Steve Worster; and Royal's team had won 19 consecutive games.

On the other hand, Notre Dame had a quarterback named Joe Theismann and a gifted receiver in Tom Gatewood, a combination that could stun any team. Texas was a predictable 7-point favorite.

The Irish, however, dominated the game, taking a 3–0 lead at the end of the first quarter and producing a 10–7 margin at halftime, the touchdown coming on a 54-yard pass play from Theismann to Gatewood.

Nobody scored in the third period, but then in the final quarter Texas wrested the lead when Ted Koy ran for a touchdown. But Notre Dame came right back, Theismann this time finding Jim Yoder free and clear for a go-ahead touchdown.

In the end it was fourth-down gambles that Darrell Royal used to sink the Irish. The first one took place on the Notre Dame 20-yard line with about four and a half minutes left. A field goal would have tied the game, but Royal disdained that and ran the ball instead. The Longhorns picked up the first down, and seconds continued to tick off the clock. The drive continued to the 10-yard line, and again it was fourth down, this time with two yards to go.

Again the field goal kicker stayed on the Texas bench. James Street took the ball from center, rolled out on an option, and then threw a fluttery pass that

Cotton Speyrer picked off his shoelaces at the two. Another first down. Notre Dame rebuffed the Longhorns on two plays, but finally, with just over a minute left, running back Billy Dale found a hole and squeezed into the end zone.

The score was 21–17 in favor of Texas, but the game was far from over. Theismann moved the Irish quickly and deftly, all the way to the Texas 38-yard line. With a half-minute left he dropped back again, and it appeared he had a receiver open at the 14, but Texas defensive back Tom Campbell stepped up and snatched the ball. The interception killed Notre Dame's dream.

Defensive Battles

In the history of the four major bowls—Rose, Orange, Sugar, and Cotton—there have only been three scoreless ties, and two of them have occurred in the Cotton. In the rain, snow and mud of 1947, Arkansas and a Y. A. Tittle–led Louisiana State ended up 0–0; and in 1959 neither Texas Christian nor the Air Force Academy could post any points. The only other scoreless tie occurred in the Rose Bowl back in 1922, when California met Washington & Jefferson.

Notre Dame quarterback Joe Theismann is ready to hand off here in 1970. Theismann threw two touchdowns that day in the Cotton Bowl, but the Irish still lost to Texas by four points.

The Hall of Fame Classic

(Birmingham, Alabama)

Date	Schools	Score
12-22-77	Maryland	17
	Minnesota	7
12-20-78	Texas A&M	28
	Iowa State	12
12-29-79	Missouri	24
	South Carolina	14
12-27-80	Arkansas	34
	Tulane	15
12-31-81	Mississippi State	10
	Kansas	0
12-31-82	Air Force	36
	Vanderbilt	28
12-22-83	West Virginia	20
	Kentucky	16
12-29-84	Kentucky	20
	Wisconsin	19

The Aloha Bowl

(Honolulu, Hawaii)

Date	Schools	Score
12-25-82	Washington	21
	Maryland	20
12-26-83	Penn State	13
	Washington	10
12-29-84	SMU	27
	Notre Dame	20

The Holiday Bowl

(San Diego, California)

Date	Schools	Score
12-22-78	Navy	23
	Brigham Young	16
12-21-79	Indiana	38
	Brigham Young	37
12-17-80	Brigham Young	46
	SMU	45
12-18-81	Brigham Young	38
	Washington State	36
12-17-82	Ohio State	47
	Brigham Young	17
12-23-83	Brigham Young	21
	Missouri	17
12-21-84	Brigham Young	24
	Michigan	17

Bowls That Never Made It

Bowl/Location	Date of First and Last Game(s)		
Alamo San Antonio, TX	1/4/47	Hardin-Simmons Denver	20 0
Aviation Dayton, OH	12/9/61	New Mexico Western Michigan	28 12
Bacardi Havana, Cuba	1/1/37	Auburn Villanova	7 7
Bluegrass Louisville, KY	12/13/58	Oklahoma State Florida State	15 6
Camellia Lafayette, LA	12/30/48	Hardin-Simmons Wichita State	49 12
Delta Memphis, TN	1/1/48	Mississippi TCU	13 9
Dixie Birmingham, AL	1/1/48	Arkansas William & Mary	21 19
	1/1/49	Baylor Wake Forest	20 7
Dixie Classic Dallas, TX	1/2/22	Texas A&M Centre	22 14
	1/1/34	Arkansas Centenary	7 7
El Paso Charity El Paso, TX	1/2/33	SMU Texas-El Paso	26 0
Ft. Worth Classic Ft. Worth, TX	1/1/21	Centre TCU	63 7
Garden State East Rutherford, NJ	12/16/78	Arizona State Rutgers	34 18
	12/13/81	Tennessee Wisconsin	28 21
Gotham New York, NY	12/9/61	Baylor Utah State	28 9
	12/15/62	Nebraska Miami (Florida)	36 34
Grape Lodi, CA	12/13/47	Pacific Utah State	35 31
	12/11/48	Hardin-Simmons Pacific	35 35
Great Lakes Cleveland, OH	12/6/47	Kentucky Villanova	24 14
Harbor San Diego, CA	1/1/47	New Mexico Montana State	13 13
	1/1/49	Villanova Nevada-Reno	27 7
Los Angeles Christmas Festival Los Angeles, CA	12/25/24	USC Missouri	20 7
Mercy Los Angeles, CA	11/23/61	Fresno State Bowling Green	36 6
New York City Charity New York, NY	12/6/30	Colgate NYU	7 6
	12/5/31	Tennessee NYU	13 0
Oil Houston, TX	1/1/46	Georgia Tulsa	20 6
	1/1/47	Georgia Tech St. Mary's	41 19
Pasadena Pasadena, CA	12/2/67	West Texas State Northridge State	35 13
	12/18/71	Memphis State San Jose State	28 9
Pittsburgh Charity Pittsburgh, PA	12/5/31	Carnegie Tech Duquesne	0 0
Presidential Cup College Park, MD	12/9/50	Texas A&M Georgia	40 20
Raisin Fresno, CA	1/1/46	Drake Fresno State	13 12
	12/31/49	San Jose State Texas Tech	20 13
Salad Phoenix, AZ	1/1/48	Nevada-Reno North Texas State	13 6
	1/1/52	Houston Dayton	26 21
San Diego East-West Christmas San Diego, CA	12/26/21	Centre Arizona	38 0
	12/25/22	West Virginia Gonzaga	21 13
Shrine Little Rock, AR	12/18/48	Hardin-Simmons Ouachita	40 12

The College All-Star Game

The College All-Star game was inaugurated in 1934, the brainchild of *Chicago Tribune* sports columnist Arch Ward. It was designed to serve as a cavalcade of the finest college football players in the nation, brought together to challenge the National Football League champions. All proceeds of the games were turned over to the Chicago Tribune Charities, which distributed millions of dollars to worthy organizations over the 43-year history of the classic.

Players for the College All-Star squad were selected by a poll conducted by the *Tribune* and more than 100 other newspapers throughout the country. Traditionally they were seniors who had completed their college eligibility the previous season, although underclassmen were selected during the war years. It was a special honor to be chosen for the starting team, though many of pro football's greatest players saw little or no action when playing as All-Stars.

The game was scheduled annually to precede the pro football exhibition season, and came to stand as the unofficial launch of the football season. A total of 42 games were played between 1934 and 1976, skipped only once, in 1974, due to the NFL players-owners dispute that year. All the games were played at Soldier Field in Chicago, except two during World War II, which were staged instead at Northwestern University's Dyche Stadium, a few miles north of Chicago.

The pros won 31 of the games, the All-Stars only 9; 2 ended in ties. Among the pros the Green Bay Packers appeared in the most, 8, with the Chicago Bears' 7 a close second. Following are the results, All-Star starting teams, and highlights of each classic.

1934

All-Stars   0
Chicago Bears 0

STARTING LINEUP

Position	Player	School
E	Eggs Manske	Northwestern
E	Joe Skladany	Pittsburgh
T	Moose Krause	Notre Dame
T	Abe Schwammel	Oregon State
G	Frank Walton	Pittsburgh
G	Bob Jones	Indiana
C	Chuck Bernard	Michigan
QB	Homer Griffith	USC
HB	Beattie Feathers	Tennessee
HB	Joe Laws	Iowa
FB	Mike Mikulak	Oregon
Coach	Nobel Kizer	Purdue

Highlights

Moose Krause recovered a Bear fumble inside the All-Stars 20 yard-line to stop a scoring drive in the second quarter.

The Bears blocked a 41-yard field goal attempt on the last play of the game.

1935

Chicago Bears 5
All-Stars   0

STARTING LINEUP

Position	Player	School
E	Don Hutson	Alabama
E	Ray Fuqua	SMU
T	Tony Blazine	Illinois
T	Jim Barber	San Francisco
G	Regis Monahan	Ohio State
G	Bill Bevan	Minnesota
C	George Shotwell	Pittsburgh
QB	Miller Munjas	Pittsburgh
HB	Bill Shepherd	Western Maryland
HB	Al Nichelini	St. Mary's
FB	Stan Kostka	Minnesota
Coach	Frank Thomas	Alabama

Highlights

Jack Manders kicked a 27-yard field goal for the Bears in the first quarter.

Bear defenders tackled Bill Shepherd in the end zone for a safety in the final period.

1936

All-Stars   7
Detroit Lions 7

STARTING LINEUP

Position	Player	School
E	Wayne Millner	Notre Dame
E	Keith Topping	Stanford
T	Dick Smith	Minnesota
T	Truman Spain	SMU
G	Paul Tangora	Northwestern
G	Vernon Oech	Minnesota
C	Gomer Jones	Ohio State
QB	Riley Smith	Alabama
HB	Jay Berwanger	Chicago
HB	Bill Shakespeare	Notre Dame
FB	Sheldon Beise	Minnesota
Coach	Bernie Bierman	Minnesota

Highlights

Babe LeVoir came off the bench for the All-Stars and raced 17 yards for a touchdown in the second quarter.

Detroit Lions halfback Ernie Caddell carried the ball 8 yards for a touchdown in the fourth quarter, and the extra point from Dutch Clark tied the game.

1937

All-Stars 6
Green Bay Packers 0

STARTING LINEUP

Position	Player	School
E	Gaynell Tinsley	Louisiana State
E	Merle Wendt	Ohio State
T	Ed Widseth	Minnesota
T	Averell Daniell	Pittsburgh
G	Max Starcevich	Washington
G	Steve Reid	Northwestern
C	Earl Svendsen	Minnesota
QB	Vern Huffman	Indiana
HB	Bobby LaRue	Pittsburgh
HB	Johnny Drake	Purdue
FB	Sam Francis	Nebraska
Coach	Gus Dorais	Detroit

Highlights

Sammy Baugh of Texas Christian connected with Gaynell Tinsley on a 47-yard touchdown pass play in the first quarter. Baugh completed a total of 7 of 13 passes for 115 yards.

Arnie Herber gained 202 yards on 14 completions for the Packers.

1938

All-Stars 28
Washington Redskins 16

STARTING LINEUP

Position	Player	School
E	Perry Schwartz	California
E	Chuck Sweeney	Notre Dame
T	Fred Shirey	Nebraska
T	Vic Markov	Washington
G	Joe Routt	Texas A&M
G	Leroy Monsky	Alabama
C	Ralph Wolf	Ohio State
QB	Andy Puplis	Notre Dame
HB	Cecil Isbell	Purdue
HB	Andy Uram	Minnesota
FB	Frank Patrick	Pittsburgh
Coach	Bo McMillin	Indiana

Highlights

Jim McDonald of Ohio State kicked a 15-yard field goal in the first quarter.

Redskin fullback Max Krause plunged in for a touchdown to give Washington a 7–3 lead.

Riley Smith booted a 30-yard field goal for the Redskins in the second quarter.

Cecil Isbell tossed a 39-yard touchdown pass to John Kovatch of Northwestern in the third quarter, but the extra point was missed. Bill Daugherty of Santa Clara intercepted a Redskin pass and ran it back 40 yards for another score. The conversion was missed again, giving the All-Stars a 15–10 lead at the end of the third quarter.

Corby Davis of Indiana carried for a touchdown in the fourth period. This time the extra point was blocked.

George Karamatic scored for Washington from the 2 to bring the Redskins within 5 points, 21–16.

Andy Uram intercepted another Redskin pass and carried it 35 yards for the game's final score.

1939

New York Giants 9
All-Stars 0

STARTING LINEUP

Position	Player	School
E	Bowden Wyatt	Tennessee
E	Earl Brown	Notre Dame
T	Joe Mihal	Purdue
T	Bob Haak	Indiana
G	Frank Twedell	Minnesota
G	Ralph Heikkinen	Michigan
C	Charlie Brock	Nebraska
QB	Davey O'Brien	Texas Christian
HB	Marshall Goldberg	Pittsburgh
HB	Bob MacLeod	Dartmouth
FB	Howard Weiss	Wisconsin
Coach	Elmer Layden	Notre Dame

Highlights

Ward Cuff kicked a 34-yard field goal for the Giants in the first quarter.

Ken Strong kicked two more field goals for New York, one in the second quarter and the other in the fourth.

1940

Green Bay Packers 45
All-Stars 28

STARTING LINEUP

Position	Player	School
E	Bill Fisk	USC
E	Esco Sarkinen	Ohio State
T	Nick Cutlich	Northwestern
T	Tad Harvey	Notre Dame
G	Jim Logan	Indiana
G	Harry Smith	USC
C	Bulldog Turner	Hardin-Simmons
QB	Ambrose Schindler	USC
HB	Nile Kinnick	Iowa
HB	Lou Brock	Purdue
FB	Joe Thesing	Notre Dame
Coach	Eddie Anderson	Iowa

Highlights

Ambrose Schindler gave the All-Stars the lead when he ran 6 yards for the game's first score.

Cecil Isbell threw 2 touchdown passes for Green Bay in the same period, one for 81 yards to Don Hutson, and the other for 26 yards to Moose Mulleneaux.

The Packers Arnie Herber hit Andy Uram on a 60-yard touchdown pass and then Isbell came back on to throw a 35-yarder to Hutson in the second quarter.

Nile Kinnick threw a 56-yard touchdown pass to Banks McFadden of Clemson.

Herber hit Hutson for a 29-yard Packers touchdown in the third period.

Schindler scored again for the All-Stars in the last quarter on a 1-yard run.

Isbell carried the ball 4 yards for another Packers touchdown, and Ernie Smith added a 34-yard field goal, giving Green Bay a total of 45 points, the most ever scored by one team in the classic. This was also the highest-scoring College All-Star game in history.

1941

Chicago Bears 37
All-Stars   13

STARTING LINEUP

Position	Player	School
E	Dave Rankin	Purdue
E	Ed Rucinski	Indiana
T	Ernie Plannell	Texas A&M
T	Nick Drahos	Cornell
G	Augie Lio	Georgetown
G	Tommy O'Boyle	Tulane
C	Rudy Mucha	Washington
QB	Forest Evashevski	Michigan
HB	Tom Harmon	Michigan
HB	Sonny Franck	Minnesota
FB	George Paskvan	Wisconsin
Coach	Carl Snavely	Cornell

Highlights

Sid Luckman completed a 34-yard touchdown pass to Ken Kavanaugh for the Bears first score.

Tom Harmon passed 22 yards to Sonny Franck to tie the game in the first quarter.

Harry Clark ran for two more Bear touchdowns, both 1-yard plunges.

Charlie O'Rourke of Boston College threw to Jackie Robinson of UCLA for a 46-yard touchdown play.

In the fourth period, the Bears Sid Luckman hit George McAfee on a 25-yard touchdown pass, and Young Bussey threw to Bob Nowaskey for another score.

1942

Chicago Bears 21
All-Stars   0

STARTING LINEUP

Position	Player	School
E	Mal Kutner	Texas
E	Judd Ringer	Minnesota
T	Jim Daniell	Ohio State
T	Al Blozis	Georgetown
G	Rob Jeffries	Missouri
G	Bernie Crimmins	Notre Dame
C	Vince Banonis	Detroit
QB	Dick Erdlitz	Northwestern
HB	Bruce Smith	Minnesota
HB	Steve Juzwik	Notre Dame
FB	Jack Graf	Ohio State
Coach	Bob Zuppke	Illinois

Highlights

Hugh Gallarneau ran 4 yards for a Chicago touchdown in the first quarter, and scored on an 8-yard run in the third quarter.

Young Bussey passed for the Bears other touchdown, a 21-yarder to Hampton Pool.

Steve Juzwik ran 91 yards from scrimmage to the Bears 6-yard line, but the collegians could not score on the ensuing four downs.

1943

All-Stars   27
Washington Redskins 7

STARTING LINEUP

Position	Player	School
E	Pete Pihos	Indiana
E	Bill Huber	Notre Dame
T	Al Wistert	Michigan
T	Dick Wildung	Minnesota
G	Felix Bucek	Texas A&M
G	Buster Ramsey	William & Mary
C	Vic Lindskog	Stanford
QB	Dick Renfro	Washington State
HB	Otto Graham	Northwestern
HB	Bob Steuber	Missouri
FB	Pat Harder	Wisconsin
Coach	Harry Stuhldreyer	Wisconsin

Highlights

Bob Steuber returned a punt 50 yards to give the All-Stars their first score.

Redskin Sammy Baugh lobbed a 6-yard touchdown pass to Joe Aguirre in the second quarter.

Glenn Dobbs of Tulsa threw to Pat Harder on a 37-yard touchdown pass.

Otto Graham ran back an interception 97 yards for a touchdown in the third quarter.

Pat Harder raced 33 yards for the All-Stars final score in the fourth quarter.

—

1944

Chicago Bears 24
All-Stars   21

STARTING LINEUP

Position	Player	School
E	John Dugger	Ohio State
E	John Yonakor	Notre Dame
T	Bill Willis	Ohio State
T	Bob Zimny	Indiana
G	Dick Barwegan	Purdue
G	Lin Houston	Ohio State
C	John Tavener	Indiana
QB	Lou Saban	Indiana
HB	Glenn Dobbs	Tulsa
HB	Charlie Trippi	Georgia
FB	Creighton Miller	Notre Dame
Coach	Lynn Waldorf	Northwestern

Highlights

The All-Stars took a 14–0 lead into the second quarter on a touchdown pass from Glenn Dobbs to Creighton Miller, and a Dobbs fumble, recovered in the end zone by teammate John Tavener.

The Bears scored twice in the second quarter: Gary Famiglietti carried from the 3, and Sid Luckman passed 12 yards to Jim Benton.

Lou Saban gave the All-Stars the lead in the third period when he carried from the 1-yard line.

Scooter McLean sprinted 19 yards for a Chicago touchdown.

Pete Gudauskas kicked a 13-yard field goal in the final period to win the game for the Bears.

1945

Green Bay Packers 19
All-Stars   7

STARTING LINEUP

Position	Player	School
E	Ted Cook	Alabama
E	Bill Huber	Notre Dame
T	Bob Zimny	Indiana
T	Ralph Foster	Oklahoma A&M
G	Damon Tassos	Texas A&M
G	Glen Burgeis	Tulsa
C	Tex Warrington	Auburn
QB	Charlie Mitchell	Tulsa
HB	Charlie Trippi	Georgia
HB	Don Greenwood	Illinois
FB	Bob Kennedy	Washington State
Coach	Bernie Bierman	Minnesota

Highlights

Don Hutson kicked a 20-yard field goal for the Packers, the only score in the first period.

Following a safety, which gave the Pack a 5–0 lead, Tex McKay added a touchdown on a 20-yard reception.

The All-Stars scored when Bob Kennedy passed to Nick

Scollard of St. Joseph's (Indiana) on a 68-yard play.

Don Hutson picked off a pass from Perry Moss of Illinois and sped 85 yards for a Green Bay touchdown in the fourth quarter.

1946

All-Stars   16
Los Angeles Rams 0

STARTING LINEUP

Position	Player	School
E	Jack Russell	Baylor
E	Ralph Heywood	USC
T	Martin Ruby	Texas A&M
T	Derrell Palmer	Texas Christian
G	Visco Grgich	Santa Clara
G	Buster Ramsey	William & Mary
C	Bill Godwin	Georgia
QB	Otto Graham	Northwestern
HB	Billy Hillenbrand	Indiana
HB	Dub Jones	Tulane
FB	Pat Harder	Wisconsin
Coach	Bo McMillin	Indiana

Highlights

Elroy "Crazylegs" Hirsch of Wisconsin came off the bench and streaked 68 yards for a touchdown in the first quarter for the All-Stars.

Hirsch and quarterback Otto Graham teamed up for a 62-yard pass-play touchdown in the third quarter.

Rams halfback Kenny Washington was tackled in the end zone for a safety in the fourth quarter.

1947

All-Stars   16
Chicago Bears 0

STARTING LINEUP

Position	Player	School
E	Horace Gillom	Nevada
E	Joe Tereschinski	Georgia
T	Dick Barwegan	Purdue
T	Joe Mastrangelo	Notre Dame
G	Alex Agase	Illinois
G	Weldon Humble	Rice
C	Paul Duke	Georgia Tech
QB	George Ratterman	Notre Dame
HB	Buddy Young	Illinois
HB	Vic Schwall	Northwestern
FB	Jim Mello	Notre Dame
Coach	Frank Leahy	Notre Dame

Highlights

A record 105,840 fans attend the game.

Jim Mello scored the first All-Stars touchdown on a 6-yard run in the first quarter, but the extra point was blocked.

Jack Zilly of Notre Dame caught a 46-yard touchdown pass from George Ratterman in the same period for the All-Stars.

Ernie Case of UCLA kicked a 21-yard field goal in the third quarter.

1948
Chicago Cardinals 28
All-Stars   0

STARTING LINEUP

Position	Player	School
E	Paul Cleary	USC
E	Len Ford	Michigan
T	George Connor	Notre Dame
T	Ziggy Czarobski	Notre Dame
G	Arnie Weinmeister	Washington
G	Howard Brown	Indiana
C	Dick Scott	Navy
QB	Johnny Lujack	Notre Dame
HB	Bob Chappius	Michigan
HB	Charlie Conerly	Mississippi
FB	Chalmers Elliott	Michigan
Coach	Frank Leahy	Notre Dame

Highlights

Elmer Angsman scored the Cardinals first touchdown on a 2-yard plunge in the first quarter.

Vic Schwall ran 14 yards for another Chicago touchdown in the second quarter.

Vince Banonis intercepted a pass by Perry Moss of Ilinois in the fourth quarter and ran 31 yards for a Cardinal score in the fourth quarter.

The final Chicago touchdown came when Charlie Trippi caught a 13-yard pass from Ray Mallouf.

1949
Philadelphia Eagles 38
All-Stars   0

STARTING LINEUP

Position	Player	School
E	Barney Poole	Mississippi
E	Mel Sheehan	Missouri
T	George Petrovich	Texas
T	Al DeRogatis	Duke
G	Marty Wendell	Notre Dame
G	Bill Fischer	Notre Dame
C	Chuck Bednarik	Pennsylvania
QB	Jack Mitchell	Oklahoma
HB	George Taliaferro	Indiana
HB	Jerry Williams	Washington State
FB	Joe Geri	Georgia
Coach	Bud Wilkinson	Oklahoma

Highlights

Steve Van Buren scored the first Eagles touchdown on a 1-yard run in the second quarter.

Cliff Patton kicked a 14-yard field goal and 5 extra points for Philadelphia.

Russ Craft scored on a 4-yard run, and Noble Doss carried another in from the 4-yard line.

Tommy Thompson hit Pete Pihos in the end zone for another Philadelphia score.

1950
All-Stars   17
Philadelphia Eagles 7

STARTING LINEUP

Position	Player	School
E	Art Weiner	North Carolina
E	Jim Martin	Notre Dame
T	Tiny Campora	Pacific
T	Bill Manley	Oklahoma
G	Porter Payne	Georgia
G	George Hughes	William & Mary
C	Clayton Tonnemaker	Minnesota
QB	Travis Tidwell	Auburn
HB	Doak Walker	SMU
HB	Hall Haynes	Santa Clara
FB	Curly Morrison	Ohio State
Coach	Eddie Anderson	Holy Cross

Highlights

Ralph Pasquariello of Villanova smashed through for the All-Stars' first touchdown.

Charlie ''Choo Choo'' Justice of North Carolina left the bench and took a pass from Pacific's Eddie LeBaron for another touchdown in the second period.

Steve Van Buren scored the Eagles only touchdown on a 1-yard plunge in the fourth quarter.

Gordie Soltau of Minnesota kicked a field goal for the All-Stars in the fourth quarter.

1951
Cleveland Browns 33
All-Stars   0

STARTING LINEUP

Position	Player	School
E	Don Stonesifer	Northwestern
E	Bob Wilkinson	UCLA
T	Bob Gain	Kentucky
T	Mike McCormack	Kansas
G	Bud McFadin	Texas
G	Lynn Lynch	Illinois
C	Jerry Groom	Notre Dame
QB	Bob Williams	Notre Dame
HB	Wilford White	Arizona State
HB	Kyle Rote	SMU
FB	Don Dufek	Michigan
Coach	Herman Hickman	Yale

Highlights

Len Ford tackled Bob Williams in the end zone to give the Browns their first 2 points.

Dub Jones ran for 2 touchdowns for Cleveland in the second and third quarters.

Lou Groza kicked a field goal and a total of 4 extra points for the Browns.

In the fourth quarter, Otto Graham threw touchdown passes to Dante Lavelli and Emerson Cole.

1952

Los Angeles Rams 10
All-Stars   7

STARTING LINEUP

Position	Player	School
E	Leo Sugar	Purdue
E	Billy Howton	Rice
T	Harold Mitchell	UCLA
T	Bill Pearmann	Tennessee
G	Don Coleman	Michigan State
G	Bob Ward	Maryland
C	Doug Mosley	Kentucky
QB	Babe Parilli	Kentucky
HB	Vic Janowicz	Ohio State
HB	Hugh McElhenny	Washington
FB	Ed Modzelewski	Maryland
Coach	Bobby Dodd	Georgia Tech

Highlights

Vic Janowicz broke through for a score in the second quarter to give the All-Stars a 7–0 lead at halftime.

In the fourth quarter, Ram fullback Tank Younger took a short pass from Norm Van Brocklin for the tying touchdown.

Bob Waterfield kicked a 24-yard field goal to win the game for the Rams.

1953

Detroit Lions 24
All-Stars   10

STARTING LINEUP

Position	Player	School
E	Bernie Flowers	Purdue
E	Tom Scott	Virginia
T	Kline Gilbert	Mississippi
T	J. D. Kimmel	Houston
G	Donn Moomaw	UCLA
G	Harley Sewell	Texas
C	George Morris	Georgia Tech
QB	Jack Scarbath	Maryland
HB	Fred Bruney	Ohio State
HB	Jim Sears	USC
FB	Buck McPhail	Oklahoma
Coach	Bobby Dodd	Georgia Tech

Highlights

Bob Hoernschemeyer carried from the 5 to give the Lions the lead in the first quarter.

Doak Walker kicked a field goal for Detroit, and Gib Dawson

of Texas booted one for the All-Stars in the second period.

Bobby Layne hit Cloyce Box for a Detroit touchdown in the third quarter.

Hunchy Hoernschemeyer plunged in for another Lions score in the final quarter.

Gib Dawson sprinted 17 yards for an All-Stars touchdown.

During the game Bobby Layne completed 21 of 31 passes for 323 yards.

1954

Detroit Lions 31
All-Stars   6

STARTING LINEUP

Position	Player	School
E	Carlton Massey	Texas
E	Dick Dietrick	Pittsburgh
T	Bob Morgan	Maryland
T	Stan Jones	Maryland
G	Jerry Hilgenberg	Iowa
G	Menil Mavraides	Notre Dame
C	Ed Beatty	Mississippi
QB	Zeke Bratkowski	Georgia
HB	Johnny Lattner	Notre Dame
HB	Chet Hanulak	Maryland
FB	Neil Worden	Notre Dame
Coach	Jim Tatum	Maryland

Highlights

The Lions scored 17 points in the first quarter on a 5-yard touchdown run by Doak Walker, a 4-yard run by Lew Carpenter, and a field goal by Jim Martin.

Johnny Lattner scored the All-Stars only touchdown on a 4-yard run in the third period.

Carpenter scored again for Detroit in the third quarter, and in the fourth quarter Jim Doran returned an All-Stars fumble 37 yards for another Detroit score.

1955

All-Stars   30
Cleveland Browns 27

STARTING LINEUP

Position	Player	School
E	Max Boydston	Oklahoma
E	Henry Hair	Georgia Tech
T	Jim Ray Smith	Baylor
T	Frank Varrichione	Notre Dame
G	Hank Bullough	Michigan State
G	Bud Brooks	Arkansas
C	Dick Szymanski	Notre Dame
QB	Ralph Guglielmi	Notre Dame
HB	Dick Moegle	Rice
HB	Dave Middleton	Auburn
FB	Alan Ameche	Wisconsin
Coach	Curly Lambeau	Retired

Highlights

Tad Weed of Ohio State kicked field goals in the first, third and fourth quarters for the All-Stars.

Quarterback George Ratterman snuck in from the 1 for a Cleveland touchdown in the first quarter.

Ray Renfro ran for another Cleveland touchdown in the second quarter.

Ralph Guglielmi threw a touchdown pass to Henry Hair for the All-Stars.

Just before halftime, Ratterman tossed to Renfro, on a 25-yard touchdown play.

Mel Triplett of Toledo ran from the 1 for the All-Stars in the fourth quarter.

Curly Morrison ran one in for the Browns before the final gun, but Cleveland was still 3 points shy.

1956

Cleveland Browns 26
All-Stars   0

STARTING LINEUP

Position	Player	School
E	Ron Beagle	Navy
E	Don Holleder	Army
T	Frank D'Agostino	Auburn
T	Bob Skoronski	Indiana
G	Hugh Pitts	Texas Christian
G	Sam Huff	West Virginia
C	Bob Pellegrini	Maryland
QB	Earl Morrall	Michigan State
HB	Howard Cassady	Ohio State
HB	Don McIlhenny	SMU
FB	Don Schaefer	Notre Dame
Coach	Curly Lambeau	Retired

Highlights

George Ratterman passed to Curly Morrison for the Browns first touchdown in the opening period.

Lou Groza kicked four field goals for Cleveland in the second and third quarters of 45, 37, 24 and 27 yards.

Gene Filipski ran from the 3 for Cleveland's last score of the game in the fourth quarter.

1957

New York Giants 22
All-Stars   12

STARTING LINEUP

Position	Player	School
E	Ron Kramer	Michigan
E	Tom Maentz	Michigan
T	Carl Vereen	Georgia Tech
T	Earl Leggett	Louisiana State
G	Dalton Truax	Tulane
G	Mike Sandusky	Maryland
C	Joe Amstutz	Indiana
QB	John Brodie	Stanford
HB	Jon Arnett	USC
HB	Abe Woodson	Illinois
FB	Don Bosseler	Miami (Florida)
Coach	Curly Lambeau	Retired

Highlights

Billy Barnes of Wake Forest got the All-Stars out to a 6-point lead in the first quarter when he carried the ball in from the 2-yard line.

A field goal by Ben Agajanian and a touchdown pass from Charlie Conerly to Ken McAfee gave the Giants a 10–9 lead at halftime.

Another touchdown pass from Conerly to McAfee in the third quarter, a field goal from Agajanian and a safety when Dick Nolan tackled All-Star back Abe Woodson in the end zone completed the Giants scoring.

Paige Cothren of Mississippi kicked two field goals for the All-Stars of 25 and 12 yards.

1958

All-Stars   35
Detroit Lions 19

STARTING LINEUP

Position	Player	School
E	Charlie Krueger	Texas A&M
E	Jim Gibbons	Iowa
T	Lou Michaels	Kentucky
T	Gene Hickerson	Mississippi
G	Jerry Kramer	Idaho
G	Bill Krisher	Oklahoma
C	Dan Currie	Michigan State
QB	King Hill	Rice
HB	Jim Pace	Michigan
HB	Bobby Joe Conrad	Texas A&M
FB	Walt Kowalczyk	Michigan State
Coach	Otto Graham	No Affiliation

Highlights

Tobin Rote passed to Jim Doran for the Lions first touchdown of the game in the first quarter.

The All-Stars amassed 20 points in the second quarter on 2 touchdown passes from Jim Ninowski of Michigan State to Bobby Mitchell of Illinois, and 2 field goals, of 19 and 33 yards, by Bobby Joe Conrad.

Bill Jobko of Ohio State sacked Tobin Rote in the end zone to give the All-Stars a safety in the third quarter.

Conrad kicked 2 more field goals in the fourth quarter, both 24-yarders.

Chuck Howley of West Virginia intercepted a Detroit pass and ran it back 29 yards for the last score of the game.

1959

Baltimore Colts 29
All-Stars   0

STARTING LINEUP

Position	Player	School
E	Buddy Dial	Rice
E	Dave Sherer	SMU
T	Gene Selawski	Purdue
T	Fran O'Brien	Michigan State
G	Mike Rabold	Indiana
G	Andy Cverko	Northwestern
C	Dan James	Ohio State
QB	Lee Grosscup	Utah
HB	Don Brown	Houston
HB	Dick Haley	Pittsburgh
FB	Nick Pietrosante	Notre Dame
Coach	Otto Graham	Coast Guard Academy

Highlights

After a safety put the Colts ahead by 2, Johnny Unitas increased the lead to 8 on a 3-yard pass to Raymond Berry.

Unitas threw 2 more touchdown passes in the second period, a 29-yarder to Jim Mutscheller and a 13-yard throw to L. G. Dupree.

Milt Davis picked off an All-Stars pass and returned it 36 yards for the Colts last score of the game.

1960

Baltimore Colts 32
All-Stars   7

STARTING LINEUP

Position	Player	School
E	Carroll Dale	Virginia Tech
E	Hugh McInnis	Southern Mississippi
T	Bob Denton	Pacific
T	Gene Gossage	Northwestern
G	Chuck Janerette	Penn State
G	Mike McGee	Duke
C	Bill Lapham	Iowa
QB	George Izo	Notre Dame
HB	Prentice Gault	Oklahoma
HB	Tom Moore	Vanderbilt
FB	Frank Mestnik	Marquette
Coach	Otto Graham	Coast Guard Academy

Highlights

Johnny Unitas connected with Lenny Moore for 3 Baltimore

touchdowns in the first half on pass plays of 4, 3 and 13 yards.

Steve Myrha kicked field goals of 38, 27, and 26 yards for the Colts.

Big Daddy Lipscomb sacked All-Stars quarterback George Izo in the end zone for a safety in the third quarter.

The All-Stars only score came on a 60-yard pass play from substitute quarterback Don Meredith of Southern Methodist to Prentice Gault.

1961

Philadelphia Eagles 28
All-Stars   14

STARTING LINEUP: OFFENSE

Position	Player	School
E	Aaron Thomas	Oregon State
E	Mike Ditka	Pittsburgh
T	Roland Lakes	Wichita
T	Jim Tyrer	Ohio State
G	Billy Shaw	Georgia Tech
G	Houston Antwine	Southern Illinois
C	Greg Larson	Minnesota
QB	Norm Snead	Wake Forest
HB	Pervis Atkins	New Mexico State
HB	Bernie Casey	Bowling Green
FB	Bill Brown	Illinois

DEFENSE

Position	Player	School
E	Earl Faison	Illinois
E	Bob Lilly	Texas Christian
T	Joe Rutgens	Illinois
T	Ernie Ladd	Grambling
LB	Frank Visted	Navy
LB	E. J. Holub	Texas Tech
LB	Fred Hageman	Kansas
DB	Tom Matte	Ohio State
DB	Ed Sharockman	Pittsburgh
DB	Claude Gibson	North Carolina State
DB	Joe Krakoski	Illinois
Coach	Otto Graham	Coast Guard Academy

Highlights

Sonny Jurgensen threw 2 touchdown passes in the first quarter, one to Tommy McDonald for 27 yards, and the other to Pete Retzlaff for 25 yards.

Tommy McDonald caught 2 more 24-yard touchdown passes, one from King Hill and the other from Jurgensen.

Billy Kilmer of UCLA came off the bench to throw a touchdown pass, and Dick Grecni of Ohio returned an interception 57 yards for a touchdown.

1962

Green Bay Packers 42
All-Stars   20

STARTING LINEUP: OFFENSE

Position	Player	School
E	Reg Carolan	Idaho
E	Charles Bryant	Ohio State
T	Fate Echols	Northwestern
T	Joe Carollo	Notre Dame
G	Dick Hudson	Memphis State
G	Roy Winston	Louisiana State
C	Wayne Frazier	Auburn
QB	John Hadl	Kansas
HB	Lance Alworth	Arkansas
HB	Curtis McClinton	Kansas
FB	Earl Gros	Louisiana State

DEFENSE

Position	Player	School
E	Frank Parker	Oklahoma State
E	Clark Miller	Utah State
T	Merlin Olsen	Utah State
T	John Meyers	Washington
LB	Bill Saul	Penn State
LB	Larry Onesti	Northwestern
LB	Frank Buncom	USC
DB	James Saxton	Texas
DB	Wendell Harris	Louisiana State
DB	T. Dellinger	North Carolina State
DB	A. Dabiero	Notre Dame
Coach	Otto Graham	Coast Guard Academy

Highlights

Earl Gros plunged in from the 1 to give the All-Stars the lead in the first quarter.

Bart Starr passed to Boyd Dowler for a touchdown of 22 yards to tie the score.

Starr connected again in the second quarter, this time with Ron Kramer, for a 4-yard touchdown.

John Hadl found Chuck Bryant of Ohio State for a 21-yard touchdown pass for the All-Stars.

Starr broke the game open with 3 touchdown passes in the second half, going to Boyd Dowler, for 22 yards, to Max McGee for 20 yards, and again to McGee for 36 yards.

Elijah Pitts ran for another touchdown from the 3-yard line.

1963

All-Stars   20
Green Bay Packers 17

STARTING LINEUP: OFFENSE

Position	Player	School
E	Pat Richter	Wisconsin
E	Bob Jencks	Miami (Ohio)
T	Bob Vogel	Ohio State
T	Daryl Sanders	Ohio State
G	Ed Budde	Michigan State
G	Don Chuy	Clemson
C	Dave Behrman	Michigan State
QB	Ron VanderKelen	Wisconsin
FL	Paul Flatley	Northwestern
HB	Larry Ferguson	Iowa
FB	Bill Thornton	Nebraska

DEFENSE

Position	Player	School
E	Fred Miller	Louisiana State
E	Don Brumm	Purdue
T	Chuck Sieminski	Penn State
T	Jim Dunaway	Mississippi
LB	Dave Robinson	Penn State
LB	Lee Roy Jordan	Alabama
LB	Bobby Bell	Minnesota
DB	Tom Janik	Texas A&M
DB	Larry Glueck	Villanova
DB	Lonnie Sanders	Michigan State
DB	Kermit Alexander	UCLA
Coach	Otto Graham	Coast Guard Academy

Highlights

Jim Taylor burst in from the 2 to give Green Bay the first score of the contest.

Larry Ferguson scored the first All-Stars touchdown in the second period on a 6-yard run.

Bob Jencks kicked a pair of field goals, 20 and 33 yards, for the All-Stars.

In the fourth quarter, Ron VanderKelen lobbed a short pass to Pat Richter, who raced for a 73-yard touchdown.

Jim Taylor muscled in from the 1 for a Green Bay score, but the Pack could not close the remaining 3-point deficit.

All-Americans of a Different Sort

Three recent presidents, Republicans all, made appearances on the college gridiron (Army's halfback, Dwight D. Eisenhower, rounds out the GOP foursome). Ronald Reagan played for Eureka College in Illinois, which was good training for when he played George Gipp as an actor in the film *Knute Rockne—All American*. (The photo shown here is taken from the film.)

Richard Nixon of Whittier College in California will probably be remembered in the football world more for his self-created role of unofficial adviser to the Washington Redskins during his presidency than for his collegiate performance.

Gerald Ford of Michigan was probably the best player of the trio, going to the College All-Star game in 1935. The beating he took as Michigan's center did, however, lead to a joke or two once he reached the Oval Office.

1964

Chicago Bears 28
All-Stars   17

STARTING LINEUP: OFFENSE

Position	Player	School
E	Chuck Logan	Northwestern
E	Ted Davis	Georgia Tech
T	Lloyd Voss	Nebraska
T	Ernie Borghetti	Pittsburgh
G	Harrison Rosdahl	Penn State
G	Dick Evey	Tennessee
C	Ray Kubala	Texas A&M
QB	Pete Beathard	USC
FL	Paul Warfield	Ohio State
HB	Tony Lorick	Arizona State
FB	Willie Crenshaw	Kansas State

DEFENSE

Position	Player	School
E	George Seals	Missouri
E	Ed Lothamer	Michigan
T	Tom Keating	Michigan
T	George Bednar	Notre Dame
LB	Wally Hilgenberg	Iowa
LB	Mike Reilly	Iowa
LB	Dave Wilcox	Oregon
DB	George Rose	Auburn
DB	Jerry Richardson	West Texas State
DB	Mel Renfro	Oregon
DB	Perry Lee Dunn	Mississippi
Coach	Otto Graham	Coast Guard Academy

Highlights

Dick VanRaaphorst of Ohio State started the scoring with a 14-yard field goal.

The Bears took the lead in the second quarter when tight end Mike Ditka scored on a 13-yard pass from Bill Wade.

Ted Davis scored for the All-Stars in the same period to give them a 10–3 halftime lead.

Bill Wade, on a quarterback sneak, regained the lead for the Bears in the third quarter.

The Bears pulled away on a 20-yard touchdown pass from Wade to Gary Barnes and a 30-yard scoring strike from Rudy Bukich to Charlie Bivins.

1965

Cleveland Browns 24
All-Stars   16

STARTING LINEUP: OFFENSE

Position	Player	School
E	Bob Hayes	Florida A&M
E	Fred Brown	Miami (Florida)
T	Ralph Neely	Oklahoma
T	Harry Schuh	Memphis State
G	Bob Breitenstein	Tulsa
G	Jim Wilson	Georgia
C	Bill Curry	Georgia Tech
QB	Roger Staubach	Navy
FL	Fred Biletnikoff	Florida State
HB	Pat Donnelly	Navy
FB	Ken Willard	North Carolina

DEFENSE

Position	Player	School
E	Jim Garcia	Purdue
E	Verlon Biggs	Jackson State
T	Joe Szczecko	Northwestern
T	Jim Norton	Washington
LB	Don Croftcheck	Indiana
LB	Dick Butkus	Illinois
LB	Marty Schottenheimer	Pittsburgh
DB	Clancy Williams	Washington State
DB	Roy Jefferson	Utah
DB	George Donnelly	Illinois
DB	Al Nelson	Cincinnati
Coach	Otto Graham	Coast Guard Academy

Highlights

Jim Brown scored from the 7 for the Browns in the first quarter.

Chuck Mercein of Yale booted a 36-yard field goal.

Stan Sczurek recovered a fumble for Cleveland in the end zone after teammate Jamie Caleb blocked an All-Star punt.

In the third period, Cleveland quarterback Frank Ryan threw a 10-yard pass to Gary Collins for another touchdown.

John Huarte of Notre Dame quarterbacked the All-Stars in the second half and threw two 5-yard touchdown passes, one to Chuck Mercein and the other to Lance Rentzel of Oklahoma.

1966

Green Bay Packers 38
All-Stars   0

STARTING LINEUP: OFFENSE

Position	Player	School
E	Gary Garrison	San Diego State
E	Milt Morin	Massachusetts
T	Dave McCormick	Louisiana State
T	Francis Peay	Missouri
G	John Niland	Iowa
G	Tom Mack	Michigan
C	Pat Killorin	Syracuse
QB	Steve Sloan	Alabama
FL	Roy Shivers	Utah State
HB	Donny Anderson	Texas Tech
FB	Johnny Roland	Missouri

DEFENSE

Position	Player	School
E	Stan Hindman	Mississippi
E	Aaron Brown	Minnesota
T	Jerry Shay	Purdue
T	George Rice	Louisiana State
LB	Doug Buffone	Louisville
LB	Tommy Nobis	Texas
LB	Don Hansen	Illinois
DB	Charlie King	Purdue
DB	S. Quintana	New Mexico
DB	Nick Rassas	Notre Dame
DB	Doug McFalls	Georgia
Coach	John Sauer	Retired

Highlights

Bart Starr hit Boyd Dowler on a 10-yard touchdown pass in the first quarter for the Packers.

Green Bay added three more touchdowns in the second period: Starr passed to Bill Anderson for one, Jim Taylor scored on a 1-yard plunge, and Herb Adderley returned an interception for 36 yards.

Don Chandler kicked a 17-yard field goal, and Jim Taylor ran 13 yards for a touchdown.

1967

Green Bay Packers 27
All-Stars   0

STARTING LINEUP: OFFENSE

Position	Player	School
E	Gene Washington	Michigan State
E	Tom Beer	Houston
T	Gene Upshaw	Texas A&I
T	Mike Current	Ohio State
G	Tom Regner	Notre Dame
G	Norman Davis	Grambling
C	Bob Hyland	Boston College
QB	Steve Spurrier	Florida
FL	Dave Williams	Washington
HB	Floyd Little	Syracuse
FB	Mel Farr	UCLA

DEFENSE

Position	Player	School
E	Leo Carroll	San Diego State
E	Alan Page	Notre Dame
T	Bubba Smith	Michigan State
T	Dave Rowe	Penn State
LB	George Webster	Michigan State
LB	Jim Lynch	Notre Dame
LB	Paul Naumoff	Tennessee
DB	Bob Grim	Oregon State
DB	Phil Clark	Northwestern
DB	Rick Volk	Michigan
DB	Henry King	Utah State
Coach	John Sauer	Retired

Highlights

Don Chandler kicked 2 field goals, 13- and 14-yarders, for Green Bay in the first quarter.

Boyd Dowler took an 11-yard pass from Bart Starr in the second period to increase the Packer lead to 10–0.

Starr threw a 22-yard touchdown pass to Bob Long later in the period.

Fullback Jim Grabowski broke free on a 22-yard touchdown run in the final period to complete Green Bay's attack.

1968

Green Bay Packers 34
All-Stars   17

STARTING LINEUP: OFFENSE

Position	Player	School
E	Bob Wallace	Texas-El Paso
E	Charlie Sanders	Minnesota
T	Mo Moorman	Texas A&M
T	Ron Yary	USC
G	Bill Leuck	Arizona
G	John Williams	Minnesota
C	Bob Johnson	Tennessee
QB	Gary Beban	UCLA
FL	Dennis Homan	Alabama
HB	MacArthur Lane	Utah State
FB	Larry Csonka	Syracuse

DEFENSE

E	Claude Humphrey	Tennessee State
E	Marv Upshaw	Trinity
T	Curley Culp	Arizona State
T	Bill Staley	Utah State
LB	Fred Carr	Texas-El Paso
LB	Mike McGill	Notre Dame
LB	Adrian Young	USC
DB	Jon Henderson	Colorado State
DB	Jim Smith	Oregon
DB	Bob Atkins	Grambling
DB	Major Hazelton	Florida A&M
Coach	Norm Van Brocklin	Retired

Highlights

Donny Anderson got Green Bay's first score with a 1-yard plunge in the first quarter.

Bart Starr tossed 2 more touchdowns for the Pack in the following period, both to Carroll Dale, for 20 and 36 yards.

The All-Stars' only score of the half came on a 22-yard field goal from Jerry DePoyster of Wyoming.

Gary Beban connected with Earl McCullouch of USC on a 7-yard touchdown pass in the third quarter. McCullouch caught another touchdown pass, a 24-yarder from Greg Landry of Massachusetts, in the final period.

Dale caught his third touchdown pass for Green Bay, a 23-yarder from Starr.

1969

New York Jets 26
All-Stars   24

STARTING LINEUP: OFFENSE

Position	Player	School
E	Jim Seymour	Notre Dame
E	Jerry LeVias	Southern Methodist
TE	Bob Klein	USC
T	Dave Foley	Ohio State
T	George Kunz	Notre Dame
G	Mike Montler	Colorado
G	John Shinners	Xavier
C	Jon Kolb	Oklahoma State
QB	Terry Hanratty	Notre Dame
HB	Altie Taylor	Utah State
FB	Paul Gipson	Houston

DEFENSE

E	Bill Stanfill	Georgia
E	Fred Dryer	San Diego State
T	Rich Moore	Villanova
T	Rolf Krueger	Texas A&M
LB	Ron Pritchard	Arizona State
LB	Bill Bergey	Arkansas State
LB	Bob Babich	Miami (Ohio)
DB	Jim Marsalis	Tennessee State
DB	Bill Thompson	Maryland State
DB	Roger Wehrli	Missouri
DB	Gene Eps	Texas-El Paso
Coach	Otto Graham	Retired

Highlights

Jim Turner kicked 2 field goals of 43 and 16 yards for the Jets in the first quarter.

Matt Snell powered in from the 3 to give New York a 13–0 halftime lead.

Greg Cook of Cincinnati came off the bench to hurl 3 touchdown passes in the second half: a 17-yarder to Gene Washington of Stanford, a 12-yarder to tight end Bob Klein of USC, and a 19-yard throw to Jerry LeVias of SMU.

Matt Snell broke loose for a 35-yard touchdown run for the Jets in the second half, and Jim Turner kicked 2 more field goals.

1970

Kansas City Chiefs 24
All-Stars   3

STARTING LINEUP: OFFENSE

Position	Player	School
E	Jerry Hendren	Idaho
E	Ron Shanklin	North Texas State
TE	Rich Caster	Jackson State
T	Bob McKay	Texas
T	Bob Asher	Vanderbilt
G	Doug Wilkerson	North Carolina Central
G	Chuck Hutchinson	Ohio State
C	Sid Smith	USC
QB	Dennis Shaw	San Diego State
HB	Bob Anderson	Colorado
FB	Art Malone	Arizona State

DEFENSE

E	Al Cowlings	USC
E	Cedric Hardman	North Texas State
T	Mike McCoy	Notre Dame
T	Mike Reid	Penn State
LB	John Small	Citadel
LB	Steve Zabel	Oklahoma
LB	Jim Files	Oklahoma
DB	Bruce Taylor	Boston
DB	Al Mathews	Texas A&I
DB	Charlie Waters	Clemson
DB	Steve Tannen	Florida
Coach	Otto Graham	Retired

Highlights

On the Chiefs first possession, Len Dawson passed to wide receiver Frank Pitts for a 36-yard touchdown.

In the second period, Warren McVea scored from the 3, and safety Jim Kearney picked off an All-Stars pass and returned it 65 yards for a touchdown.

1971

Baltimore Colts 24
All-Stars   17

STARTING LINEUP: OFFENSE

Position	Player	School
E	J. D. Hill	Arizona State
E	E. Jennings	Air Force
TE	Bob Moore	Stanford
T	Marv Montgomery	USC
T	Vern Holland	Tennessee State
G	Steve Lawson	Kansas
G	Henry Allison	San Diego State
C	Warren Koegel	Penn State
QB	Jim Plunkett	Stanford
HB	Mike Adamle	Northwestern
FB	John Brockington	Ohio State

DEFENSE

E	Jack Youngblood	Florida
E	Richard Harris	Grambling
T	Julius Adams	Texas Southern
T	Tony McGee	Bishop
LB	Ron Hornsby	Southeast Louisiana
LB	Isiah Robertson	Southern
LB	Jack Ham	Penn State
DB	Clarence Scott	Kansas State
DB	Ike Thomas	Bishop
DB	Jack Tatum	Ohio State
DB	Charles Hall	Pittsburgh
Coach	Blanton Collier	Retired

Highlights

Earl Morrall of the Colts started the scoring in the first period with a 24-yard strike to wide receiver Ray Perkins.

John Brockington burst in from the 1 to give the All-Stars their first score.

Morrall hit Tom Matte with a 15-yarder to regain the lead in the second quarter.

In the fourth quarter, Morrall passed for his third touchdown, a 44-yarder to tight end Tom Mitchell.

Jack Ham scooped up a Colts fumble in the fourth period and carried it 47 yards for an All-Stars touchdown.

1972

Dallas Cowboys 20
All-Stars   7

STARTING LINEUP: OFFENSE

Position	Player	School
E	Mike Siani	Villanova
E	Glenn Doughty	Michigan
TE	Riley Odoms	Houston
T	Lionel Antoine	Southern Illinois
T	Dan Yockum	Syracuse
G	Reggie McKenzie	Michigan
G	Steve Okoniewski	Montana
C	Bob Kuziel	Pittsburgh
QB	Jerry Tagge	Nebraska
HB	Jeff Kinney	Nebraska
FB	Franco Harris	Penn State

DEFENSE

E	Walt Patulski	Notre Dame
E	Sherman White	California
T	John Mendenhall	Grambling
T	Pete Lazetich	Stanford
LB	Willie Hall	USC
LB	Jeff Siemon	Stanford
LB	Mike Taylor	Michigan
DB	Willie Buchanan	San Diego State
DB	Tommy Casanova	Louisiana State
DB	Thom Darden	Michigan
DB	Craig Clemons	Iowa
Coach	Bob Devaney	Nebraska

Highlights

After a 31-yard field goal by Mike Clark, the Cowboys added an 18-yard touchdown pass from Craig Morton to wide receiver Ron Sellers, for a 10–0 halftime lead.

In the third quarter, Morton passed to Bob Hayes for 24 yards and another Dallas touchdown.

The All-Stars' only score came in the fourth period when fullback Robert Newhouse of Houston carried from the 1.

1973

Miami Dolphins 14
All-Stars   3

STARTING LINEUP: OFFENSE

Position	Player	School
E	Barry Smith	Florida State
E	Steve Holden	Arizona State
TE	Charles Young	USC
T	Paul Seymour	Michigan
T	Jerry Sisemore	Texas
G	Pete Adams	USC
G	John Hannah	Alabama
C	Dave Brown	USC
QB	Bert Jones	Louisiana State
HB	Terry Metcalf	Long Beach State
FB	Chuck Foreman	Miami (Florida)

DEFENSE

E	Wally Chambers	Eastern Kentucky
E	John Matuszak	Tampa
T	John Grant	USC
T	Richard Glover	Nebraska
LB	Jim Merlo	Stanford
LB	Jim Youngblood	Tennessee Tech
LB	Gary Weaver	Fresno State
DB	Mike Holmes	Texas Southern
DB	Burgess Owens	Miami (Florida)
DB	Jackie Wallace	Arizona
DB	J. T. Thomas	Florida State
Coach	John McKay	USC

Highlights

Larry Csonka scored for the Dolphins in the first period on a 3-yard run.

The All-Stars first and only score of the game came on a 10-yard field goal by Ray Guy of Southern Mississippi.

Csonka scored again in the fourth quarter, on a 7-yard run.

1974

The game was canceled because of a collective bargaining dispute between the NFL Players Association and the team owners.

1975

Pittsburgh Steelers 21
All-Stars 14

STARTING LINEUP: OFFENSE

Position	Player	School
E	Pat McInally	Harvard
E	Emmett Edwards	Kansas
TE	Russ Francis	Oregon
T	Dennis Harrah	Miami (Florida)
T	Kurt Schumacher	Ohio State
G	Ken Huff	North Carolina
G	Lynn Boden	South Dakota State
C	Kyle Davis	Oklahoma
QB	Steve Bartkowski	California
HB	Walter Payton	Jackson State
FB	Stan Winfrey	Arkansas State

DEFENSE

E	Mike Fanning	Notre Dame
E	Robert Brazile	Jackson State
T	Mike Hartenstine	Penn State
T	Randy White	Maryland
LB	Glenn Cameron	Florida
LB	Ralph Ortega	Florida
LB	Richard Wood	USC
DB	Louis Wright	San Jose State
DB	Neal Colzie	Ohio State
DB	Marvin Cobb	USC
DB	Charles Phillips	USC
Coach	John McKay	USC

Highlights

Steve Bartkowski tossed a 26-yard touchdown pass to Pat McInally in the first quarter for the All-Stars.

From the 2-yard line, Terry Bradshaw hit tight end Randy Grossman for a Steeler touchdown in the second period.

Virgil Livers of Western Kentucky returned a punt 86 yards for a touchdown before the half ended.

Joe Gilliam of the Steelers threw 6 yards to Rocky Bleier for a touchdown and then connected with wide receiver Frank Lewis on a 21-yarder to win the game.

1976

Pittsburgh Steelers 24
All-Stars 0

STARTING LINEUP: OFFENSE

Position	Player	School
E	Duriel Harris	New Mexico State
E	Brian Baschnagel	Ohio State
TE	Bennie Cunningham	Clemson
T	Mark Koncar	Colorado
T	Dennis Lick	Wisconsin
G	Tom Glassic	Virginia
G	Jackie Slater	Jackson State
C	Pete Brock	Colorado
QB	Mike Kruczek	Boston College
HB	Joe Washington	Oklahoma
FB	Tony Galbreath	Missouri

DEFENSE

E	Troy Archer	Colorado
E	James White	Oklahoma State
T	Lee Roy Selmon	Oklahoma
T	Dewey Selmon	Oklahoma
LB	Kevin McLain	Colorado State
LB	Ed Simonini	Texas A&M
LB	Larry Gordon	Arizona State
DB	Mario Clark	Oregon
DB	Aaron Kyle	Wyoming
DB	Ed Lewis	Kansas
DB	Shafer Suggs	Ball State
Coach	Ara Parseghian	Retired

Highlights

Roy Gerela kicked 3 field goals of 29, 32 and 23 yards for the Steelers in the first half.

After Pittsburgh picked up a safety in the third quarter to make the score 11–0, fullback Franco Harris charged 21 yards for a Steeler touchdown.

Reserve back Tommy Reamon of Pittsburgh scored the game's final touchdown from the 3 in the fourth quarter.

With one minute and 22 seconds remaining, the game was suspended when a sudden thunderstorm flooded the field, and with that the 43-year history of the College All-Star football game came to a close.

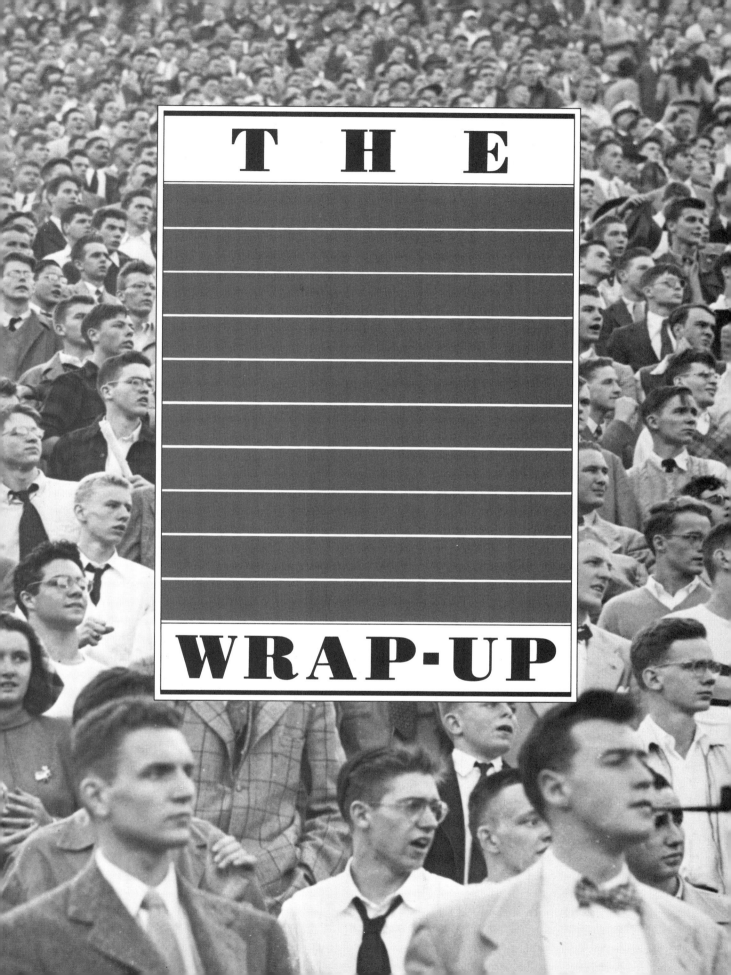

NCAA Division 1-A Records

CAREER

Total Offense

Yards

Doug Flutie	Boston College	(1981–84)	11,317
Jim McMahon	Brigham Young	(1977–78, 80–81)	9723
John Elway	Stanford	(1979–82)	9070
Ben Bennett	Duke	(1980–83)	9061
Steve Young	Brigham Young	(1981–83)	8817

Average Yards Per Game

Tony Eason	Illinois	(1981–82)	299.5
Steve Young	Brigham Young	(1981–83)	284.4
Doug Flutie	Boston College	(1981–84)	269.5
Jim Plunkett	Stanford	(1968–70)	254.4
Randall Cunningham	Nevada-Las Vegas	(1982–84)	249.2

Rushing

Yards Gained

Tony Dorsett	Pittsburgh	(1973–76)	6082
Charles White	USC	(1976–79)	5598
Herschel Walker	Georgia	(1980–82)	5259
Archie Griffin	Ohio State	(1972–75)	5177
George Rogers	South Carolina	(1977–80)	4958

Average Yards Per Game

Ed Marinaro	Cornell	(1969–71)	174.6
O. J. Simpson	USC	(1967–68)	164.4
Herschel Walker	Georgia	(1980–82)	159.4
Tony Dorsett	Pittsburgh	(1973–76)	141.4
Mike Rozier	Nebraska	(1981–83)	136.6

Passing

Passing Efficiency (minimum 325 completions)

Jim McMahon	Brigham Young	(1977–78, 80–81)	156.9
Steve Young	Brigham Young	(1981–83)	149.8
Danny White	Arizona State	(1971–73)	148.9
Gifford Nielsen	Brigham Young	(1975–77)	145.3
Tom Ramsey	UCLA	(1979–82)	143.9

Yardage

Doug Flutie	Boston College	(1981–84)	10,579
Ben Bennett	Duke	(1980–83)	9614
Jim McMahon	Brigham Young	(1977–78, 80–81)	9536
John Elway	Stanford	(1979–82)	9349
Mark Herrmann	Purdue	(1977–80)	9188

Completions

Ben Bennett	Duke	(1980–83)	820
John Elway	Stanford	(1979–82)	774
Mark Herrmann	Purdue	(1977–80)	717
Doug Flutie	Boston College	(1981–84)	677
Jim McMahon	Brigham Young	(1977–78, 80–81)	653

Receiving

Receptions

Howard Twilley	Tulsa	(1963–65)	261
Darrin Nelson	Stanford	(1977–78, 80–81)	214
Ron Sellers	Florida State	(1966–68)	212
Keith Edwards	Vanderbilt	(1980, 82–84)	200
Gerald Harp	Western Carolina	(1977–80)	197

Average Receptions Per Game

Howard Twilley	Tulsa	(1963–65)	10.0
Neal Sweeney	Tulsa	(1965–66)	7.4
John Love	North Texas State	(1965–66)	7.2
Ron Sellers	Florida State	(1966–68)	7.1
Barry Moore	North Texas State	(1968–69)	7.0

Yardage Gained

Ron Sellers	Florida State	(1966–68)	3598
Howard Twilley	Tulsa	(1963–65)	3343
Gerald Harp	Western Carolina	(1977–80)	3305
Rick Beasley	Appalachian State	(1978–80)	3124
Chuck Hughes	Texas-El Paso	(1964–66)	2882

Scoring

Total Points

Luis Zendejas	Arizona State	(1981–84)	368
Tony Dorsett	Pittsburgh	(1973–76)	356
Glenn Davis	Army	(1943–46)	354
Kevin Butler	Georgia	(1981–84)	353
Art Luppino	Arizona	(1953–56)	337

Average Points Per Game

Bob Gaiters	New Mexico State	(1959–60)	11.9
Ed Marinaro	Cornell	(1969–71)	11.8
Bill Burnett	Arkansas	(1968–70)	11.3
Steve Owens	Oklahoma	(1967–69)	11.2
Eddie Talboom	Wyoming	(1948–50)	10.8

Touchdowns Rushing

Steve Owens	Oklahoma	(1967–69)	56
Tony Dorsett	Pittsburgh	(1973–76)	55
Ed Marinaro	Cornell	(1969–71)	50
Mike Rozier	Nebraska	(1981–83)	50
Herschel Walker	Georgia	(1980–82)	49

Touchdowns Passing

Jim McMahon	Brigham Young	(1977–78, 80–81)	84
Joe Adams	Tennessee State	(1977–80)	81
John Elway	Stanford	(1979–82)	78
Dan Marino	Pittsburgh	(1979–82)	74
Doug Flutie	Boston College	(1981–84)	67

Touchdowns Receiving

Elmo Wright	Houston	(1968–70)	34
Howard Twilley	Tulsa	(1963–65)	32
Gerald Harp	Western Carolina	(1977–80)	26
Emanuel Tolbert	SMU	(1976–79)	25
Phil Odle	Brigham Young	(1965–67)	25

Field Goals

Louis Zendejas	Arizona State	(1981–83)	78
Kevin Butler	Georgia	(1981–84)	77
Fuad Reveiz	Tennessee	(1981–84)	71
Larry Roach	Oklahoma State	(1981–84)	68

Interceptions

Al Brosky	Illinois	(1950–52)	29
John Provost	Holy Cross	(1972–74)	27
Martin Bayless	Bowling Green	(1980–83)	27
Tom Curtis	Michigan	(1967–69)	25
Tony Thurman	Boston College	(1981–84)	25

Kickoff Returns Best Average

Forrest Hall	San Francisco	(1946–47)	36.2
Anthony Davis	USC	(1972–74)	35.1
Overton Curtis	Utah State	(1957–58)	31.0
Altie Taylor	Utah State	(1966–68)	29.3

Punt Returns Best Average

Jack Mitchell	Oklahoma	(1946–48)	23.6
Gene Gibson	Cincinnati	(1949–50)	20.5
Eddie Macon	Pacific	(1949–51)	18.9
Jackie Robinson	UCLA	(1939–40)	18.8

Punting Best Average

Marv Bateman	Utah	(1970–71)	46.9
Ricky Anderson	Vanderbilt	(1982–84)	45.6
Reggie Roby	Iowa	(1979–82)	45.6
Randall Cunningham	Nevada-Las Vegas	(1982–84)	45.6
Ray Guy	Southern Mississippi	(1970–72)	44.7

IN A SINGLE SEASON

Total Offense

Yards

Jim McMahon	Brigham Young	1980	4627
Steve Young	Brigham Young	1983	4346
Robbie Bosco	Brigham Young	1984	3932
Todd Dillon	Long Beach State	1982	3587
Doug Flutie	Boston College	1984	3603

Average Yards Per Game

Steve Young	Brigham Young	1983	395.1
Jim McMahon	Brigham Young	1980	385.6
Jim McMahon	Brigham Young	1981	345.8
Bill Anderson	Tulsa	1965	334.3
Robbie Bosco	Brigham Young	1984	327.7

Rushing

Yards

Marcus Allen	USC	1981	2342
Mike Rozier	Nebraska	1983	2148
Tony Dorsett	Pittsburgh	1976	1948
Herschel Walker	Georgia	1981	1891
Ed Marinaro	Cornell	1971	1881

Average Yards Per Game

Marcus Allen	USC	1981	212.9
Ed Marinaro	Cornell	1971	209.0
Charles White	USC	1979	180.3
Mike Rozier	Nebraska	1983	179.0
Tony Dorsett	Pittsburgh	1976	177.1

Passing

Passing Efficiency

Jim McMahon	Brigham Young	1980	176.9
Jerry Rhome	Tulsa	1964	172.6
Steve Young	Brigham Young	1983	168.5
Brian Dowling	Yale	1968	167.0
Dave Wilson	Ball State	1977	164.2

Yards Gained

Jim McMahon	Brigham Young	1980	380.9
Jim McMahon	Brigham Young	1981	355.5
Steve Young	Brigham Young	1983	354.7
Bill Anderson	Tulsa	1965	346.4
Marc Wilson	Brigham Young	1979	338.2

Completions

Steve Young	Brigham Young	1983	306
Bill Anderson	Tulsa	1965	296
Todd Dillon	Long Beach State	1982	289
Jim McMahon	Brigham Young	1980	284
Jim McMahon	Brigham Young	1981	272

Receiving

Receptions

Howard Twilley	Tulsa	1965	134
David Williams	Illinois	1984	101
Jay Miller	Brigham Young	1973	100
Keith Edwards	Vanderbilt	1983	97

Average Receptions Per Game

Howard Twilley	Tulsa	1965	13.4
Jerry Hendren	Idaho	1969	9.5
Howard Twilley	Tulsa	1964	9.5
David Williams	Illinois	1984	9.2

Scoring

Total Points

Mike Rozier	Nebraska	1983	174
Lydell Mitchell	Penn State	1971	174
Art Luppino	Arizona State	1954	166
Bobby Reynolds	Nebraska	1950	157
Fred Wendt	Texas-El Paso	1948	152

Touchdowns Rushing

Mike Rozier	Nebraska	1983	29
Ed Marinaro	Cornell	1971	24
O. J. Simpson	USC	1968	22
Marcus Allen	USC	1981	22
Tony Dorsett	Pittsburgh	1976	21

Touchdowns Passing

Jim McMahon	Brigham Young	1980	47
Dennis Shaw	San Diego State	1969	39
Robbie Bosco	Brigham Young	1984	33
Steve Young	Brigham Young	1983	33
Jerry Rhome	Tulsa	1964	32

Touchdowns Receiving

Tom Reynolds	San Diego State	1969	18
Howard Twilley	Tulsa	1965	16
Clay Brown	Brigham Young	1980	15
Howard Twilley	Tulsa	1964	13
Jerry Hendren	Idaho	1969	12

Field Goals

John Lee	UCLA	1984	29
Paul Woodside	West Virginia	1982	28
Luis Zendejas	Arizona State	1983	28
Fuad Reveiz	Tennessee	1982	27
Chuck Nelson	Washington	1982	25

Interceptions

Al Worley	Washington	1968	14
George Shaw	Oregon	1951	13
Tony Thurman	Boston College	1984	12
Terry Hoage	Georgia	1982	12
Frank Polito	Villanova	1971	12
Bill Albrecht	Washington	1951	12
Hank Rich	Arizona State	1950	12

Kickoff Returns Best Average

Forrest Hall	San Francisco	1946	38.2
Tony Ball	Tenn.-Chattanooga	1977	36.4
George Marinkov	North Carolina State	1954	35.8
Bob Baker	Cornell	1964	35.1

Punt Returns Best Average

Bill Blackstock	Tennessee	1951	25.9
George Sims	Baylor	1948	25.0
Gene Derricotte	Michigan	1947	24.8
George Hoey	Michigan	1967	24.3
Floyd Little	Syracuse	1965	23.5

Punting Best Average

Reggie Roby	Iowa	1981	49.8
Kirk Wilson	UCLA	1956	49.3
Zack Jordan	Colorado	1950	48.2
Reggie Roby	Iowa	1982	48.1
Marv Bateman	Utah	1971	48.1

Best Games

Total Offense

Virgil Carter	Brigham Young (vs. Texas-El Paso)	1966	599
Dave Wilson	Illinois (vs. Ohio State)	1980	585
Marc Wilson	Brigham Young (vs. Utah)	1977	582
Jim McMahon	Brigham Young (vs. Utah)	1981	552
Archie Manning	Mississippi (vs. Alabama)	1969	540

Rushing

Rueben Mayes	Washington St. (vs. Oregon)	1984	357
Eddie Lee Ivery	Georgia Tech (vs. Air Force)	1978	356
Eric Allen	Michigan State (vs. Purdue)	1971	350
Ricky Bell	USC (vs. Washington State)	1976	347
Ron Johnson	Michigan (vs. Wisconsin)	1968	347

Completed Passes

Sandy Schwab	Northwestern (vs. Michigan)	1982	45
Jim McMahon	Brigham Young (vs. Colorado State)	1981	44
Gary Schofield	Wake Forest (vs. Maryland)	1981	43
Dave Wilson	Illinois (vs. Ohio State)	1980	43
Rich Campbell	California (vs. Florida)	1980	43

Yards Passing

Dave Wilson	Illinois (vs. Ohio State)	1980	621
Marc Wilson	Brigham Young (vs. Utah)	1977	571
Jim McMahon	Brigham Young (vs. Utah)	1981	565
Tony Adams	Utah State (vs. Utah)	1972	561
Greg Cook	Cincinnati (vs. Ohio)	1968	554

Receptions

Jay Miller	Brigham Young (vs. New Mexico)	1973	22
Rick Eber	Tulsa (vs. Idaho State)	1967	20
Howard Twilley	Tulsa (vs. Colorado State)	1965	19
Howard Twilley	Tulsa (vs. Southern Illinois)	1965	18

Yards Receiving

Chuck Huges	Texas-El Paso (vs. North Texas State)	1965	349
Rick Eber	Tulsa (vs. Idaho State)	1967	322
Harry Wood	Tulsa (vs. Idaho State)	1967	318
Jeff Evans	New Mexico State (vs. Southern Illinois)	1978	316
Tom Reynolds	San Diego State (vs. Utah State)	1971	290

Points Scored

Jim Brown	Syracuse (vs. Colgate)	1956	43
Arnold "Showboat" Boykin	Mississippi (vs. Mississippi State)	1951	42
Fred Wendt	Texas-El Paso (vs. New Mexico State)	1948	42
Dick Bass	Pacific (vs. San Diego State)	1958	38
Jimmy Nutter	Wichita State (vs. Northern State)	1949	37

Touchdowns

Arnold "Showboat" Boykin	Mississippi (vs. Mississippi State)	1951	7

Field Goals

Mike Prindle	Western Michigan (vs. Marshall)	1984	7

Extra Points

Terry Leiweke	Houston (vs. Tulsa)	1968	13

The Longest of All

Run from Scrimmage

Kelsey Finch	Tennessee (vs. Florida)	1977	99
Ralph Thompson	West Texas State (vs. Wichita State)	1970	99
Max Anderson	Arizona State (vs. Wyoming)	1967	99
Gale Sayers	Kansas (vs. Nebraska)	1963	99

Pass Play

Scott Ankrom to James Maness	TCU (vs. Rice)	1984	99
Cris Collinsworth to Derrick Gaffney	Florida (vs. Rice)	1977	99
Terry Peel to Robert Ford	Houston (vs. San Diego State)	1972	99
Terry Peel to Robert Ford	Houston (vs. Syracuse)	1970	99
Colin Clapton to Eddie Jenkins	Holy Cross (vs. Boston)	1970	99
Bo Burris to Warren McVea	Houston (vs. Washington State)	1966	99
Fred Owens to Jack Ford	Portland (vs. St. Mary's)	1947	99

Interception Return

(47 players have returned interceptions 100 yards)

Kickoff Returns

(147 players have returned kickoffs 100 yards)

Punt Returns

Jimmy Campagna	Georgia (vs. Vanderbilt)	1952	100
Hugh McElhenny	Washington (vs. USC)	1951	100
Frank Brady	Navy (vs. Maryland)	1951	100
Bert Rechichar	Tennessee (vs. Washington & Lee)	1950	100
Eddie Macon	Pacific (vs. Boston)	1950	100

Field Goal Returns

Richie Luzzi	Clemson (vs. Georgia)	1968	100
Don Guest	California (vs. Washington State)	1966	100

Punts

Pat Brady	Nevada-Reno (vs. Loyola Marymount)	1950	99
George O'Brien	Wisconsin (vs. Iowa)	1952	96
John Hadl	Kansas (vs. Oklahoma)	1959	94
Carl Knox	Texas Christian (vs. Oklahoma State)	1947	94
Preston Johnson	SMU (vs. Pittsburgh)	1940	94

Field Goals

Joe Williams	Wichita State (vs. Southern Illinois)	1978	67
Steve Little	Arkansas (vs. Texas)	1977	67
Russell Erxleben	Texas (vs. Rice)	1977	67
Tony Franklin	Texas A&M (vs. Baylor)	1976	65
Russell Erxleben	Texas (vs. Oklahoma)	1977	64

Roster of People

Roster of Schools

Picture Credits

p. 1: The Bettmann Archive, Inc.; p. 3: Hy Peskin, LIFE Magazine, © 1947 Time Inc.; pp. 6-7: Pro Football Hall of Fame.

The Kickoff

p.11: Princeton; p.14: The Bettmann Archive, Inc./Pro Football Hall of Fame; p. 15: The Bettmann Archive, Inc.; p. 16: The Bettmann Archive, Inc.; p. 18: Pro Football Hall of Fame; p. 19: Harvard/Pro Football Hall of Fame; p. 20: Culver Pictures, Inc.(2); p. 21: The Bettmann Archive, Inc./Pro Football Hall of Fame; p.22: The Bettmann Archive, Inc./Pro Football Hall of Fame; p. 23: U. of Chicago/Harvard/Pro Football Hall of Fame/U. of Minnesota; p. 24: Pro Footbal Hall of Fame(2); p. 25: Pro Football Hall of Fame; p. 26: The Bettmann Archive, Inc./AP-Wide World/Pro Football Hall of Fame; p. 27: Brown; p. 28: Chicago Bears; p. 29: Pro Football Hall of Fame/Notre Dame; p. 31: U. of Michigan/U. of Chicago; p. 32: Lafayette College/Notre Dame; p. 33: Notre Dame(2); p. 34: Pro Football Hall of Fame/Photo Archives-Ohio State/U. of the Pacific; p. 35: AP-Wide World(2); p. 36: U. of Texas/U. of Kansas; p. 37: Pro Football Hall of Fame/Brigham Young(2); p. 40: Notre Dame/Oklahoma/Wichita State/U. of Arkansas/Georgia Tech; p. 41: U. of Nebraska/AP-Wide World/U. of Illinois.

The League

p. 42: Wake Forest; p. 43: AP-Wide World; p. 44: Joe Di Paola, Jr., Sunpapers. Courtesy LIFE Picture Service; p. 46–47: AP-Wide World(3); p. 48: AP-Wide World; p. 50: AP-Wide World; p. 51: Hy Peskin, LIFE Magazine, (c) 1948 Time Inc.; p. 52: Hy Peskin, LIFE Magazine (c) 1948 Time Inc.; p. 53: Pro Football Hall of Fame; AP-Wide World(2); p. 54: AP-Wide World/Sugar Bowl Classic/AP-Wide World; p. 55: Courtesy Supreme Court of the U.S./U. of Colorado; pp. 56–57: AP-Wide World(3); p. 58: U. of Chicago; p. 59: U. of Illinois; p. 60: Joe Scherschel, LIFE Magazine (c) 1947 Time Inc.; Minnesota Historical Society; p. 61 U. of Michigan; p. 62: AP-Wide World; p. 63: USC; p. 64: AP-Wide World; p. 66: Pro Football Hall of Fame(3); p. 67: S. Frinzi, Yale; Pro Football Hall of Fame; p. 69: Pro Football Hall of Fame/David Ottenstein, Yale/The Bettmann Archive, Inc.; p. 70: Cornell/Otto Hagel, LIFE Magazine (c) 1938 Time Inc.

"Coach"

p. 76: Culver Pictures, Inc.; Hart Preston, LIFE Magazine (c) 1939 Time Inc.; p. 77: U. of Chicago; p. 78: Stanford; p. 79: AP-Wide World; p. 80: AP-Wide World/U. of Michigan; p. 81: AP-Wide World; p. 83: U. of Pennsylvania/Georgia Tech; p. 84: USC/AP-Wide World; p. 85: AP-Wide World; p. 86: The Bettmann Archive, Inc./Notre Dame; p. 87: Pro Football Hall of Fame; p. 88: Notre Dame(3); p. 89: AP-Wide World; p. 90: U. of Illinois; Pro Football Hall of Fame; p. 91: Pro Football Hall of Fame(2); p. 92: Duke(2); p. 94: US Military Academy Archives; p. 96: US Military Academy Archives/Notre Dame Archives; p. 96: Notre Dame; p. 97: Notre Dame; p. 98: AP-Wide World; p. 99: Princeton University Library, Manuscripts Division(2); p. 100: Western History Collections, U. of Oklahoma/U. of Oklahoma; p. 101: Sugar Bowl Classic; p. 102: U. of Texas; p. 103: AP-Wide World; p. 104: Notre Dame/Bill Ray, LIFE Magazine (c) 1964 Time Inc.; p. 105: Notre Dame; p. 107: Ohio State/AP-Wide World; p. 108: AP-Wide World; p. 109: Grambling/AP-Wide World.

The Big Game

p. 114: Courtesy of the Harvard University Archives; p. 115: Yale; pp. 116-117: Pro Football Hall of Fame; p. 118: Pro Football Hall of Fame/Yale; p. 119: Yale/Havard; pp. 120-121: AP-Wide World(3); p. 122: The Harvard Crimson; p. 123: Alfred Eisenstaedt, LIFE Magazine © 1944 Time Inc.; p. 124: US Military Academy Archives/The Bettmann Archive, Inc.; p. 125: UPI-The Bettmann Archive, Inc./AP-Wide World; p. 126: US Naval Academy; p. 127: Pro Football Hall of Fame; p. 128: US Military Academy

Archives/AP-Wide World; p. 129: George Silk, LIFE Magazine © 1950 Time Inc.; p. 130: U. of Alabama; p. 131: AP-Wide World; p. 132: The Birmingham News; p. 133: AP-Wide World; p. 134: Frank Armstrong-U. of Texas at Austin/U. of Oklahoma; p. 135: AP-Wide World; p. 136: Barker Texas History Center; p. 138: USC; p. 139: Leonard McCombe, LIFE Magazine © 1952 Time Inc./Notre Dame; p. 140: University of Southern California Libraries, USC; p. 141: AP-Wide World; p. 142: USC Libraries/AP-Wide World; p. 143: AP-Wide World; p. 144: U. of Michigan; p. 145: AP-Wide World/Ohio State; p. 146: AP-Wide World; p. 147: Ohio State(2); p. 148: Ohio State; p. 149: AP-Wide World; p. 152: USC/AP-Wide World; p. 153: USC; p. 154: USC Libraries; p. 155: U. of Minnesota/USC Libraries/U. of Minnesota.

Halftime

pp. 158-159: Cornell/Princeton/Nebraska/Cornell; pp. 160-61: Pro Football Hall of Fame/Nebraska; pp. 162-63: Pittsburgh/Northwestern/Yale/Cornell/UCLA/Colorado/Kansas/Nebraska; pp/ 164-65: Museum of Modern Art; pp. 166-67: Northwestern/US Naval Academy/Stanford/Notre Dame/Indiana University.

The Greatest

p. 172: AP-Wide World; p. 174: US Military Academy Archives/Culver Pictures, Inc.; p. 175: Culver Pictures, Inc.; p. 176: U. of Chicago; p. 177: The Bettmann Archive, Inc.; p. 178: Culver Pictures, Inc./Notre Dame; p. 179: Notre Dame; p. 180: The Bettmann Archive, Inc.; p. 181: Culver Pictures, Inc.; p. 182: AP-Wide World; p. 183: Yale; p. 184: U. of Minnesota; p. 185: Fordham; p. 186: Pro Football Hall of Fame; p. 187: Notre Dame; p. 188: Notre Dame; p. 189: US Military Academy Archives; p. 190: AP-Wide World; p. 191: Notre Dame; p. 193: US Military Academy Archives; p. 194: US Military Academy Archives; p. 195: US Military Academy Archives; p. 196: Bob Huddleston, Notre Dame; p. 197: U. of Oklahoma; p. 198: AP-Wide World; p. 199: Mark Kauffman, LIFE Magazine © 1966 Time Inc.; p. 200: Bob Gomel, LIFE Magazine © 1966 Time Inc.; p. 202: AP-Wide World; p. 203: U. of Nebraska/U. of Oklahoma; p. 204: U. of Nebraska; p. 205: USC; p. 206: USC Archives; p. 207: Stanford; p. 209: U. of Nebraska; p. 211: Boston College; p. 212: U., of Nebraska; p. 213: Ohio State; p. 216: AP-Wide World/Notre Dame(2); p. 217: AP-Wide World; p. 218: US Military Academy Archives; p. 219: U. of Pittsburgh.

New Year's Day

p. 224: Pasadena Tournament of Roses(3); p. 225: The Bettmann Archive, Inc./Pasadena Tournament of Roses; p. 228: Pasadena Tournament of Roses(2); p. 229: Pasadena Tournament of Roses; p. 230: Pasadena Tournament of Roses; p. 231: Pasadena Tournament of Roses; p. 232: Pasadena Tournament of Roses; p. 233: Pasadena Tournament of Roses/University of Southern California Library; p. 236: Orange Bowl Committee(3)/all program covers courtesy Orange Bowl Committee; 237: Orange Bowl Committee(2); p. 238: Orange Bowl Committee; p. 239: Orange Bowl Committee(2); p. 240: Notre Dame; p. 241: Orange Bowl Committee; p. 244: Sugar Bowl/The Bettmann Archive, Inc./ all program covers courtesy Sugar Bowl; p. 245: Sugar Bowl; p. 246: Sugar Bowl; p. 247: Sugar Bowl; p. 248: Sugar Bowl; p. 249: Sugar Bowl; p. 251: Sugar Bowl; p. 252: Art Rickerby LIFE Magazine © 1970 Time Inc.; p. 253: Penn State; p. 251: Cotton Bowl Classic/The Bettmann Archive, Inc./all program covers courtesy Cotton Bowl Classic; p. 257: Cotton Bowl Classic; p. 258: Cotton Bowl Classic; p. 259: Cotton Bowl Classic(2); p. 260: Cotton Bowl Classic; p. 261: Cotton Bowl Classic; p. 262: Southern Methodist University; p. 263: Pittsburgh/SMU; p. 282: Michigan / Museum of Modern Art/US Military Academy Archives; p. 304: Bill Ray, LIFE Magazine © 1964 Time Inc.